The
11-Year-Old
Man

The 11-Year-Old Man

His Fight and Flight to Freedom and Liberty

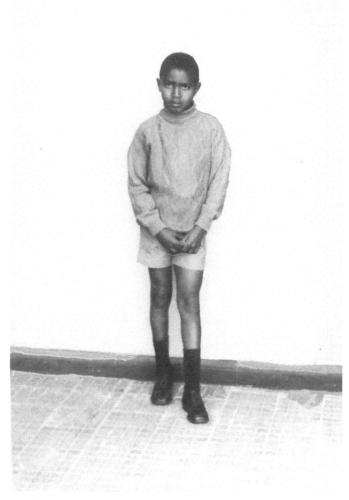

An Inspiring Story of a Child Fighter's Journey,
as Narrated at 40,000 ft

MULUGHETA ABRAHA(M)

The 11-Year-Old Man

Mulugheta Abraha(m)

ISBN: 978-0-578-39221-9
Independent Publishing
Printed in USA

www.M-Abraham.com

Cover & book design
Mulugheta Abraha(m)

Dedication

Throughout the years, many individuals have played a large role in shaping my future in one way or another. Most were strangers I met during my journey who felt responsible to take care of me in my vulnerable years.

Many Eritreans made life-changing decisions on my behalf with incredible compassion, generosity, and care that only the devotion of a parent can match. The love and sympathy exhibited by those (seemingly) strangers who acted as my custodians is heartwarming. Thanks to them, I made it to where I am today. Yet, sadly most of them did not get the opportunity they created for me to survive and flourish in life.

Once I left the continent of Africa, the Dutch people, in particular the volunteers, gave me a second chance at life. Their guidance, compassion, and empathy for the situation I found myself in at such a young age made an immense difference in helping me navigate the treacherous roads of life in Europe.

Hence, I dedicate this book to all those individuals who felt called upon to contribute to my well-being and made me who I am today.

The 11-Year-Old Man

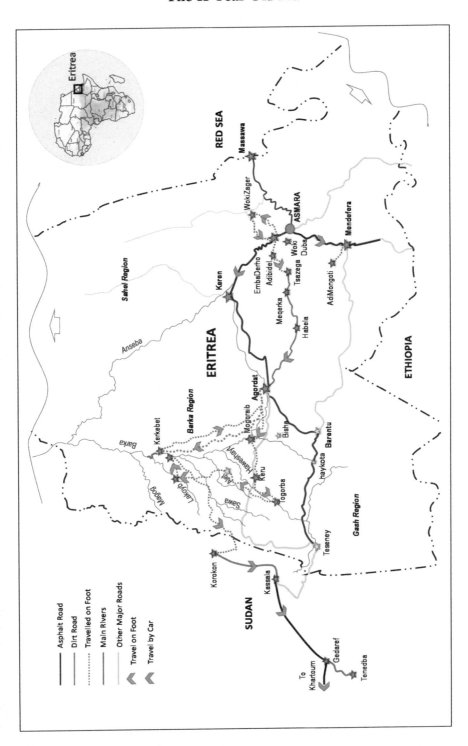

Contents

Preface

This book tells the story of an 11-year-old Eritrean boy - Mulugheta - who grew up in Asmara, the charming capital city of Eritrea, (known as *La Piccola Roma* – Africa's Little Rome) filled with Roman architecture and Italian gelato. The serenity of this Italian colonial city disappears as Mulugheta flees the capital, only to find himself in the jungle, an AK-47 on his hip, being hunted by the mightiest army in Africa, with the support of Russia and Cuba. In a war that cost the lives of hundreds of thousands of people, Mulugheta navigates a life of war and music, and finds an opportunity to leave the country, he jumps at the chance, landing in the middle of Rosse Buurt , the Red Light District in Amsterdam.

Confronted with an unfamiliar culture and social order, he struggles to overcome the new challenges of assimilating to European life. Isolated and lonely but supported by dedicated volunteers in the small town of Mepple in the Northern part of Holland, he sets his eyes on further unrealistic goals.

This story tells a thrilling tale of a young Eritrean child soldier's journey, from bush warfare in Eritrea, human smuggling operations in Khartoum, to navigating the social and cultural complexities of European life, and finally his path to tasting the American dream.

Written from 40,000 feet, the story is expertly recounted whilst traveling en-route, as the Regional Marketing Director at the world's largest airplane manufacturer, The Boeing Company. This fascinating story of hardship, fate, love, and perseverance reminds us that sometimes luck can not only be stumbled upon but even mined from your deepest and darkest moments.

Introduction

Eritreans are very humble people. Telling your own story is considered boastful and self-aggrandizing. It is therefore hard to find books of Eritreans who tell their personal experiences. This was highlighted to me when I met with the Eritrean Minister of Transportation, Mr. Andemichael. His story is fascinating. He served as a pilot in the Ethiopian air force. He eventually escaped with his MiG Jet Fighter to Saudi Arabia and joined the Eritrean liberation movement. He fought his whole life and eventually ended up becoming a minister. When I asked him why he didn't write a book, his answer was, "There are many other people who have a much more powerful memoir to write; mine is nothing." He passed away a few years ago and so did his story. That is when I realized – we have to change the culture and start writing our truth and personal accounts.

Thanks to all the friends, coworkers, family members, and even strangers who, after hearing a limited version of my story, urged me to share it with the world, writing this book helped me reflect on my journey and appreciate the blessings awarded to me by the almighty God. At times, just like Mr. Andemichael, I resisted the idea of writing a book, convinced that my story is not worth writing a book about, because so many stories of many people I know are much more dramatic and inspiring. Nevertheless, I gathered the energy to write this book with unusual transparency and vulnerability, primarily to document my life and pass it on to my descendants.

Yet, it doesn't escape me that many refugees and immigrants who in their journey encounter difficulties might relate to my journey. Also, many other ordinary people who face daunting challenges in life tend to draw inspiration from books they read and stories they hear. As such, it is my sincere hope that this book will serve as a reminder and inspiration to those who sometimes face obstacles that may seem unsurmountable.

Many of the events I wrote about in this book took place decades ago. I am not known for the best long-term memory; however, I did my best to stick to the events recorded in my memory that could be retrieved in the airplane flying at 30,000 ft with a certain degree of confidence. There may be some omissions or minor errors here and there, but nothing is added or omitted to intentionally dramatize the content. However, I did use fictitious names for real characters to protect the privacy of those who weren't able to permit me to mention their names.

I hope that you will find this book interesting and draw your positive outlook on life from it. The future is never written based on the challenges we encounter today. Today's challenges and hopeless conditions may in many cases be a prelude to greater things to come next. Your resilience, perseverance, and positive outlook toward life are key ingredients that get you through tough times.

The least you could get out of this book, however, is not to underestimate what kids in their preteen years are capable of. Typical traits like naivety, wild imagination, daring to prove courage, bravado, curiosity, obsession with self-image, intense focus, desire to grow faster and be respected, in combination with chaotic environments, can drive kids to do unimaginable things.

Lastly, I will be honored if this book inspires you to learn more about Eritrea. I hope that it gives you a glimpse into the history of the Eritrean people, their magnanimity, and extraordinary struggle for freedom which no single book could possibly do justice.

Restless

Eritrean liberation fighters seen 16 km (10 miles) away
from Asmara (Photo Credit EPLF)

I

Restless

1. Shielded

Higg above the north pole, close to Iceland, "Welcome, Mr. Abraham. Thank you for being a Diamond Medallion member. May I offer you a glass of champagne?" a flight attendant asked as I settled into my recliner seat on a flight from Amsterdam to Seattle. "What would you like for your main course?"

I decided to decline one of the best elite services that any business traveler enjoys when flying first or business class with the largest airline in the world. I spend 50% of my life travelling across the globe, and in-flight food, even in first or business class, becomes monotonous eventually.

No main meal for me today. The first course with an appetizer, a grilled Thai red curry shrimp starter, the second course a mixed green salad bowl with cucumber, tomato, olives, and feta cheese, followed by a dessert of my choice felt too much for me. After a two-week stay at some of the most luxurious hotels in Dubai and having enjoyed the best food and vodkas Moscow has to offer, I had had enough of being pampered for the time being.

Furthermore, I had just received an email from one of the sales directors requesting my attendance at meetings with several executives and engineers of various airlines in Dubai, Muscat, and Jordan. This meant I would soon be traveling back on Delta's first-class seats and staying in meticulously designed hotels in the oil-rich countries where luxury knows no limit – at places only the uber-rich can afford.

When I check into any of the innumerable plush and extravagantly designed hotels and restaurants around the world, a plastic card with 16 digits on the front and a magnetic strip in the back is all I need to carry to pay for all my expenses. I never have to worry about not having enough cash in my bank

When the flight attendant interrupted me with her pleasant request, I was reading a Dutch newspaper, *de Volkskrant*, that reminded me it was time to continue writing my book. I was ignited by the picture I saw in the newspaper depicting a child soldier with an AK-47 held firmly in his arms. He was staring at the camera with nearly lifeless eyes that revealed to me so much about what this young boy must have been going through at the very moment when the photographer, Tim Hetherington, took that picture.

I read the newspaper with deep interest and realized that the article was reporting the photographer's death in the civil war in Misrata, Libya. So, the story was not about the young African boy I saw in the picture, but about the photographer who had passed away documenting war-ravaged places. Nevertheless, the picture was fascinating. My Dutch is very good, and I read the article with intense concentration. So many memories floated up from the recesses of my mind as I saw a reflection of myself in that little boy who, under normal circumstances, would have then been in middle school under the warm protection and tutelage of his parents and teachers.

The caption read that he was a child soldier. I was unsure what that meant. He was a child and a soldier, but the words have so much of a negative tint to them that it didn't sound fair to the kid in the picture. If someone told the kid that he was a child soldier who needed to be rescued from his commanders, he might even get offended. At least, in my opinion, the words "child soldier" hadn't applied to me and I would have been offended.

As a child, for almost five years I had roamed with an AK-47 on my back. I never considered myself a child soldier and never expected sympathy nor did I want anyone to try to save me from a perceived misery. I considered myself a full-fledged freedom fighter. Yes, by any civilized standards, it would be considered over-achievement for a 13-year-old to claim that title. But I truly believed, and still believe, that I was not a child soldier. If I have to compromise, I will accept that I was a child freedom fighter, fighting for something that was so much bigger than me that I may have not understood all its complications at the time.

Now, at 40,000 feet above the surface of our blue planet and so far from what I once called home, my memories of my life as a child fighter are as vivid as the photograph I see.

The man sitting next to me on the flight was an executive at a large US company that provides and manages industrial power plants in the Middle East. He was flying back from Dubai to Seattle through Amsterdam. He noticed me reading the Dutch article and couldn't help but be curious. He seemed perplexed by the fact that he saw a black man reading a Dutch magazine, intensely interested in an African story while traveling to the USA and speaking with an accent very difficult to associate with a given ethnicity or country. It simply didn't make any sense to him and he had a hard time reconciling these unusual observations.

After making a few gestures indicating that he wanted to chat, he finally broke the silence and asked directly if I were Dutch, from Holland. I told him that I had carried four different nationalities but I consider myself primarily Eritrean. Like most Americans, he didn't know what or where Eritrea is. I gave him my usual canned description of the country I love so much. My pride and fascination with my country Eritrea made him more inquisitive and we launched into a deeper conversation. As much as I hate to be interrupted reading, I like to talk about Eritrea, and my energy level rises when I explain what the country has gone through to achieve its rightful place on the world map. In fact, in this particular situation, talking more about Eritrea helped me get into the right mood to write my book.

As soon as we concluded our conversation, I unpacked my laptop to start drafting my book about my journey in life, an idea that was proposed to me by my father in 1991 when he observed that I couldn't tell him everything I had gone through during my teenage years.

As I write my story, the contrast between what my brain is recalling from my deepest memory cells and my real-time experience in the Delta business class cabin is so stark that I question the validity of what I am seeing, or, sometimes, what I am remembering. While I come in and out of the real world at 40,000 ft and my memory-world in the 1970s, I realize I am so lucky to have such a contrasting experience in life. It almost feels as if I am one of the actors in *Avatar* who were in an alternate reality world until they were relieved from it and brought back to reality (at least that is how I understood the essence of *Avatar*). At this point, I am lucky to have the option to go in and out at will. So, for now, I will leave the luxurious business-class cabin of Delta Airlines and go into the world that was mine at age 10.

When I was young, I was a very shy and pleasant boy. I could never say no to the mothers of my neighborhood when they asked me to do something for them, so they loved me very much. Although, we were living in a quiet and safe communal neighborhood in the suburbs of Asmara called North Paradiso, my mother would never allow me to play outside with friends as often as I would have liked. Most of the time I would stay at home, or sometimes watch my friends play soccer from behind the fence or from the top of our garage balcony. I did this watching so often that I had a favorite observation corner that shielded me from the wind and the afternoon sun. Occasionally, when my mother went away for an extended period, I snuck out and played with my friends, but I was always watchful of her returning while I was outside.

My mother was very strict in enforcing rules at home and outside of the home. For her, it never mattered if the kids were hers or that of the neighbors. She treated us all in the same way. Hence, in her presence, all the kids in the neighborhood behaved remarkably well. To be fair, it was not just my mother; any adult seemed to have the right to interfere in every kid's business.

I remember our neighbor who heard I smoked a rolled-up paper, resembling a cigarette, came into our house in the absence of my parents, took me to a room, and spanked the hell out of me. Another neighbor whom I occasionally used to encounter on my way back from school checked my classwork in the middle of the street and gave me an earful of "advice" wrapped with threats to make sure I stayed on top of my game.

So, the culture, in general, was based on communal upbringing. Therefore, any parent had the right to interfere and take action when the kids misbehaved. My mother was just an extreme case because she was outspoken by nature and very demanding. That was just her. She would even occasionally become aggravated if she saw parents not disciplining their kids to the standard that she thought was acceptable. Yet, as strict as she was with kids, she was very funny and entertaining with her peers.

Like many Eritrean girls in the old days, she was forced to interrupt education to get married off. My father married her when she was only 13, and she had her first child at age 17. But this doesn't explain her unique nature as many Eritrean women had gone through the same experience of getting married early on. She was just naturally very demanding in running the house and the neighborhood to perfection.

My father never interfered with house rules; he was very focused on education. The only time we kids got in trouble with my father was when we didn't get good grades or didn't do our homework on time. Since I was a reasonably good student, I never had a problem with my father. Yet, he was a very serious man who observed every detail and made up his mind based on thorough observations. He always listened more than he spoke and was not emotional or loud. In the rare moments he raised his voice, it was terrifying to the kids. When he had time to be at home, he usually read newspapers and listened to his radio. I don't remember him ever playing with the kids. He was too serious and too occupied with work to play.

He was the youngest of his siblings and grew up in very harsh conditions after both his parents died, which left him to be raised by his two older sisters. Despite the absence of his parents, he turned out to be a very successful and well-educated man. He was one of the few Eritreans who obtained his education abroad to become an air traffic controller. His photographs astride an elephant and next to the Giza pyramids of Egypt were some of the few impressive pictures I had seen as a kid. These were also facts that reminded me my father was a special person. At one point in his career, he became the airport manager at Asmara International Airport located in my hometown. So, by all standards, my father gained success from his commitment to hard work and his craft. To him, nothing tops education.

Sadly, when I was between the ages of 10 and 13, my father was often sent on long-term assignments to Addis Ababa, Ethiopia, 800 miles away from Asmara, the city where we lived. When he was in Addis, I don't think he worried too much about me or my siblings. At least, not to the extent that I might do stupid things that other teenagers with less strict mothers might do. After all, I was only a 10-year-old, and as long as my mother was strong enough to keep me shielded and disciplined , what could go wrong?

Unfortunately, the strict nature of my upbringing only made me develop resistance to harsh conditions. When I did something wrong and got spanked by my mother, I'd vow to retaliate by doing more wrong things. I developed a habit of scoring even with my mother, especially when I felt the punishment was unfair or not proportional, which to my judgment at the time was often the case. If my father had known my resentment to strict rules, considering what was going on in Eritrea at the time, he would have been incredibly worried.

A Little History and Context

In case your knowledge about Eritrea's history is limited, all you need to know for now is that it is a small country located in East Africa and was very significant to the world powers due to its strategic location allowing it to control the flow of oil through the Red Sea. The Red Sea was a vital shipping lane that the world powers wanted to keep open at all costs. The interest in this region was such that even ancient powers like the Egyptians and Ottoman Empire had set their eyes on it and were one of the first to occupy parts of Eritrea. In recent history, however, the most significant colonizers were the Italians. Before the Second World War, Italy occupied Eritrea for about 60 years on a quest for raw materials in Africa. During that time, the Italians treated the Eritrean people as second-class citizens. At the same time, they built Eritrea to be one of the most advanced industrialized countries in Africa. Benito Mussolini wanted Asmara, the capital city of Eritrea, to be the Piccola Roma of Africa. With unlimited design regulations, the architects unleashed their wildest creativity and designed a marvelous city with modern hotels, cinemas, and cafes that are now designated as World Heritage sites and protected by UNESCO.

During the Second World War, Britain invaded Eritrea from Sudan and defeated Italy. Britain then colonized Eritrea for another 10 years, during which it looted and destroyed what was built by the Italians, as well as taught us to drive on the wrong side of the road. Britain had no desire to keep Eritrea as a colony. In 1952, the United Nations decided that Eritrea should be federated with its southern neighbor, Ethiopia, to serve the interests of the United States. During the deliberation at the UN, in 1952, the US Secretary of State, John Foster Dulles, made the following unforgettable remarks in his attempts to justify the forced and arranged marriage between Ethiopia and Eritrea:

"From the point of view of justice, the opinions of the Eritrean people must receive consideration. Nevertheless, the strategic interests of the United States in the Red Sea basin and considerations of security and world peace make it necessary that the country be linked with our ally, Ethiopia."

With this misguided foreign policy, Dulles and his colleagues in the State Department laid the foundation for another dark chapter in Eritrea.

Within a few years, the emperor of Ethiopia annexed Eritrea, and the dream of becoming an independent nation was stolen from the Eritrean people. The US strategic interest was served by controlling the most critical sea from where the majority of oil from Arab countries flowed to the rest of the world. The emperor of Ethiopia, in return for the gift, allowed the US to establish the largest intelligence center ever built by the US on Eritrean land. More than 3,000 US soldiers were stationed in the city of Asmara to operate the center called "Kagnew Station".

In the meantime, the Ethiopians tightened their grip on Eritrea and became ever more oppressive. Any resistance was met with deadly force. With the help of the US and Israel, Ethiopia boasted one of the most advanced armed forces in Africa. An armed struggle by a few Eritreans against a formidable power seemed an impossible task, incapable of even making a dent in the armor. Yet, as the Ethiopian aggression and atrocities against the Eritrean people worsened, the Eritreans' resolve to fight for their freedom intensified.

In reaction to the Ethiopian aggression and after waging a long nonviolent struggle, in September 1961, the Eritrean people began an armed struggle for independence. A few brave individuals with ragtag equipment decided to take on one of the largest armies in Africa supported by the mightiest superpower in the world.

2. *Hadmo Debate - Woki Zager*

Despite my shy demeanor as a kid, I was a very adventurous boy. The contrast between my actions and my shy character was sometimes so strong that people wouldn't even believe I could be guilty of the things I was reprimanded for. Yet, if I heard rumors that something was going on outside my neighborhood or even outside Asmara, I would be the first one to take the risk and go see it. Despite my mother's strict rules, taking off to unknown places at a moment's notice gave me a thrill I could not resist as a child. I developed a sense of confidence and normalcy when encountering extraordinary things. Partly, this could have been due to the long distance I had to travel to go to my school every day.

When I joined middle school, the influx of Ethiopian soldiers was so high they used many of the schools as their living quarters. As a result, I was assigned to go to a middle school that was located on the other side of the city. Each day, I had to walk alone for more than one hour to get there. The shortest route to my school was straight through the rough streets of downtown Asmara. Because of this, at a very early age, I was exposed to all the bad and good that took place in the city. But I never felt unsafe.

October 5, 1974; it was early morning, my friend Geremeskel and I went for a walk toward Keren road, a major artery that leads to the checkpoint located north of Asmara. The road was unusually crowded and we were eager to figure out why. Hundreds of people were heading north to the outskirts of the city, while very few seemed to be going south toward downtown Asmara. This was odd – for the time of the day, the flow should have been the other way around because many villagers should have been heading to downtown Asmara to sell their goods and go to work.

We quickened our pace in anticipation, eager to understand what was going on. As we approached the main road, we noticed overcrowded buses heading north. Many cars trailed them, packed to capacity. We wondered at the traffic, at what could be going on, and sat down by the roadside to observe. As the day wore on, the traffic and crowds intensified. The buses plying now were carrying people not just inside but also on the roof – a space normally allocated to cargo. We noticed that the small cars too were now crowded beyond capacity, many even carrying more than five people inside. Everyone was headed north using every means of transportation – buses, cars, horses, motorcycles, and bicycles – and many were walking on foot. We wondered if evacuation had been ordered.

But the people had no luggage with them and there was no perceptible sense of panic. They were all smiling, cheering, and laughing. It seemed that they were heading to a major festival.

After observing the crowd for a long time with bewilderment, we started asking some people what was happening. Then someone said that people were going out to see the freedom fighters (or *Jebhas* as they were called in Arabic). We were told that the *Jebhas* were a Muslim tribe who lived far away from the city, and they could be identified by three long scars on each of their cheeks. This description, which turned out to be wrong as I discovered later, fascinated me.

But something didn't seem right. Why would all of these people head out to see the freedom fighters on the same day? It worried me to think of what the Ethiopian soldiers would do to them if they found out what was going on.

Confused as we were, no other reason was rumored for the massive crowd of people all heading out in the same direction on the same day. So, we looked at each other and decided to go with them. As kids, we were not allowed to wander off too far from our neighborhood. But we were too excited to wonder whether we were breaking rules or worried about what punishment we would receive from our parents when we returned – or worse, whether we would even be able to return. We had no clue what the destination was. It could have been 5 miles outside Asmara or 50 miles. We simply didn't know and didn't care. We just wanted to follow the crowd and see what was going on.

So we began walking toward the northern security checkpoint less than a mile away. With us, hundreds of people were walking, cycling, driving, horse-riding ... you name it. The Ethiopian checkpoint was overwhelmed with the massive crowd heading out. Not knowing what was going on and not having received any instructions out of the ordinary, the soldiers let everybody go. After all, people coming into the city were their main security concern, not people going out.

Once we had passed the checkpoint, the scene became very chaotic. Everyone seemed to be in a hurry. Buses, loaded beyond capacity with chanting people and their speakers blasting popular music, raced through the winding two-lane highway. It wouldn't be surprising if the bus drivers were making multiple trips that day. It was as if a movie was about to start and we were going to be very late. We felt that unless we got on one of the buses, we would not make it to wherever we were supposed to be going. We began to feel anxious and desperate.

So Geremeskel and I collected large rocks from the roadside and lined them up across the highway to force the buses to stop or at least slow down so that we could hop on. Overloaded as they were, if a bus slowed down, people would climb up to sit on top of the bus, elbowing everyone for room to sit. Compared to the people who were on the road, I was most likely the youngest and the weakest of all.

I tried to climb a bus a few times but was thrown off by more muscular guys and never made it up. It was the survival of the fittest. Geremeskel, however, after several failed attempts, managed to hop on to a bus, and before I knew it, he was gone. After a while, the larger buses started to simply drive over the rocks we had laid out. The rocks started flying like projectiles when hit by the tires, which turned the area into a dangerous place to be standing in.

With my friend gone, my only choice now was to keep walking, following a huge crowd of mostly men. When it became clear that it was not possible to board a bus, people started to walk away off the highway and onto a dirt road that was a shortcut. The road took us through valleys, mountains, bushes, rivers, and villages. We walked for miles, but I don't remember being tired. I was blindly following the crowd in whatever direction the invisible first person seemed to be leading us. We reached a small village along the dirt track. I recall an old lady coming to me and giving me water. She asked me to take off my sweater and she wrapped it tightly around my waist. This was meant to support my back for the long haul. That was an indication to me that I still had a long way to go before reaching the destination.

After hours of walking, I sensed that we were getting close to our destination. People began to walk faster, their faces elated as if they were about to meet a long-lost friend or family member. The main asphalt road that we had departed from a few hours earlier was now visible and seemed to have ended at a single focal point with hundreds of vehicles. From there, a dirt road branched off the highway and led the way through a winding road resembling a slithering snake. We could see the plume of dirt thrown into the air by the hundreds of buses and cars that were heading toward the top of the hill. The road led to the town of Woki Zager.

The long queue of cars and buses winding around the hills was barely moving. As we got closer, we could see people jumping off the buses and starting to walk. Our path eventually intersected with that of the buses. The only difference was that the buses and cars were not moving anymore but we still were.

The town of Woki Zager had never seen such a crowd and concentration of automobiles since its inception. It was only a small town at a top of a hill. Its master plan, if there was one, was designed to accommodate animal traffic, not buses and cars. The hundreds of cars and buses couldn't find parking, so they were stranded on the road. The town, for that single day of its existence, became the Mecca of Eritreans. Every Eritrean who could afford to be there was there. Even I, a 10-year-old boy who knew nothing about the purpose and goal of this gathering, was determined enough to make it there.

Once I entered the town, I tried to figure out where I was supposed to go, but it looked very chaotic to me – everyone was going off in different directions. It seemed as though everyone was searching for something.

Soon, for the first time, I saw a freedom fighter directing the crowd to a location in the town. I was fixated on the freedom fighter. I didn't care where I was heading – I just wanted to look at him for as long as I could. Then more freedom fighters joined, and a little later a few more appeared. They looked like they were from a different planet. They had bony cheeks and thick afro hair. Their military gear didn't look like that of a conventional army; the fighters wore tight shorts and plastic sandals. Some of them had large vertical scars on their cheeks, caused by deep cuts they endured as part of their tradition in the lowlands of physically marking one's identity on their face. To me, these marks made them look like they were different creatures. Some of them spoke different languages. Yet, these were Eritreans from the lowlands whom I had never seen before and never known existed.

The scene, the fighters, traditional homes, goats, cows, chickens, the smell of manure, and everything I could see across the landscape was new to a city boy like me. The impression that the town of Woki Zager left on me was so strong that as I write this book, 46 years later, I vividly remember the feeling ... I was enjoying all that was new to my eyes.

Unknown to me, serious activity was underway. While everyone was quietly sitting and standing around, a few freedom fighters were standing on top of traditional homes called *hidmo*s and loudly debating. The discussion, I learned later, was about how to settle the ideological differences between two groups of freedom fighters so they could join hands in defeating the Ethiopian army.

Thousands had traveled from Asmara to attend a historic moment where the two groups – the Eritrean Liberation Front (ELF) and the Eritrean People's Liberation Front (EPLF) – would merge into a single organization. As a 10-year-old boy, I didn't understand the significance of what was at stake or what was taking place, let alone the differences between the two groups.[1]

But for all those who took a day off and risked their lives to come to this town to reconcile the two movements, it was a monumental task. For if they succeeded in uniting the two groups, it would go into the books as one of the most significant achievements ever recorded in Eritrean history.

My time in Woki Zager felt short and somewhat insignificant compared to the journey to get there. After a long day of debating, the meeting ended, and it was time to go back to Asmara. By then the sun had set, and walking back through the shortcut in the darkness was no longer an option. So, people started walking on the main road back to Asmara.

I tried hard to find Geremeskel in the crowd. But the place was so crowded I was unable to find him. I worried that my trip back home would be difficult. It was getting dark and I dreaded the idea of heading home on foot.

Fortunately, thousands of other people were headed back home to Asmara, and all I needed to do was follow the crowd, just as I had in the morning. We left the town and made our way down the hill toward the main asphalt road. The narrow dirt road that was built to serve horse buggies was completely jammed with cars and buses. Since it was dark, people were no longer taking the risk of climbing onto the roofs of already crowded buses. They preferred to walk.

I felt comfortable in the crowd. Before reaching the asphalt road, it was slow-moving traffic, similar to the traffic after a football game in the US. The dust coming off the tires made it very difficult to walk alongside motorized traffic, but we had to – there was no other choice. So, covering my nose with my sweater, I walked down the hill and made it to the main asphalt road.

---

[1] The difference between the two groups is complex to explain. The ELF was established in 1961. It was the oldest and largest armed liberation movement in Eritrea. The EPLF was established in 1970 by a handful of fighters who split from the ELF due to serious mismanagement and wrong strategy pursued by the ELF leaders. The difference was not ethnic or religion-based. Often, you would find sibling fighters on both sides.

Once we reached the asphalt road, the buses started to speed up and disappear into the distance toward Asmara. While thousands of people were walking to Asmara, a few smart people were walking in the other direction toward Keren. They would catch a bus coming from Keren before it reached the intersection point where hundreds of people were waiting.

Amid all the noise and chaos, a man suddenly approached me and asked in a concerned tone, "Whose son are you, boy?" [2] I told him that I am the son of Abraha Tesfaghiorghis. He asked, "Abraha? The air traffic controller who works at the airport?" I nodded, "Yes."

Shocked, he immediately grabbed my arm and instructed me to stay by his side, adding that he would not allow me to walk back to Asmara, but would get me on a bus with him. He explained that he knew my father, and would ensure my safe passage home.

I felt like an angel had descended from the heavens to save me from what could have been a very long and exhausting walk. We turned around and walked toward Keren for about half a mile to catch a bus before it reached the crowd. After a long wait, a nearly empty bus came from Keren and we hopped in.

As we reached the intersection where the crowd was waiting for a bus, while others were walking toward Asmara, I could only imagine how lucky I was to have met this man. To this day, I don't remember his name or how we were related. But, when I was cruising on the bus and passing by the crowd that was moving on foot like a snail in the darkness, I appreciated him so much.

Moments later, we arrived in Asmara. As the bus slowly moved through the crowded road, I saw hundreds of people lined up on both sides of the road, waving hands to the triumphant heroes who had managed to unite the two groups of freedom fighters. The scene was very similar to that of Ethiopia's King Haile Selassie's visit to Asmara when thousands of people were forced to line up to greet

---

[2] In Eritrea, typically if they want to know who you are, they don't ask for your name, they ask for your parents' name.

him. The only difference this time was that nobody had forced the people to greet the "kings of Woki Zager". Amongst the hundreds of expectant were my parents and the entire neighborhood who were eagerly awaiting my return.

For a child of my age to disappear for a full day in such a tense situation must have been extremely worrisome for my parents. This was exhibited when I jumped off the bus and appeared in front of the crowd and my family. My family started crying with relief. I can only imagine now what they would have felt. I have a 12-year-old daughter now when I'm writing this, and can't fathom her in any way doing what I did then. But at the time I was so proud of my accomplishment. I had attended a historical event, while many of my friends and family had simply stayed at home or hadn't even known of the event.

Just like a wildebeest calf, traversing the plains of the Serengeti under the protection of the herd, I had miraculously returned home safely - but not unaffected. With my mind full of idealistic fantasies, and visions of an independent Eritrea, the Hidmo Debate and everything I had seen during this trip sparked an obsessive fire which would alter the trajectory of my life. More importantly, it shaped my perception of myself. Nobody could say I was just a little boy anymore. I felt like I was the toughest kid in the neighborhood – a full-fledged adult who had managed to take on a challenge that few can claim to have done.

Although my return to Asmara was uneventful, I learned later it could have been a bloodbath of unprecedented proportions. Later that day, the Ethiopian generals had realized what had happened and had ordered their soldiers to kill everyone who was coming back from visiting the fighters. It was rumored that military leader Aman Andom later overruled the order and averted the disaster. Andom was the highest-ranking Ethiopian general of Eritrean descent. He was later killed during a coup d'état by the brutal Mengistu Haile Mariam who later ruled Ethiopia with an iron fist.

ሐ C ነ ት

LIBERATION

PUBLISHED MONTHLY BY ERITREANS FOR LIBERATION IN NORTH AMERICA

Vol. 4, No. 2   �   ታሕሳስ፡74-ጥሪ·75   Dec.1974-Jan.1975

On October 5, 1974, more than 20,000 Eritreans assembled on a outskirts of Asmara. Coming from all over Eritrea, they were the to discuss and resolve the fratricidal war waged among the two Eritrean liberation forces, namely Kiada el Ama and the Eritrean People's Liberacion Forces.

The EPLF has issued a statement on the events, the translatic of which EFLNA is hereby presenting with full responsibility for any discrepancies.

* * * *

RECENT EVENTS CONFRONTING OUR ADVANCE UNITS

It has been explained that a cease-fire had been effected an that a committee selected by the people had been working to reco cile the two forces.

The following is the subsequent development and events that took place since then.

As soon as the committee of the people started its task, our comrades presented eight points:

1) There should be a cease-fire between our forces.

2) The two forces should observe and respect the cease-fir not only in their own areas but throughout all other pa of Eritrea as well.

3) The people's committee should supervise the cease-fire sending its delegation all over Eritrea.

4) The two forces should remain, temporarily, operating in specific areas. (However, we are opposed to a permanen demarcation between us.)

5) All our guns should be directed against the Ethiopian occupation army.

6) There should not be any propaganda campaigns by one for against the other in the towns or in the countryside.

7) Eritreans who support us or the other side should live peace and not be subjected to any kind of reprisals on either their property or their lives.

8) To implement the preceding points a democratic dialogue should be started directly.

Woki Zager conference and its outcome as reported in the US

1977: Woki Zager conference location, Hidmo (traditional designed home)

2021: Woki Zager conference location upgraded as a historical monument

3. *Friday Evening - Asmara*

On the evening of January 31, 1975, a Friday, Asmara's peace was suddenly disturbed by a streak of nonstop gunshots and explosions. My father was not home yet. He had gone from work to the city center to buy me shoes in preparation for our trip planned the following day to visit his birthplace some 60 km outside Asmara. It was to be an exciting trip. A Land Rover was already parked in our garage loaded with gifts and other necessities we planned to take to the village.

But the gunfire wouldn't stop, and my mother and a few adults in the house visibly began to worry about what was going on, and, more importantly, whether my father was safe. They locked all the doors and waited for my father to show up. I had no clue what was happening. This was the first time I had ever heard gunshots and I was simply too young to comprehend the situation. I was just eager for my father to come home so that I could see my new shoes.

Late in the evening, my father arrived home and everyone was elated. I too was happy, but for a different reason. While my father was narrating his ordeal to the adults, I quickly unboxed the new shoes, put them on, and burst into the living room. I excitedly bowed down to each adult asking for their blessings. This was a tradition kids learn from an early age: for any gift you receive, you have to bow to your elders and ask for their blessings. That was what well-mannered children did. But this time the reaction I got seemed to indicate otherwise. In a matter of seconds, the mood in the room changed from sober and concerned to laughing at me. They were terrified for their lives and there I was, completely oblivious to the shootings, concerned about my new shoes and the protocol for blessings. This made me feel like the clown of the evening. Needless to say, the next day, the long-awaited trip was canceled and the Land Rover remained parked in our garage for a long time.

That Friday evening heralded a new reality in Asmara and my personal life. From that day on, the sound of machine guns and mortar became part of my day-to-day life and those of many millions of Eritreans. Over the following few days, Ethiopian soldiers went on a rampage through the city. Civilians were dragged out of their houses and executed. According to sources, up to 3,000 people were killed in the city, making it the bloodiest moment in the history of Asmara. Life in Asmara changed forever, and what followed was repression and the unleashing of deadly force against any civilian that was suspected of aiding Eritrean fighters. Death roamed the once-peaceful and calm streets of Asmara.

The fighting, which originally started with poorly armed fighters in remote areas, expanded tremendously and reached the outskirts of every major Eritrean town, including the capital, Asmara. Ordinary people who knew nothing about the war that had been raging in remote mountains started to take notice. It was at this point that the otherwise tranquil and peaceful Asmara started to feel the tension. For me and many other kids, it was impossible to understand how high the stakes were and just how horrible the situation was about to become.

The daily fight that took place mainly at night was a source of deep curiosity for me. Although the sounds of ear-piercing machine guns and rocket-propelled grenades were terrifying and everyone in the neighborhood was praying, I started to idealize the fight that took place in the darkness and I wanted to hear more of it every day. The sounds of mortars, rocket launchers, and heavy machine guns started to become music to my ears, especially when it was at a safe distance from where I lived. I got very disappointed when the city was occasionally silent in the evenings.

Many homes in Asmara were hit by bullets and few homes were demolished by artillery. To me, this was sensational. The bullet holes on the walls of a home signified the family's involvement in the battle. Obviously, I wanted to see our family be involved as well. Every morning, as soon as I woke up, I ran to the front of our house and scanned the walls for a bullet hole. To my disappointment, after months of waiting, no bullet had hit our house.

Nevertheless, I was so desperate to see a bullet mark on our house that I decided to make it happen. One day, I grabbed a key and started to dig a hole resembling a bullet mark next to the living room window. I figured the closer I place the hole to the window, the more exciting the story was going to be. I finished my artwork as best as I could and it was time to hear the reaction of my family members. Every guest who came to our home was shocked to see how close the "bullet" came to entering our house.

Apparently, I did such a great job, my father has been telling the story for more than 40 years confidently. When I recently broke the news to him, the look on his face was not amusing. His expression read "you are a stupid kid, you made me tell a false story for my entire life". He is right; I was a stupid kid who thought war was a game. After all, I was only 11 year old, I had no idea of the pain others were going through or the people being killed every time. I enjoyed the sound of machine guns. Yet, every evening, people were dying, and tremendous suffering engulfed the city.

Every time an Ethiopian soldier got attacked by Eritrean fighters, the soldiers caused terror and bloodshed among the civilian population of the city. In search of hidden freedom fighters, they would go door to door terrorizing and killing people. Dead bodies were transported in trucks to mass graves. In every corner and every major building, Ethiopian soldiers were stationed to guard and bring order. The Ethiopian government brought so many soldiers to Eritrea that local schools were converted to military camps. The asphalt roads started to disintegrate due to the heavy traffic of tanks and trucks going in and out of the city. The Ethiopian soldiers didn't speak any Eritrean languages and were unable to communicate, and as such, they had no understanding of what the population thought of them or just how much they were hated. All they knew was that the source of the freedom fighters were the Eritrean people and therefore the people were the enemies of the soldiers and had to be punished.

The soldiers were stationed everywhere in and around Asmara city. Traveling outside the city was a very dangerous thing to do.

Asmara was under military curfew and surrounded by heavily armed Ethiopian soldiers who lived in constant vigil due to the daily attacks mounted on them by the Eritrean fighters who dug trenches around Asmara, poised to take control of the city any time. Given that our house was on the outskirts, we were in a danger zone. I remember at one point the soldiers taking positions so close to our home that my father decided to evacuate the family in a rush. Just before the curfew hit, he borrowed a car, a Volkswagen beetle, from our neighbor, loaded the entire family – six kids and my mother – and drove us to the center of the city to drop us off at a friend's house deemed safer.

It was a thrilling ride! There was not even a single car in the streets of Asmara and my father was racing through the streets as fast as he could. I didn't want the ride to end. We stayed there for two weeks while my father and other men stayed back. Fortunately, nothing happened and we returned home. But the tension was felt everywhere and in every home.

Many youngsters began to leave the city, some to escape the danger and others to join the freedom fighters; the news of people disappearing never stopped. Every day I went to school there was fascinating but terrible news about my peers, ranging from "someone left the city to join the fighters" to "someone got killed". Eventually, older boys whom I looked up to, as well as my closest family members, began leaving Asmara to join the liberation front. Two of my uncles and a young man who rented the extra room in my childhood home also left. The horror stories I heard every day at school, coupled with the pictures forming in my mind about the nightly battles fought by my uncles and friends, brought me to one conclusion: I wanted to be a part of it. I wanted to join the freedom fighters and avenge the bloodshed.

I recall drawing pictures of how I imagined the war to be. My pictures would show one single Eritrean fighter burning many tanks and the Eritrean flag being raised in Asmara and so on. My mother would immediately tear up these pictures and burn them since the

Ethiopian soldiers were performing routine searches. These pictures being found in our home could result in my parents being executed on the spot. But, as a kid, I didn't see the danger or the suffering of my people. All I could see was the "bright side" of the war. I had dreams of going out to join the freedom fighters and coming back triumphantly. I never thought of myself dying or not making it back. I dreamed that Eritrea would be free and I would be one of the first fighters to enter my hometown, with an AK-47 strapped on my shoulder. So, at 11 years old, I was desperate to join the freedom fighters and find out if my imagination could turn into reality.

Researching how to search for and find freedom fighters became my primary preoccupation. In the absence of the Internet and social media, I would listen intently when adults spoke about the freedom fighters and stories of battles. My favorite person to learn from was my grandfather, Aboy Tseghay, whose two kids had joined the liberation front.

In the mornings, after his night shift at the famous building Fiat Talero, he would often come to our home on his shiny bicycle and bring us freshly baked Italian bread (*bani samarco*). My mother would make him traditional coffee – which is a ceremony that takes a few hours to complete. They would chat about how things were going and what the latest developments were on the battlefields. To avoid getting into trouble or having the children overhear them, they would use obvious code words to refer to the liberation movement and most often refer to them as "our sons".

These coffee ceremonies were my favorite moments. I would get to hear some grown-up talk and inflate them with my augmented imagination. The stories I heard at home and school made me more determined to join the freedom fighters at all costs.

4. Foolishness - Mendefera

The trip I took to Woki Zager only emboldened me. I was invincible and I felt like nothing could stop me from exploring new locations. As the months passed, the fighting around Asmara intensified. More people joined the liberation front, and schools now became places where unconfirmed news would circulate. These stories always highlighted the heroism of Eritrean fighters while making fun of the Ethiopian soldiers. Many songs were written to highlight the political situation in Eritrea, but they would always contain hidden meanings. The interpretation of songs became an art of its own. Any love song could be twisted to also mean love for Eritrea. Initially, the Ethiopians were oblivious to how these songs were strengthening nationalism, patriotism, and heroism amongst the young generation.

As the songs became popular and people started talking about them more openly, the Ethiopians banned these songs from being played on the radio. People could only hear them on a tape recorder if they had one. Then, even tapes were forbidden, and if you were found listening to any Eritrean songs, you ended up in jail. The tightening of control over the population made things worse. Youngsters started to organize themselves to support the liberation movement in any way they could, from getting supplies out of Asmara to collaborating with the fighters to assassinate Ethiopian leaders in the city. The city became a haven and a nest for the freedom fighters.

If any Eritrean was discovered to be collaborating with Ethiopian soldiers, they would receive warning letters from the liberation movement instructing them to stop their activity or face assassination. For those who refused to stop working with the Ethiopians, after three warning notices an assassination squad was sent to seal their fate. The assassinations of both Ethiopian leaders and Eritrean collaborators were often conducted in broad daylight.

Mr. Tesfatsion, our neighbor, who was suspected of collaborating with the Ethiopians, was gunned down in front of my eyes, only 300 ft away from our house. During lunch hour, he was coming back from work on his bicycle. In Asmara, all offices close during lunch hour and everyone goes home for lunch. Right as he reached the intersection of our home, two men, also on a bicycle, approached him from behind and I heard two gunshots. As I focused my attention on the scene, I saw Mr. Tesfatsion, who was a very heavy man, fall off his bicycle. Realizing that this was a murder, I ran to my home. Sadly, the only way to go to my home was to pass his fallen body. As I ran past Mr. Tesfatsion's body, I couldn't help but take a quick curious look. Blood was streaming from his head and being soaked into the brown dirt. It was not my place to help. I don't know how long Mr. Tesfatsion lay there before he died. The two assailants disappeared. At Mr. Tesfatsion's funeral, his son vowed to avenge the death of his father and joined the list of collaborators. A few months later, he too met the same fate as his father.

The freedom fighters tasked with assassination missions would often use bicycles to move around the city and escape fast. So bicycles became the next target of Ethiopian soldiers and the population was forbidden to ride bicycles. This brought immense hardship to the majority of people who used bicycles as their mode of transportation. Ethiopian soldiers could no longer trust any Eritrean in the city. Villagers who brought their load of goods to the city to sell were suspected of helping freedom fighters smuggle weapons into the city.

All these restrictions made the city very uneasy to live in. People started complaining openly, and whenever there was an opportunity to chat safely, the conversation would be about what the freedom fighters were doing.

My grandfather, who used his bike to come and visit us frequently, could no longer do so. He could neither afford the bus fee nor walk the long distance. He used to always let me ride his bicycle when he came home. The ban on bicycles affected me personally and I became very angry. I became a victim of this rule directly, which fueled my frustrations.

The once beautiful and enjoyable city of Asmara became hell on earth. The freedom fighters began targeting the industry sector, destroying facilities, and creating a shortage of goods in Asmara. This certainly helped the liberation movement in many ways. The Ethiopians struggled to supply their army with basic needs. Many young people also began to join the freedom fighters after seeing that they had the upper hand. On the flip side though, civilians living in Asmara no longer had access to necessities like water, sugar, oil, and grain. In every house, mothers gathered the family for a daily choir and evening prayer, pleading loudly with Saint Mary and every other saint that they thought God might listen to. With each passing day, despite the overflow of prayers, the city became more unsafe to live in, and thousands began to flee to the nearby villages and towns.

For me, all these problems were a source of curiosity and excitement, but for my parents and others, living in these conditions was unmanageable. Fortunately, my father worked at the airport as a traffic controller and he asked pilots and his friends to bring supplies for him from Addis Ababa, the capital of Ethiopia. This meant that, unlike my family members and neighbors, we had no noticeable shortage of supplies at home, at least not to me. Our immediate family members were also fortunately not affected from the brutal Ethiopian secret service who made the killing of young suspected Eritreans their daily routine.

Living in a city teeming with horror stories and rumors, it was very easy for me to have an open discussion with my friends about my obsession with leaving the city to see the fighters. One day, I asked my friend Tedros to accompany me to the city of Mendefera to find the fighters. Mendefera was a large town occupied by Ethiopian soldiers. I had never been to Mendefera before, and it was a challenge to figure out how to get there. The exit checkpoint to Mendefera was on the other side of Asmara. I had very little knowledge about the area and I needed someone to help me out. Tedros was one of my best friends and his mother was ten times stricter than my own. She was a tough lady, and all the kids in the block were afraid of her. Just one look directed from the angle of her eyebrow would terrify any of us. So, messing around with Tedros was not such a good idea. But adventures were what made things fun for me. So, Tedros became the first friend whom I convinced to share my journey. Yet, my choice of Tedros was coincidental, not planned. If I were to be sensible, Tedros would be the last person I would want to take on adventures like the one I was planning. He was a city boy who was used to living a luxurious life. His parents were relatively rich and his life was too regulated for what I had planned. Still, he was my favorite friend and destined to taste what I had in store.

After a short discussion, Tedros and I agreed to head to Mendefera located 45 miles southwest of Asmara. With Tedros being a rich boy, and me knowing the location of my mother's purse, there was no issue with finding enough money to sustain us for a day. So, we decided to go to the bus station and purchase a bus ticket for Mendefera. This decision for two 12-year-olds was outrageous by any standard in Eritrea but we did it anyway.

The last time I had boarded a regional bus was before the war situation in Asmara had intensified – when our entire school was going on an excursion to Keren. The memory of that trip had left me with an incredible feeling that was still fresh in my mind. The popular songs playing in the bus, as it drove up and down the winding roads to Keren, left me with an impression that was hard to describe in words. That made me forget that I was embarked on a very dangerous adventure this time. I was excited to experience a great bus ride to Mendefera.

Tedros and I didn't know what to expect once we got to Mendefera, a city we had never been to. We had no idea where we would go after reaching Mendefera to find the fighters. The fighters could have been 10 miles outside Mendefera or 40 miles – we had no clue. But for me, the idea of experiencing the unknown was all the motivation I needed.

We boarded the bus together with more than 50 other people. The cargo in this bus was very different from the one I had taken during my excursion to Keren. Most people were going home after a business trip to Asmara or were heading to Mendefera to do business. This meant that people had all kinds of luggage. The most annoying load was chickens stuffed in the overhead compartment. The smell of the chickens combined with 50 people packed in a small bus with no air conditioning was too much for us two city boys. On top of this, the road to Mendefera entailed some sharp turns and ravines that had ended many lives. Hastily planted crosses at many curbs served as a reminder of the lives lost.

Some people suffering motion sickness started throwing up as the bus drove. The vomit thrown up out of the windows carried on the wind and smashed onto the windows behind, creating a pretty disgusting painting. To add to it all, the songs that I was looking forward to listening to were not being played since by then the Ethiopians had forbidden any Tigrinya songs from playing anywhere. So, the bus trip was not pleasant at all.

After a few hours of driving, we arrived at the Mendefera bus station safely. We were happy to get out of the stinky bus and get some fresh air. But a few minutes later, we were confronted with the jarring reality that this was not our destination and that we would now have to find a way to get out of the city to the remote villages to meet the fighters.

Upon our arrival in Mendefera, achieving our goal of meeting the fighters seemed impossible. The city was too large and maze-like. We felt overwhelmed. But despite all the distraction and sense of being lost, we never lost sight of the purpose of our visit – to see the fighters and possibly join them.

We didn't have a map of the city and we didn't know who and what to ask for. In addition, time was not on our side. Even with all the odds stacked against us, we were in a good mood. After a short discovery walk in the city, we decided to rent bicycles. Luckily for us, bicycles were not forbidden in Mendefera at that time. Bicycle rental was by the hour and we didn't have enough money for a full day. In addition, our goal was to move out of the city. If everything went well, we might never return to the city. So, we decided to take a very bold step that could have been very dangerous and landed us in jail.

We stopped two teenagers we met in the city and asked them if they knew where the Eritrean fighters were in the vicinity of Mendefera. For any person with common sense, the expected answer to our question for obvious safety reasons would be, *"No, we don't know,"* followed by *"How stupid can these two dorks be?"* However, teenagers seem to share the same inherent stupidity everywhere. After a short deliberation, the two boys told us to go to the nearest town called Adi Mengoti – that we might be able to find them there. If we did not, we would have to try another town a few miles further.

Encouraged by the cooperation we received, we further asked, "What is the best way to get there?" They gave us directions and told us how long it was going to take on foot. But with some cash in hand, we were in no mood to walk. The best idea we could come up with was to rent bicycles. But how would we return them if we decided to go further on? So, we asked them if they would ride with us to the town so that they could return the rented bicycles for us. Ironically, we were concerned about who was going to return the bicycles to the renter, but we were not concerned whatsoever about who was going to return us home. The two teenagers volunteered to return the bicycles and agreed to join our game of innocent adventurism, thereby risking their lives as well.

We rented two very old cycles. The renters, I am sure, thought that we would rent the bicycles for an hour of pleasure ride. With two persons on each bicycle, we started our journey to the nearest exit checkpoint. Since the teenagers were older than Tedros and me, we trusted them unconditionally. They knew the way to Adi Mengoti and they rode the bicycles. As we zigzagged through Mendefera, Tedros and I were enjoying the city as if we had come sightseeing. As we reached the outskirts of Mendefera, the checkpoint became visible and the crowd of people on the streets thinned. It was only then that it hit us that this was no picnic but a serious trip that could change or end our lives forever.

At the checkpoint, none of the guards detected the very unnatural composition of our team or the nervousness we were feeling. I am not sure what my friend Tedros, who had never crossed any checkpoints before in his life, was thinking, but he surely didn't look nervous or shifty, else we would have been in trouble. So, we passed the checkpoint and headed toward Adi Mengoti, riding across rolling hills that seemed to never end.

We reached the town and started asking the villagers where the liberation fighters were in the area. None of the villagers was willing to tell us since they were suspicious that we might be operating on the instructions of the Ethiopian soldiers in Mendefera. After we told them our story – that we had come from Asmara – the villagers became even more suspicious. For them, this was an unlikely, unbelievable, and stupid story that could only be made up by teenagers. So, our chance of getting any information was nil.

Frustrated by the lack of cooperation and unavailability of other options, we decided to return to Mendefera and head to another town on the other side of Mendefera. On the way back, there was little conversation and excitement. Our butts were sore from riding on the unpaved roads sitting on cushion-less bicycle seats.

By the time we reached the city, it was already getting late and we were very hungry. After a lot of arguments, we decided on a sensible course of action. We told the two teenagers to return the bicycles and that we would come back another day to try out another town. We thanked the boys for their help, gave them money to pay for the rental, and headed toward the bus station. At that moment, we were not sure what we were going to do next. Would we stay in Mendefera for the night or go back to Asmara?

It was getting late and for safety reasons buses did not depart after 4 p.m. The steep ravines and sharp turns of the road to Asmara were very dangerous. So, we seriously contemplated finding a cheap hotel to stay the night in Mendefera. Little did we know that hotels would never accept 12- and 11-year-old boys without adult supervision, not to mention the exorbitant amount of money they would ask.

Luckily, while we were looking for a food place, we saw a small bus on the main road to Asmara loading people. Instantly, we ran to the bus and asked the driver if he was heading to Asmara. He said it was the last bus heading to Asmara for the day. We immediately boarded the bus and headed to Asmara despite our empty stomachs.

Once on the bus, Tedros and I realized we had serious work to do on what we were going to tell our parents. Especially for Tedros, this was a very important consideration. He was afraid his mother was going to tear him apart for the irresponsible action he took. Realizing our houses were located next to each other with only a fence separating them, I feared the violence could easily spill over to my house. I started to worry about how my mother was going to react. The proximity of Tedros's house would affect how I was going to be inducted back into my own home. Unfortunately, with the packed bus, we couldn't talk loudly about our problem, so we suffered quietly for hours thinking of the many horrendous scenarios that might unfold once we reached our respective homes.

We arrived at the Asmara bus station safely and rushed to our homes, a 30-minute walk away. We were pressed for time for two reasons; first, we only had 30 minutes to get our stories straight in case we were cross-examined by our mothers. Secondly, the 7 p.m. evening curfew was approaching fast and we couldn't afford to walk slowly or take time to think about our story. As such, the walk which would have otherwise seemed very long felt like seconds. Before we knew it, we arrived at the front doors of our homes and it was time to say goodbye and wish each other good luck.

As I walked alongside the fence, past our main villa toward the two service rooms in the backyard, I could imagine the yelling and screaming in Tedros's house. The shear thought of what could happen to Tedros sent chills down my spine. I was terrified that his mother would come into our house roaring and that soon I too would join the screaming. Luckily, his mother refrained from taking this quite plausible action and I was spared.

As I faced my mother, I could tell she felt helpless. With my father gone for an extended work assignment in Addis, she could only handle so much. I had a nonviolent welcome from my mother. However, I paid a big price for my actions. Tedros was now forbidden from going outside or playing with me for an indefinite time. Not surprisingly, I was seen as a very dangerous kid who had to be avoided. I would have done the same if I were in his mother's position.

The Mendefera visit was not a successful undertaking. On the contrary, I lost my privileges to play with my best friend and learned that finding freedom fighters was not a simple undertaking.

5.   *MiG21 Down - Keren*

18 June 2009, Iberia flight from Palma Majorca to Madrid: I am returning from Majorca, one of Spain's best islands in the Mediterranean. With its gorgeous coastline and natural setting, I expected this trip to be a memorable one. Memorable it was, but for a different reason. Normally, I travel in casual outfits and my luggage is checked in to avoid dragging it through transit airports. This time, KLM lost my luggage on the way to Majorca. With my meeting being the next morning, I had no choice but to go from the airport straight to the shopping center. With less than an hour left to close, I went on a shopping spree for full business attire, including a belt and shoes. I tested my shopping skills under pressure and managed to show up at the meeting with Air Europa presentable. Going forward, there will be no checked-in baggage for me.

In the absence of my good friend Tedros, I started looking for other friends to play with and share my adventurous dreams with. My cousin Amine lived only 2 miles away. He was a nice and pleasant boy to be around. He was raised in a very religious environment and a very loving family. He was very quiet and had never been in harm's way before, so the odds of getting him to join my next adventure were not that great. Yet, the only option I had was to befriend him and see if I could get him to join me in my plans.

As I gave attention to Amine, he would find it enjoyable to come to my home on his way from school and go to church together with me on Sundays. One day, I proposed that we try to go out of town and meet with the freedom fighters. Surprisingly, Amine agreed, and his only worry was what we were going to tell our parents when we came back. Knowing that I had never been punished for my actions before, I told him we would make up a credible story so that he wouldn't get into trouble.

My primary concern was actually where to take him so that we could have a successful trip. I suggested we travel to Keren (about 56 miles from Asmara) by bus and see what was out there. My obsession with exploration and the confidence with which I was trying to go out of my limits must have had an impact on him. He agreed, and we managed to save enough money for our bus tickets.

We planned to take the bus from downtown Asmara on the following Saturday morning. We boarded the bus and sat on my favorite seat in the back so that I could see the entire bus in front of me. As the bus started its journey to Keren, we realized that it would pass through our neighborhood, since our home was located on the main road to Keren. The name of our street was "Keren Road." This was risky because if some of our neighbors boarded the bus then we would be caught in the act. We were also afraid that we would be spotted by our friends as we passed by. So, we agreed to duck out of sight until we passed our neighborhood.

Our bus crossed our neighborhood without any incident, reaching the checkpoint, which was less than a mile from my home. We heaved a sigh of relief and sat in our seats more comfortably now. Checkpoints were very interesting to me, in that I would witness the brutal action of the Ethiopian soldiers against our people first-hand. I would also have an up-close view of the weapons they carry. This fueled my desire to join the freedom fighters even more.

We passed the checkpoint, and the bus started to drive through the rolling hills. As we headed deeper into the no man's land, I scouted for signs of battle, looking for burned tanks, trucks, or dead soldiers. For more than a 30-minute drive, we saw nothing but barren land and occasional cattle grazing. Then, suddenly, everyone began looking out of the right-hand-side windows of the bus and the gasps and exclamations of astonishment grew louder. Amine and I fought our way to the right side of the bus to get a glimpse of the action.

This was what I had always waited for and dreamt to see. Perfectly positioned on the mountainside facing the road, lay a monument of the heroism of the freedom fighters, completely charred but still, a visible trophy that no one could take away – an Ethiopian jet fighter (most likely a Northrop F-5 or MiG21) shot down by the freedom fighters – like a museum piece for every traveler to see. The driver slowed down just enough to give us the full view, but not too slow to be noticed by the Ethiopian army that might have been in the area.

With this incredible early pay-off to my adventure, my hopes were high that this trip was going to satisfy my thirst for what I had imagined taking place on the battlefield. As we drove deeper toward Keren, the asphalt road got rougher. The damage caused by the metal chain tracks of the Ethiopian tanks was unforgiving, and the bus started rattling.

We came across a bridge (Tekor Bridge) that had been wrecked so badly that the bus had to go around the bridge crossing a dry riverbed. This was very exciting. Further down the road, we saw burned trucks and a couple of tanks stuck in cliffs from where they couldn't get out.

Now, my 12-year-old brain was working very hard to interpret the sights and imagine what could have taken place in the area. I pictured my uncles and family members who had joined the freedom fighters burning these tanks and trucks. The exciting news that I used to hear from my grandfather Aboy Tseghay about the heroism of the fighters was now laid bare for me to see in this amazing landscape. We had a long way to go to Keren, but with this scenery, Amine and I were not bothered about time or what would happen after our arrival.

After a grueling but very exciting trip of four hours, we arrived in Keren. The bus would remain at the stop for one hour before heading back to Asmara through the same route. Normally, I would continue the journey to find the fighters, but with the exclusive scene of the road littered with damaged tanks and trucks waiting for me on the way back, there was no question that I would be the first to step on the bus returning to Asmara.

So, we entered the same bus we had come in. During the one-hour layover, we managed to see people who looked and dressed very differently than us. Keren is a predominantly Muslim city, and many of the lowlanders have different customs than highlanders. Our stay in Keren was short, but the scenery was picturesque.

With empty stomachs, we sat in our favorite seat that allowed us to see the jet fighter better. After all, there were no cell phones or cameras in those days – it was all about having a photographic memory. On the way back, we enjoyed the scenery even more since we knew where to look this time.

Whenever there wasn't much to see, Amine and I had to engage in an intense argument cooking a story on what to tell our parents. After exploring so many ideas, we agreed to tell our parents that we got arrested by the Ethiopian soldiers and spent the entire day in prison. After all, the soldiers were the bad boys that were terrorizing the city. Why not join them virtually and in our imagination – that would make a believable story.

We got back home way before curfew and told the story. To our surprise, no one believed us. To add to it, Amine was such a disciplined and a good Christian boy that cooking a story like that was deemed impossible to come from him. So, we got the benefit of the doubt and made it out unscathed, but with no visible sympathy from our parents. Until this day, I do not know what our parents must have thought when we told them this stupid story that no one should believe. Regardless, this trip was one of my most memorable ones and served as a catalyst for my next adventures.

Except for my first adventure of heading to Woki Zager at age 10, my father never knew about my deepest emotions and desire to join the freedom fighters. However, at this point, my mother must have informed him that I was going outside of Asmara in search of freedom fighters. One day, he asked me to join him for a one-on-one chat in the formal living room where only adults were allowed to go. He was very worried about me. He advised me not to try to go out of the city ever again. He said he would have been the first to join the fighters if it was not for the love he had for our family. Many of his friends had joined the struggle for freedom and the only reason he was staying behind was to raise us.

The conversation felt unreal and odd to me. I never imagined my father openly speaking to me about all that was happening in Eritrea. Through my bold actions, I had forced my way into adulthood to a point where my father, the man I feared and respected the most, was talking to me about a topic that no one dared to mention.

My father, unlike my mother, was a calm and composed gentleman who spoke with a serious tone. There was depth behind every word he chose. And in my heart, I felt guilty for causing him so much trouble, but I was fascinated by the fighters and wanted to fight against the Ethiopian soldiers. So, for me, despite my father's advice and call to focus on my education, there was no choice. I was determined to join the struggle, a struggle that, in my humble judgment, would not last long.

For me, joining the struggle meant that I would meet all the young family members and neighbors who had left Asmara to fight for the liberation of Eritrea. I pictured us fighting side by side against the Ethiopian soldiers in a movie-like setting where only the enemies die and suffer defeat. If something happened to me, so be it. After all, at age 11, I had experienced a horrible accident where a half-inch-thick metal rod had pierced my thigh on one side and come out on the other. I knew what it meant to be wounded and in pain, or so I thought.

On a Sunday afternoon, I climbed a wall that divided our home from our neighbors and stood on the edge facing down. I was talking to my friends who were on the street 20 feet below me. Directly to my left, about 5 feet below where I stood, a metal railing had been installed on top of our garage balcony, separating our home from the street. Facing upward a row of hundreds of spikes, each ½-inch thick and 10-inch-long, were welded on top of the balcony railing to prevent intruders from climbing into our house. I don't remember how it happened, but as I tried to climb down, I slipped and fell.

My body plummeted toward the ground head down. Miraculously, my right leg flung and hit one of the spikes. The spike entered my upper thigh and protruded on the lower end, stopping my inertia toward the ground. Suspended in the air, held up by a few muscle fibers that refused to tear apart, my body dangled on the outside of the railings. If my thigh muscles tore, I would have certainly plummeted to the ground, which would have meant certain death.

Helpless, my friends screamed in horror and banged on the door to alarm my family. I managed to hold on to the railings supporting my upper body weight until adults came to rescue me. Finally, my uncle and my mother lifted me off the spikes and saved my life. I remember a single trail of blood was dripping from the gaping wound that the spike protruded from. The entry wound however didn't have blood, it looked like it was stuffed with chicken breast meat. They rushed me to the hospital using our neighbor's Volkswagen. A six months' rehabilitation followed, and I made it without any disability, just two "battle scars" on my thigh.

So, armed with this experience, I felt I could handle anything on the battlefield. I never realized that, in that very moment, some of the family and friends who had joined the struggle for freedom had already lost their lives and that I would never see them again. I was eager to join the struggle before it was all over. As far as my imagination goes, the war was about to end soon and it would end with the fighters marching through the road from Keren to Asmara, straight through my neighborhood in victory. So, I continued my search for fighters.

6. *Fiat Talero - Woki Duba*

Triggered by my adventurous trip to Woki Zager, and emboldened by my experience in Keren and Mendefera, I managed to make several more trips to remote towns in search of fighters: Woki Zager, Mendefera, Keren, Woki Duba, Adi Shmagle, Adi Kuncy, Tsazega, and Emba Derho. Mostly, I would go alone or with only one friend at a time. An exception was the trip to Emba Derho, for which I managed to convince three of my friends to join me. But the last trip I made to Woki Duba and Adi Shmagle was something special.

It was one early morning in October 1977, a month before I turned 13 years old. My mother wanted me and my uncle, Fitsum, who had a sleepover at our home that night, to go to Fiat Talero, the iconic petrol station in downtown Asmara, to fetch the gasoline my grandfather had saved for us. She gave us an empty metal container to take with us that we could leave behind so that my grandfather would use it the next time he got a chance to save some for us. With the city being under siege, there was a severe scarcity of all necessities. Water and gasoline were especially difficult to come by.

My mother told us to go on foot to the petrol station – which was about a 30-minute walk – and to take the bus on the way back since then we'd be carrying 20 gallons of gasoline. I felt that was not fair since the empty metal container we had to carry was heavy and we deserved to go by bus both ways. So, I started a little argument about that, and my mother was not happy. In her strict way, she ordered us to walk anyway. Noticing the uncompromising attitude of my mother, my uncle and I, mumbling and whining, started to head to our destination to fetch gasoline.

A few minutes later, before we turned a corner, my mother came out of the house and started yelling my name in a bid to get me back to talk to her. Not knowing what she wanted and being as angry as I was, I refused to listen to her and kept walking. As her voice got louder to get my attention, I visibly refused by waving my arm as a sign of angry rejection. This was the first time I ever stood up against my mother and refused her orders so publicly.

Perplexed by my refusal to listen, my mother shouted, "I will show you what you deserve when you come back." At that point, I realized the gravity of my mistake, instantly concluding that going back home any time soon would not be a pleasant experience. I dropped the metal container on the ground and told my uncle that I was fed up and would no longer go back home. As impulsive as that, I went off to a place that I always wanted to go.

Leaving my uncle and the container behind, I started to walk off the paved roads and head toward the checkpoint on the west side of the city. My uncle, not knowing what hit him, walked back home to my mother to find out why she had been calling us back. She had changed her mind and wanted to give us more money, meeting my request to take a bus both ways.

Unfortunately, I didn't know this, and, having committed an offense, I embarked on a few-hour walking adventure to see my favorite friends, the liberation fighters. This time, I headed to a place called Woki Duba and vowed to never return home.

Woki Duba was a town located on a hill a few miles away, which overlooked the Ethiopian barracks set up on the outskirts of Asmara, a former US military station for massive radars, known as the Deep Space Intelligence Center. The town had changed hands many times between the fighters and the Ethiopian army. As a result, the houses in the town had been destroyed by aerial and artillery bombardments. The Ethiopian soldiers had also committed heinous crimes against the inhabitants by deliberately burning houses, killing men and women.

Often, the battles took place in the fields between Asmara and Woki Duba. In fact, from my house, we had an unobstructed view of the battlefield. We used to see explosions and smoke billowing from the fields right from our balcony above the garage. I had a panoramic view and saw the village Woki Duba burn, sometimes for days, the smoke rising above the village in slow motion, reaching various heights, intensities, and shades of gray. It was as if the smoke clouds were stretching as high as possible to alarm God of what was happening to Woki Duba.

That day, however, Woki Duba was calm and occupied by the fighters, and served as the center of frontline trenches surrounding Asmara. My adventure now would entail walking through the killing field that both sides normally observe for any suspicious movements. I crossed the checkpoint uneventfully. I worked hard to shift gears from visiting a gas station in the heart of the city to walking on a dirt road directly toward the town of Woki Duba in broad daylight. After 30 minutes of walking, I felt the sun get hot. The city noise was replaced with a terrifying silence. The only sound I heard was that of my footsteps. I started questioning my decision, and for a moment, the thought of going back crossed my mind.

Suddenly, on the right-hand side of the field, I saw hundreds of Ethiopian soldiers moving out of their barracks in a formation that resembled military training. They were probably about 500 meters away from the road where I was walking. I was afraid that they would catch me and send me back to Asmara. But fortunately, their advance was much slower than my pace of walking and I managed to get to the town of Woki Duba.

In the highlands of Eritrea, most of the villages have a church that towers above all the homes. Woki Duba's church was built on top of a hill, overlooking the town and the fields around the town. The fighters used this hill as an observation post to command the fields around Woki Duba and to give them a direct line of sight at the Ethiopian barracks on the outskirts of Asmara.

The town was deserted and I was the only person walking in the open. Right as I started walking up the hill toward the church, I heard very loud shots. For a minute, I was completely disoriented and didn't know what to think. As I got closer to the top of the hill, a civilian carrying an AK-47 came out and asked me what I was doing in the town. I told him that I had come to see the fighters and I had an uncle named Tesfalem who had joined the fighters a few years back. I don't remember vividly what our discussion was as he walked me to the observation post. He handed me over to the fighters there and he disappeared.

The fighters were observing the Ethiopian army's movements and had shot a few rounds to let the soldiers know that they would be better off staying back. The Ethiopian army's movement and the subsequent warning shots triggered an alert for every unit in the vicinity of the town. From all directions, the fighters kept moving into the town, taking positions to confront the forward-moving army.

The movement of the army, coinciding with my arrival at the location of the fighters, complicated my situation. The fighters suspected that I might be an informant linked to the Ethiopian army movement. So, one of the fighters took me into a dark room and interrogated me in a threatening manner. Since I was a young boy, he probably thought scaring me would make me confess the real reason I came to the place. After about 10 minutes of interrogation, I was declared safe and handed over to the commander of the unit.

The commander was a nice-looking, skinny gentleman with a Palestinian scarf around his neck. He carried a foldable AK-47 on his back with the barrel pointing down. He was always accompanied by a younger fighter who was a radio operator. I stayed with him during the entire time of preparation for the eventual attack from the Ethiopian army. The commotion and alert however turned out to be false – the Ethiopian army was simply training and did not threaten the town at all.

As a child, this was one of the happiest days of my life. I received full attention from the fighters and had a chance to smell, touch, carry and admire their armaments. After many attempts to see some action, this time I even had the opportunity to imagine what a battle with the Ethiopian army could look like. Unfortunately (or fortunately) for me, no battle took place, and the fighters were instructed to go back to their bases. The commander and I followed.

On the way back to their base, a few miles behind the town Woki Duba, I remember the fighters talking about how they would have trapped the Ethiopian army in the hills around the town had the army dared to take them on. They talked about this as if it was some sort of a game where you get to have fun fighting each other. It reinforced my desire to join them. The seemingly inconsequential depiction of how they would fight the army gave me the impression that fighting was a lot of fun.

The walk from the first line trenches to the base was very scenic with small rolling hills covered with brushes and a small pedestrian road that wound through the hills. The view of fighters trekking along this narrow winding road against the backdrop of the setting sun and expansive, orange skies left me with an image that I have not forgotten until this day. It was stunningly beautiful.

Once we arrived at the base, a place called Adi Shmagle, everyone relaxed. As a child, I had never been given so much attention by young Eritrean men and women. I sang for them and told them stories. Some of them tested my education level by asking questions like "What does environment mean?" in English. This was the first thing we were taught in seventh-grade science class and we were expected to know the answer. I regurgitated, "Environment is things around us ...." They all enjoyed my stories and were happy. After all, it was one of few moments that they would have a chance to see a child from the heart of Asmara, reminding them of the childhood they had deprived themselves of.

After a fun-filled evening under a kerosene lamp, it was time to go to bed. Of course, there was no bed or cover to keep me warm nor was there a pillow to rest my head. One of the fighters untied a thin sheet from his waist and shared it with me as our bedsheet. He gave me his military gear, a leather holster filled with hundreds of bullets, and told me to use it as a pillow. The choice for my pillow was between using the leather holster or my shoes. I thankfully accepted his offer to use the holster as a pillow.

The night was rough. The room we slept in was infested with fleas called *qunchi*, and it was very cold. Although it was a sleepless night, I fell in love with the fighters and became even more determined to join their ranks.

In the morning, the fighters told me that fighting requires physical strength and that I was not up to the task. To prove their case, they asked me to carry the full military gear that a typical fighter would put on as he runs through the hills for days. I was very excited to carry the bullets, hand grenades, foldable AK-47, and a spare RPG rocket. I felt like Rambo! Too bad selfies weren't a thing back then! The fighters must have been both bewildered and sorry for such a young boy to come out of the city alone in search of fighters. Knowing the truth about living as a freedom fighter and the hell they went through to stay alive, I can only imagine, their hearts must have been filled with sadness at my naïve dreams.

It didn't take long for the commander to decide I needed to return home. But, given my exceptional desire and eagerness to work for them, he didn't want to let this opportunity go either. So, he said that I could work for them from within Asmara. To get a detailed plan which suited my age, they asked me to come back a week later to meet the man in charge of Asmara operations.

After a night with the fighters, returning to Asmara once again was a huge disappointment, but I felt very proud this time. At least I had stayed a night outside my home demonstrating my commitment to join the fighters at whatever cost. With tears streaming down my cheeks, it was time for me to leave Adi Shmagle and return home. The commander walked me to the edge of the town and suggested that I avoid the Woki Duba observation post since the Ethiopian soldiers monitor the location using binoculars.

As I began the walk down the winding road leading toward the checkpoint at Asmara, I was deeply immersed in planning my next trip and how to best convince the fighters to take me into their fold. As I got closer to Asmara, I also began thinking about how my return home would go. Would my mother beat the hell out of me for refusing to obey her orders the day before? Or, would she be shocked and thrilled that I was back home?

As a mother, she must have been terrified to lose her child in such a silly way. Now that I am a father of three daughters, I cannot begin to imagine the pain she must have gone through to lose her son for two days while her husband was gone and in a city where killing was a daily occurrence. After my father was relocated to Addis, raising seven kids as a single mother was already very difficult for her. I was the second-oldest kid and the oldest boy in the house, and by threatening to disappear I was in no way helpful.

As I approached our neighborhood, many kids who had been terrified by my disappearance were elated to see me back again. Some of them ran toward me and others ran to my home to tell my mother the good news. I am not sure what I was thinking, but I remember entering our home flanked by many young boys full of curiosity. I felt very proud of what I had accomplished, but at the same time ashamed that I had returned home with nothing to show for my trip – again.

My adventurous behavior had impressed my friends As for my mother, she was relieved and very happy to see me come home after two days. I knew her subdued reaction hid so much pain, agony, and a sense of helplessness, but I was also fighting a demon in me that didn't care about her feelings.

7. The Alternative - Emba Derho

Back in Asmara, I couldn't sleep, and the week that passed felt like years. I was so impatient to go back and meet the fighters again. But I was not happy with what they wanted me to do, which was to stay in Asmara while working for them. This work typically consists of intelligence-gathering and occasionally executing high-ranking Ethiopian officers. This was not what I was interested in, regardless of my competence, or the lack thereof, in executing the work. I wanted to join the fighters and come back at night to attack the Ethiopian soldiers as was the case every evening. But I had no choice. This was my best chance of somehow establishing a connection with them. So, I was determined to return a week later to Adi Shmagle to meet the man in charge of Asmara "operations".

In the meantime, something exciting happened. I found a pistol magazine fully loaded with bullets lying on the road. I kept it under my mattress, and every time I was alone in my room, I would take out the bullets and admire their golden shininess, not realizing how dangerous it was to have guns or bullets at home. The forbidden charm of deadly tools added more fuel to my desire to meet with the fighters again. I could smuggle the bullets and claim that I helped provision the fighters with bullets. Since the fighters' motto was "We fight our enemy with its weapons," smuggling enemy bullets to the fighters would be a major accomplishment, so I thought.

Unfortunately, around the time I was supposed to go back to meet with them, a heavy battle broke out around Woki Duba and Adi Shmagle that lasted for days, making it impossible to head to that area. The battle intensified daily and there was no end in sight.

Determined, I decided I would head to another area where no battle was taking place. I made a plan to take the road that leads to the town of Emba Derho, about 15 miles northeast of where the battle was taking place. This was the same road I took during my first trip to Woki Zager, so I was familiar with the area.

A few days before my planned departure, I told a few of my friends the details of my experience meeting the fighters in Adi Shmagle. Three of my friends were so excited they were willing to join me. I told them that we need to strategize and make sure that this time we would succeed and never come back to Asmara.

The four of us met very early in the morning and started our journey. Because of the battle that was raging on the west side near Adi Shmagle, we thought it was risky to pass through the checkpoint as a group. We were afraid the soldiers would be suspicious of four boys leaving town early in the morning. So, we decided to sneak out between two checkpoints – which was very risky for two reasons. One, if the soldiers saw us, they could fire at us thinking we were smuggling weapons. Two, the place between the two checkpoints could potentially have landmines planted to prevent fighters from entering Asmara. Also, unknown to my friends, I was carrying a pistol magazine with eight bullets in my pocket. I planned to give it to the fighters and hopefully show them my bravery. I never bothered to consider that if the soldiers caught me with bullets in my pocket, it would result in unfortunate consequences. Yet, for a young mind, and at that point, any risk seemed acceptable.

We walked to a church that was located on the edge of the city together with early-morning worshippers. Once we reached the church, we started walking slowly away. Fortunately, no soldier noticed our movement, or if they did, they must have correctly assessed that we were kids. Also, no landmines were present. We slipped out of the city safely.

After walking for two hours, we finally arrived in Emba Derho. Here, we asked the local kids if Eritrean fighters were present and they took us to an observation point in the town where we found a group of fighters from the EPLF (Eritrean People Liberation Front). The EPLF was a splinter organization that was different from the ELF (Eritrean Liberation Front). All I knew about the EPLF was that one of my uncles was with them. My previous encounter in Adi Shmagle where I had stayed the night was with the ELF fighters. But, for me, all that mattered at that point was to be part of any one of them.

Although, I was not the oldest of all four of my friends, I was physically bolder and had a better chance of being accepted by the fighters. After talking to the fighters and explaining our intention of joining the movement, I found out that even with the physical advantage I had, the EPLF fighters were not interested in me at all. Presenting them with the pistol magazine holding eight bullets that I had smuggled from Asmara didn't move the needle. They took the magazine and told us to go back to Asmara and work on our physical condition before they would accept us. In their words: "Go back, eat another quintal of food and come back." We were too young, we were told. I don't even recall them thanking me for the eight bullets I got for free.

I was 13 years old at the time. At that age I was the most experienced of all, considering the number of encounters I had had with the fighters in the years before. So, I felt that the fighters should at least accept me and send my friends back to Asmara. I tried my best to convince the fighters of that but to no avail. With no sympathy, the EPLF fighters chased us out of their post.

I almost felt disrespected. I told my friends that it was their fault that the fighters were not accepting us. I felt that they behaved like kids and were too young to be my friends for this mission. I suggested that they go back to Asmara while I stayed there to see what my chances were of being accepted.

To my surprise, they listened to me and agreed to return to Asmara. By then, it was almost 3 p.m. and we hadn't had any food. So, we decided to go to the center of the town to see if we could ask someone to give us food.

While we were waiting in a small shop where they sell tea, we met a young boy named Abdu who also was looking to join the fighters. We told him our experience and that I planned to separate from the younger-looking boys who were spoiling my chance of being accepted by the fighters.

Abdu was around 15 years old and physically stronger than any one of us. He came from a town 40 miles away. He was happy that he had found a friend in this unknown situation. I was also happy that I had found someone who might increase my chances of being accepted.

So, we started asking the villagers where else could we find fighters. Some of the youngsters advised us to go to the towns west of the main road. The problem with that idea was that the battle was still raging in the west and we were afraid that we would get caught in the crossfire. We could hear the sounds of heavy artillery and mortar in the distance. However, the villagers told us that we didn't have to walk that far west. They said within an hour of walking we should be able to meet some of the fighters in the vicinity.

Although Abdu was a total stranger to me, I trusted him fully and decided to stick with him and let my other friends go back to Asmara. Abdu and I decided to separate from the team. Casually, we hugged each other and waved goodbye to the three younger-looking boys. I didn't feel bad ditching them because I was convinced their presence did not help my case.

Abdu and I started our journey hoping we would find a willing group of fighters, but after traveling for more than an hour, we found none. We were very frustrated and I started thinking about how to get back home. By now, my friends might have reached Asmara and would be telling my mother about what they did and where I was. Abdu and I decided to return to Emba Derho before darkness set in.

Fearing that it would get dark, we started walking fast, but I was tired and very hungry. Abdu kept telling me that we would be okay, we had nothing to fear. "Even if it gets dark," he said, "there is nothing to worry about since there are no hyenas in this area" – a scary idea I hadn't thought of before.

As we were approaching Emba Derho, we saw a group of fighters approaching us from the opposite direction. Since they were coming from Emba Derho, we thought these were the fighters that were in the town who had refused to accept us. When we got closer, however, we could not believe what we saw. Amongst the group of fighters who were walking in an orderly line, we could recognize my three friends who were supposed to go back home. Shockingly, they were all carrying a Kalashnikov (AK-47) on their shoulder.

Apparently, after we left Emba Derho, my friends encountered a unit of ELF fighters who were willing to accept them and in the process, they allowed them to carry their guns for fun. As the fighters started interrogating Abdu and me, we started laughing at each other and the fighters became suspicious. After we told them the whole story, they allowed us to join them and started our journey west where we had just come from. What a happy ending!

But, I was jealous that I didn't have a weapon to carry while the other three younger boys were showing off their load. After noticing my curiosity, a young fighter by the name Mulugheta Wodi-Batsi (translation: boy from Massawa) offered his weapon to me to carry, which I accepted delightfully.

The Kalashnikov was one with a folding metal butt. The curved bullet case, a signature look of Kalashnikov, was not made from metal; instead, it was one of the rarely seen cases with orange-brownish color made of reinforced glass fiber and marble texture. I felt that the weapon was the most attractive toy I had ever held in my hand. I loved every look of the weapon. I curiously looked at every detail and found it to be the best toy again and again. When I carried it on my right shoulder while holding the forward-pointing barrel in my hand, the curved case hugging my shoulder helped the gun balance perfectly. I had no problem carrying it for miles.

After a long walk, we stopped for a break. It was almost dark. Some of the fighters spread away from the main road to do their business in the bushes. Just like little kids who refuse to go to the bathroom, I said "I don't need to." I wanted to sit and have all the time to admire the Kalashnikov.

My other friends came to join me and by then they had given their Kalashnikovs back to the owners and wanted to admire the one

I had. We all started pulling and pushing on it. It was like three lions wrestling for a pound of meat. Before we knew it a bullet was loaded and someone pulled the trigger and *boom!* it went.

The sound was deafening and one of my friends was so scared that he couldn't talk for a few minutes. For me, it was very amusing to see my friends being scared. I did not realize how close we had come to being killed on the first day of our adventure. The fighters took away the guns from us and that was the end of touching a gun before training.

We continued our journey on foot, and late in the evening, we reached a town called Tsazega. Once in Tsazega, the fighters told us that they would have to leave us there. They would have to continue their journey to where the battle was raging while we would stay there waiting for other fighters to take us. Although I did not like to see Mulugheta Wodi-Batsi, who was my mentor for the trip, go, I was fine staying in the town as long as they didn't send me back home.

There was only one serious problem. The town was the birthplace of my mother. So, if any family members in the town were told by my family that I was missing, they might come to check for me. If they knew I was there, they could plead with the fighters to return me home. Fearing that I would be discovered by the family members, I did my best to stay out of sight and remain inconspicuous.

Late in the evening, a Fiat N3 loaded with corrugated metal arrived in Tsazega and we were told to climb up the truck. Once I boarded the truck, I sat next to a young boy named Yonas, a typical 13-year-old Asmarino boy from Akriya district, a densely populated part of Asmara. He asked me to sit closer to him so we could talk. I moved closer, a move that cost me my pants. The corrugated metal tore my pants and there went my only pants. The tear was so large that the only thing covering my butt was the bright red underpants I was wearing.

I had loved the pants. I usually wore shorts, but those were my first pair of pants. My father had brought them from Addis Ababa a year ago for himself, but my mother had hated them. She felt they didn't match my father's age and status, so she altered them and gave them to me. She was a great tailor.

While my father was working in Addis, he would come back to Asmara once a year to see us. He was expected to come to Asmara two days later for a special occasion, the birth of my sister Simret. I left on the same day a small party was organized to celebrate the arrival of my baby sister. Traditionally, the event is called Ge'at and celebrates the third day of a baby's life. The entire neighborhood and family were expected to come to congratulate my mother.

I planned my departure deliberately on that day. I wanted to avoid my mother noticing that I was gone. Sometimes, if she knew I was not around, she would dispatch a search team in the surrounding villages and I would get caught before I even reached the fighters. But this time, she had just given birth and was in a weak condition. With the Ge'at celebration, I knew she would be so distracted she would neither notice my absence nor be in a position to dispatch a search operation on time.

I didn't realize how much pain I would be causing her by leaving at this celebratory moment, unfortunately. For my father, it was even more painful. My father normally brought a lot of gifts from Addis for everyone, including me. But he would find out I was not there anymore. He had not seen me for a year because of his assignment and two days before he came home I was gone.

In hindsight, that was the worst moment for my mother and father to hear such devastating news. I destroyed their happy moment, the birth of my sister. But with no regard for such emotional pain, I decided to carry out the departure as planned.

8. *Point of No Return - Meqerka*

Sitting on top of the corrugated metal that was loaded on the Fiat N3 truck, we traveled late in the evening from Tsazega to a town called Meqerka. Meqerka was a central location where the new boys and girls like me would be gathered from various towns and be registered formally to join the liberation movement.

Later, I learned that my grandfather had arrived in Tsazega just minutes after we left. Based on the description he gave them, he was told that I might have been in the truck that departed to Meqerka minutes before his arrival. It was too late and too far for him to go to Meqerka. My mother, despite the distraction Ge'at party, managed to dispatch the search operation for her son, but this time she was just a few minutes too late.

After spending the night in Meqerka, we met about 60 young people in the morning who were being drafted. We lined up to get registered. It was a very embarrassing morning for me since my red underpants flashed from a good distance through my ripped pants. All I could do was limit my movement and exposure by staying put in one place as much as possible.

After our names were registered, they told us to mentally get ready for a long trip, but it would take a few days before we departed. In Meqerka, while I was feeling more comfortable with each day that passed, my three other friends started to become nervous and dislike the adventure I had sucked them into. They asked me in a serious tone, "Wouldn't it be better if we were to return home?"

That was a non-starter for me, I told them resolutely "no." This was my chance and the closest I had come to be who I wanted to be in life – a liberation fighter. The pain and suffering of my mother and family at that time was not something I considered, even less the challenges ahead of me. They were very unsettled with my response.

For the first time, I officially registered as a volunteer fighter with the ELF. I never understood or bothered to learn what the difference was between ELF and EPLF at that time. The only thing

I knew was that EPLF was the organization that my uncle Solomon was with and ELF was the one that another uncle named Tesfalem was with. It was that simple and I didn't care which group I joined. They both were fighting to liberate Eritrea from the brutal occupation of Ethiopia.

Late in the afternoon, two Fiat N3s, one blue and one red, showed up to pick us up. Loaded with more than 60 young Asmarino boys and girls, the trucks started to move. It was dusk and I was on the second N3 that was following the first one at a reasonable distance, most likely to stay away from the dust plume generated by the tires of the first truck. We started a long journey toward the west, catching the last minutes of the sunset behind the cascade mountains of the highlands.

I had never been so far away from my home. I never asked where we were going. The ride was very uncomfortable, but it felt adventurous and exciting. Late in the evening, we reached a place called Habela. The trucks stopped and everybody was given a chance to take a break. Most of them went to buy a cup of tea and some bought bread or fruit. My friends and I had no money so we were hanging out around the trucks until everybody was done eating or drinking.

My three friends, realizing the danger of traveling so far from home better than me, started to get very serious about returning home. They insisted that we stop now and return to Asmara. Also, the comments we were getting from some of our fellow travelers for being too young made the situation worse. We argued heavily. I told my friends, "*As far as I am concerned, I would see Asmara the day it is liberated, not earlier*". My friends, however, although they were aware of what my mother would say to them when they returned to Asmara without me, made up their minds to go back to Asmara anyway.

When we were in Meqerka, one of my friends had received a blue bedsheet to use as a cover at night. Since it was a small sheet, only he could use it. Now that they decided to return to Asmara, I asked them if I could have the blue sheet to take with me. For some reason, they refused and took it back with them to Asmara. Until this day, I struggle to understand how they couldn't understand I needed it more than they did at that time. They were going back to their cozy homes and I was heading to languish in the jungle for God knows how long. Yet, no sympathy. The only answer I can think of is: we all were teenagers with little common sense.

Soon, the trucks started to blow their horn to signal departure time. My three friends started walking away from the trucks. I asked my friends to tell my mother that I was okay and gave each of them a hug, not realizing that that could be the last hug I would ever get from them. I climbed up the truck and off we disappeared into the darkness of the night.

After long hours of discomfort and bouncing like a tennis ball from left to the right of the truck's metal walls, we finally came to a stop in the middle of nowhere. The engines were working harder, but the truck was not moving. The truck was stuck in the sand of a dry riverbed.

We all jumped down and started pushing the truck to aid its movement. After a long fight, moving the truck inch by inch, we crossed the river. This problem repeated several times in the hours to come. On one occasion, while we were struggling to push the truck, one of the fighters instructed us to get some large tree branches and put them under the wheel of the truck as the wheel was spinning in the dry riverbed. This helped the tires get traction and move the truck along well.

One of the fighters remarked that if the load of the truck had been ammunition that was badly needed by our fighters on the other side of the river, he would have asked each one of us to lay down in front of the wheel so that the truck could make it to the other side and victory could be achieved. One girl asked him, "Do you want all of us to die before we even kill one Ethiopian soldier?" He replied, "You will then have sacrificed your life to save your fellow fighters who will continue the struggle and kill many Ethiopian soldiers." He continued, "This happened in Vietnam where tens of bodies had to be laid underneath a truck's wheel to get the load to those who were fighting the Americans." That was a very frightening thought, and it was my first exposure to radical and revolutionary ideas. Well, the load of the truck this time was just us. Let someone else sacrifice his life to get us across the river, we joked as the truck started to move.

The sun started to rise, and finally, we could see the landscape that I had never seen before. For the first time in my life, I could see the tall trees of *arkobkobay* (Doum Palm) trees in the distance. It was beautiful. I didn't know that these trees were the source of *Akat*, the dry fruit that I used to enjoy eating in Asmara. The sun quickly started to become unbearable and the temperature became hot and humid. I have never been exposed to such temperatures before – 100°F with 70 percent humidity was normal for that time of the year.

As we made our way through the rugged roads, we finally started to see signs of life, but not the ones I was used to. The people looked different, the way they dressed was different, and above all, the way they talked was different. I was so ignorant about my country that I didn't even know some people spoke a different language than Tigrinya in Eritrea, a language spoken in the highlands of Eritrea and the city of Asmara.

I was a bit intimidated by too many unknowns around me. I had no idea where we were going and I started to ask myself why we were going so far away. What I expected was that I would get trained in the neighborhood of Asmara and deployed back to the outskirts to liberate Asmara. For me, Eritrea meant Asmara, nothing else. So, I was confused. But everyone was enjoying the ride and no one was asking any questions, or if any of them were asking questions, they were silent questions directed at themselves. So, my only choice at that moment was to go with the flow and not show any sign of weakness.

We approached a major city. I heard that it was called Agordat. Agordat was one of the major towns that had been liberated from Ethiopian soldiers a few months before. I hated Agordat to the fullest. It was the hottest and most humid place I have ever experienced so far. I had no money to buy myself a cold drink. At this point, I was 110 miles away from home and had traveled for two days through impassable and tortuous roads of more than 125 miles. My body was sore. I needed to rest and stayed the whole day in a bunker of former Ethiopian soldiers while everyone was touring the town. It was a little cooler inside the bunkers.

After a few hours in Agordat, a girl in her early twenties in our group offered me some tangerines to eat. I gladly accepted, not having eaten anything for hours. It felt nice to be noticed by a stranger. Until then, I had felt that I did not belong to the group. No one cared where I was nor did they ask who I was. I don't think anyone noticed that my three friends had left us in Habela. During the trip, I had been able to establish a friendship only with Yonas. But this girl, whose name I can't remember anymore, was an angel sent by God to take care of me. The tangerines were sweet and cool. So was the girl's attitude toward me – she treated me like her little brother.

She must have been concerned to see so young a city boy who had not yet even grown a beard to be heading to an unknown world in the jungle. She asked me what part of the city I was from and if I had older brothers. I explained that I was the oldest and that my mother had just had a baby a few days before. She felt sad for my parents, especially my mother. She knew, unlike me then, that I would be owned by a military machine that knows no sympathy and will most likely never let me go back home. Her reaction and the sadness on her face introduced fear and doubt in me. I felt insecure, but there was nothing I could do anymore. My mother may have just gotten a new baby that would replace me forever. At age 13, I had left for good, never to return to my mother. The realization of being so far from home and never belonging to anyone, in particular, started to sink in. I started to question my decisions that had seemed very brave earlier but now had me being carried away by a fast-flowing river with an unknown destination. After eating the cool tangerines, I went back to the bunker and slept for a few hours.

It was about 4.00 p.m. The heat and humidity were still hanging over the city. I came out of my bunker and noticed many younger people milling around the buildings. They all had one thing in common: they were all people like me who gathered from all over the country wanting to join the struggle for the liberation of Eritrea. It must have been difficult logistically to accommodate all these youngsters and guide them through the induction process in an orderly fashion.

My class at Saint Bernardos Catholic school (I am at the center top)

A family photo without my father (He was in Addis Ababa)

ERITREA/ROBERTS   (c) 1975 Financial Times, London   (2nd of 3)
LOndon: Two U.S. servicemen, Tom Bowidowicz(left) and David Strickland
(right), held hostages by the Eritrean Liberation Front. They were
encountered by British journalist Gwynne Roberts a few days after they
had been kidnapped from an American communications base near Asmara, capital
of Eritrea. (Exclusive story to follow. Not for use before Sunday, Nov.2)
NYT05103175

Americans taken hostage by ELF

WokiDuba seen in the distance behind the US Deep Space Intelligence Collection Center

My parents in 1958

The home I grew up in Asmara, Eritrea

The first Eritrean Air Traffic Controllers trained in Egypt, my father is sitting second from right.

Toward The West

Negotiating Eritrea's arid planes and landscape on foot
(Photo Credit EPLF)

II

Toward The West

August 2011, Delta Flight Honolulu–Seattle: I am on the last leg of the longest trip I have ever had so far – a two-week marathon trip that took me around the globe: Seattle–Amsterdam–Bangkok–Sydney–Hawaii–Seattle. The highlights of this trip undoubtedly were Bangkok and Hawaii, the two places I visited for the first time and I happened to have time to spend an extended weekend. Bangkok was fun, I saw all the touristy locations on a motorcycle taxi. I felt I was the attraction for the locals – from elementary school children wanting to take a picture with me to university students asking me to interview for their research projects! My meeting in Hawaii was planned for Friday but got moved to Tuesday. So, with a long weekend in between, my wife flew in to spend quality time with me which was incredible! It was great to visit what I think is the most beautiful city in the world –Sydney – for the fourth time. Staying at the glamorous Park Hyatt that is tucked underneath the Sydney Harbour Bridge with an incredible view of the Opera House made my visit all the more special. To compensate for all of these, I got to spend time with Qantas Airlines and Hawaiian Airlines which in my opinion were very demanding airlines to do business with.

9.   *Keep Moving - Jeharek*

A loud whistle caught everyone's attention. We were told to gather outside of one of the buildings and stand in two lines. When one of the fighters told us where we were headed, he did it in two different languages: in Tigrinya, my mother tongue, and another unfamiliar language. Overwhelmed by the situation, I did not pay attention and ended up knowing nothing about where we were heading.

But there was one thing I noticed which was different from the day before. We were accompanied by many fighters, heavily armed and with military bags strapped on their shoulders. At the end of the line, many camels were kneeling and screaming without end, lodging a roaring protest. They were being loaded with wheat, sugar, and utensils that were meant for our journey ahead. I could tell that the camels didn't like what was happening. Neither did I.

Just when I thought our journey had ended in Agordat, the line of loaded camels gave me a bad feeling that a long journey was ahead of us. I was not desperate, but I won't deny I was somewhat anxious. My teenage brain started to resent what I was about to experience and had started looking for a way out. Escaping, however, was not an option – I would just have to stick it out. So, bravely, I convinced myself to act strong, face what may come next, and not feel inferior to anyone in the group.

The line of camels started moving and we made our way west of Agordat. Approximately 100 young men, women, and a few kids like me, accompanied by camels and many fighters formed a long winding line that slowly but surely negotiated the terrain. I was walking just ahead of the camels that brought up the rear of our convoy. There were a few camels in the front as well, leading the pack.

As we walked, I could see the long line of people ahead of us making their way across the valleys, mountains, riverbeds, and flat terrain. With the sun setting, so close to the horizon, and the incredibly red skies, this was a spectacular view that would be engraved in my mind for the rest of my life.

After hours of walking, the line started to disintegrate. The energetic young men were way ahead of the weak people who could not keep up the pace. So, the fighters had to stop the fast-walking men, asking them to wait for the weak to catch up.

The transition from the beautiful sunset scenery to the frightening dark of the night was almost instant. The darkness set in and it was time to walk slower and closer to each other. It was a scary experience to walk at night with no flashlight or sense of direction. Your only focus was that the person ahead of you remained linked to you. There were some frightening moments when we had to cross bushes at night, tightly grasping each other's hands. The occasional slip of the hand from the person ahead gave me the instant, terrifying feeling of getting lost and finding myself being the lead.

It was late night when we finally stopped walking. We were told to line up about 2 meters from each other and form a circle in open flat terrain. That was the position we would sleep in on the ground. I had nothing to sleep on, not even a single sheet to cover my face. Most of the people were prepared and had a sheet to cover their bodies or the traditional local bed sheet called *Netsela*. But before I could contemplate asking someone to share a sheet, I fell asleep. I was exhausted.

Hours later, I was awoken by an ear-splitting noise that sounded like someone was involved in a life or death struggle. For a moment, I didn't know where I was and couldn't figure out what was going on. It was dark, and all I could see on the blurry horizon were small hills surrounded by the silhouettes of evenly spread trees. The screaming continued with various intensities and then I recognized the noise. I realized that I was still in the middle of my adventurous trip and that the camels being loaded with our supplies were the source of the noise.

It was time to line up again. There was no water or food, it was time to start walking again in the darkness of the morning. The fighter who was in charge of the contingent would walk along the line and repeatedly call out, *"Teharek! Teharek!,"* meaning "move on" in Arabic. After a while, I started to hate the word *"Teharek!"* for it meant no time to rest and no time to eat.

After hours of walking, the sun was well up in the sky and it started to get hot. The shadow that had loyally followed me since dawn was getting shorter and shorter, indicating that the sun was almost above my head.

Around afternoon, we finally reached a small village on a dirt road. We were ordered to stop there and prepare our food. The wheat flour and cooking utensils were unloaded from the camels. I can't remember who was doing what, but before I knew it, the team had cooked food and it was time to eat. The food was plain traditional flatbread called *kicha* made from flour and water. That was it. There was no tea or sauce. Those who had money bought tea or other necessities from the small shops in the tiny village.

We rested for a few hours and then a Fiat N3 truck appeared on the road. It was fully loaded with supplies and heading west. They decided to load the women, kids, and the weakest among us on the truck that was heading to our destination.

Fortunately, I was eligible to board the truck. As people started climbing the truck to sit on top of the load, I decided to quickly run back to the makeshift kitchen where the food had been prepared to fetch some more *kicha* before I hopped on to the truck. There was not much bread left there. While I was trying to collect the leftover crumbs, a man approached me and warned me that the truck would depart soon.

I ran back to the truck as quickly as I could, but the truck started moving and was gone in no time. All I could see was the thick black smoke from the exhaust pipe and the yellowish plume of dust kicked up by the truck tires in the distance. Shocked, I didn't know what to make of this unfortunate moment.

For a minute, I hoped that the girl that gave me the tangerines and took care of me in Agordat would notice and somehow stop the truck. But I was out of luck. The truck and its thick red dust trail slowly disappeared into the sunset.

I was left behind with *kicha* crumbs in my hands, as the only kid in a group of strong and tough men. My friend Yonas, the girls, and other men who were considered weak were allowed to board the trucks. They were lucky.

The men were ordered to line up. By now, I knew exactly what was required from me when it came to following orders. It was the beginning of my transformation from a young boy with a lot of personal freedom to a brainwashed and disciplined young fighter. A few of our guards had gone with the truck. The majority of them, however, had stayed with us. We were told that since we were now the strongest men of the group, we would break a record by being the first to walk nonstop to Kerkebet, the final destination. Kerkebet was a camp that was approximately 100 miles away from Agordat and was a major military training center for ELF fighters. At that moment, however, no one knew where Kerkebet was or how far we would have to walk.

The young men were very enthusiastic and excited about the challenge. Many of them believed, "If these fighters carrying their weapons and ammunition can walk nonstop to Kerkebet, what is our excuse?" I did not object, feeling like a real man for a moment. The line was instructed to move and the men started to walk taking big steps at a time. I don't recall any of the men being concerned about me being so young. This was going to be looked at as a personal challenge, not a group challenge.

We walked for hours without talking. The sunset was beautiful. The landscape of Barka was flat, with occasional mountains. In the distance across the horizon, the tall *Arkobkobay* (Doum Palm) trees formed an impressive silhouette against the orange sky. I was doing very well. My legs were moving at a rhythmic pace that allowed me to hum my favorite songs in sync. That was a good distraction. As the hours slipped by and darkness set in, the temperature began to cool, making it ideal for walking long distances.

After a long walk, the line started to disintegrate, and a clear distinction could be made between the weak and strong men. The sun disappeared, leaving just a full moon and stars to illuminate the fields of Barka. The moon was so bright that the entire line of people who walked in front of me was visible to me. When it was clear that a group of young men were too far behind, the leader ordered us to park ourselves and wait for the group to catch up. I was hoping that he would let us sleep for a while and then continue. But to my dismay, he called out *"Teharek! Teharek!"* very soon and everyone got up again.

We hadn't walked for even half an hour before the weak men were far behind once more. Again, we had to wait for them. As soon as they caught up, *"Teharek"* was heard again. This would happen a few more times. Eventually, the slower group started to complain that they were not getting a chance to rest for even a minute since every time they caught up with us, the leader would order us to continue. Although I was not part of the slow group, I, too, started to hate this leader who would order "*Teharek*" time and time again.

The leader, Mr. *Teharek*, as some jokingly nicknamed him, was a skinny but stiff guy in his forties, hailing from the lowlands where the majority of the Muslim population was settled. He had a very dark face with three large scars on each of his bony cheeks that ran vertically from just below his eyes down to his chin – a typical Beni-Amer tribe member. He had oversized eyes, of which the sclera, the white part of his eyes, gave way to a brown iris with tiny blood vessels that streamed down from the center to disappear below the eyelids, making him look tough and uncompromising. He wore oversized khaki shorts, white protective sleeves, and old-fashioned military gaiters called *gambale* around his ankles. His attire was covered with an oversized green military jacket that the Ethiopian soldiers typically wore. His thick dark-green military waist belt carried two large leather holsters symmetrically separated as to be supported by the outer sides of his buttocks, one holster containing bullets and the other recognizably shaped just like the three curved magazines it contained, separated by his bedsheet that was perfectly folded into a small brick-shaped square positioned in the middle of his lower back supporting the half-filled military backpack he carried of which the color perfectly matched that of his khaki shorts.

On the front of his belt, two grenades, one on each side, were affixed to the same green military belt, leaving no space around his waist. He carried his AK-47 mostly on his right shoulder with the barrel pointing at a downward angle with the curved magazine slightly resting on one of the holsters. His AK-47 was dark purple and smaller than the one Mulugheta Wodi-Batsi had allowed me to carry when I had first met the fighters in Emba Derho. Later, I learned the fighters called this type of gun "Kalashin-Checky" since it was made in Czechoslovakia. Although its shape resembles that of an AK-47, it is not an AK-47 – it is known formally as Sampol vz. 58.

The leader barely spoke Tigrinya, a language spoken in the highlands where I come from, and he showed no sympathy at all for the weaker people. Although we were very tired, he gave us no moment to catch our breath. His job was to get us in Kerkebet as soon as possible. It is mind-boggling how the man who carried so much military gear, primarily on his waist, was able to travel so long and drive the pace.

The rhythmic pace that had allowed me to hum my favorite songs earlier had long been disrupted, my mouth was parched and gritty, and my legs started to tremble with exhaustion whenever we stopped to wait for the slow team. As we walked by the small villages and nomads, now and then we were terrorized by encounters with the cattle of Barka. In the dark, the cattle tend to stick together at whatever cost. Afraid of wild animals, when they sense anything that moves at night, the cattle panic and wildly start running. If one of them runs in the wrong direction, they all follow, and they could easily have overrun us. This was a very dangerous and terrorizing experience for me since there was no warning to the stampede.

The moon and the stars started to fade eventually and darkness began being replaced by light. Albeit my exhaustion, I still was able to appreciate and be impressed by the process of transformation from darkness to light that seemed to take place within just half an hour. It looked like everything on earth became a different color during the transition from darkness to light, before settling on its natural color. The smell of the morning hours in Barka (low land region) was very distinctive because of the combination of dust, cattle, and camels.

At one point, our leader asked us to take a break and he disappeared for a while. Fifteen minutes later, he came back and took two men with him. When they returned, they were carrying skim/buttermilk and water. The water was in a leather container made from goatskin. The buttermilk was in a large wooden dish. The men, recognizing that I was the youngest, told me to drink first from the wooden dish. I didn't know what I was getting. I tasted for the first time in my life buttermilk made in the lowlands called *Birah*. It tasted very good and I couldn't stop drinking. The leader suggested drinking water afterward to clear the taste of buttermilk in my mouth while the dish passed from one person to another. No one cared about transmitting disease from one person to another – we were all thirsty and needed to hydrate.

Then, I was presented with the water-skin. I couldn't believe I was expected to drink water from the dark-brown leather container. It had the shape of the baby goat or lamb from which it had been made. The end of the four legs and the back were each tied so that no water could leak, just like the body mass that had been contained there once. The main opening from which the water could be accessed was the neck of the goat. The leather soaked with water felt like oily jelly and was disgustingly slimy when you touched it. However, drinking from the leather was considered a privilege. The water tasted fresh and very cold, but the smell and the sliminess of the wet leather were awful.

Later, I was told that the skin keeps the water cool during the day when temperatures soar above 40°C. Honestly, I would have rather had hot water than drink from that smelly water-skin. What I didn't realize at that moment was that the water I got was a luxury that I would not get to enjoy in the following years of my life. Water in the desert was a scarce commodity, and when desperate for it, the color and smell wouldn't matter, you would drink it to keep yourself hydrated. The next day would be my first encounter with that grim reality.

After a long walk in the sweltering heat of Barka, we finally reached a dry riverbed. From a distance, one could see a lot of activity on one side of the river. These were cattle, camels, and goats that had been brought down to the river to drink water. We started moving toward the water well and I realized we were heading there to drink water just like the animals.

This time the water was light brown and that was all there was for us to drink. At the bottom of the man-made water collector, you could see small species swimming. The fighters showed me how to drink this kind of water. You use your t-shirt as a filter. As you suck through the improvised filter, the dirt and species get filtered out and you drink what was considered clean water. Then you shake the shirt to shed off the dirt and tiny species that remain stuck to the T-shirt filter. That was not fun at all, but in a place where water was hard to come by, I was happy that we got to drink something.

A long walk along the riverbed ensued, and we finally reached Kerkebet late in the evening. Everyone was excited, and yet we had no idea what to expect in Kerkebet. We veered off the riverbed and entered the thick forest to the right. This was a relief since the sandy river bed was extremely tiring to walk on.

As we walked through the bushes to enter the main body of the forest, we felt as if we had entered a city bursting with life but entirely covered by massive trees. Walking by, we could see a few men here and there who seemed to be quietly working hard. The place was lit with small fires everywhere. It felt as if we were in a busy factory where many men were doing the same work everywhere. Later, I realized these were youngsters preparing food. I didn't understand why people would make food at night in the darkness. It turned out, it was to prevent the enemy fighter jets from noticing smoke during the day, revealing the location where the fighters were hiding.

After about a 20-minute walk in the camp that was set up entirely under thick forest, we reached a small hut where we were received by a gentleman wearing a tight military outfit and a flashy blue watch. His name was Osman. Osman didn't talk to us, but he chatted with the leader of the group in Arabic, and then the famous word was heard again – "*Teharek*". This was really bad news for me because I was tired and just wanted to sleep. But now we had to move again, and this time I didn't know where we were going.

Fortunately, we walked only 5 minutes before reaching the edge of the bushes that connected to the dry riverbed. We were told to form a circle and sleep on the riverbed. The sand was still warm and for once it felt really good to sleep in the open looking at the bright stars. I had clocked more than 200 miles of traveling, two-third of which had been on foot and the rest an excruciating off-road ride, standing on a cargo truck. It didn't take me long to fall asleep; I was knocked out on the warm sand.

10. *Training Camp - Kerkebet*

2011. Flight BA-48 from London to Seattle. I never liked the seating of the 747-400 British Airways business class cabin. Just like the train seats, some of them face front and others back, making it awkward to face your travel partner all the time, unless you pull the privacy panel. Honestly, in this flight specifically, the seat issue wouldn't pass as bad compared to the service. The flight attendant is an older man, heavyset, with a partially gray beard. He served me the appetizer I ordered and his partner removed the empty plates after I finished. I was waiting for my main meal patiently. It took a little longer than usual. The traveler next to me received his main meal and was already set for his dessert.

As expected, the flight attendant started serving dessert and asked "What would you like for dessert, sir?". I nicely explained, "I am not ready for dessert yet since I am still waiting for my main meal," to which he replied, "I served you your main meal, sir." I respectfully told him that I didn't get it. He angrily responded, "Sir, I served your meal myself, for certain – I cannot serve you twice." His voice was loud and carried a malicious intent to embarrass me. I am not a big eater and I can perfectly skip the main meal. However, this was ridiculous. I had paid over 9,000 USD for a business ticket – which should have made him think twice before confronting me with "You ate two meals." Fortunately, the gentleman next to me interfered and said, "He didn't get his main meal. His plate was empty while I was eating my main meal." He continued, "Besides, even if a business class passenger wants a second meal, you should accommodate his request." I thanked the witness for interfering and getting me served. I have no idea what the ending would have been had he not interfered. Uncomfortable sittings, overcrowded Heathrow, a mileage program that sucks, and a disrespectful flight attendant were enough justification to never fly BA again. So, this story is written on my last BA flight ever.

The quiet riverbed from the night before turned into an unbelievably noisy place in the morning. It felt like the earth was shaking. The sun was about to rise soon but the camp was still dark. Young men grouped by the hundreds were jogging in concert while stomping the ground hard on every fourth step. It was like a competition where one group had to be louder and more dominant than the other. The instructors were screaming and singing loudly to keep the mood of the young men right. I wanted to see them, but I couldn't see clearly since it was dark. But the noise was literally and figuratively music to my ears.

It was a stunning experience. I was delighted to see so many young men and women who had the same desire as I did to fight for Eritrea. These were the hundreds of young men from all over Eritrea (who had joined the fighters before I did) and were getting military training. Amongst them were doctors, engineers, nurses, police officers, students, construction workers, farmers, businessmen, and people from all walks of life. Every one of them had joined the liberation movement voluntarily. Many of my schoolmates and friends who had left Asmara before me to fight for Eritrea were amongst them.

A few minutes later, a profoundly different noise began to crescendo, emerging from a different direction of the riverbed, a much brighter and higher pitch than that of the men. When coupled with the men's noise, it was like a music symphony where multiple instruments play high and low to form a harmony. These were hundreds of women who had joined the men to fight for Eritrea. To my surprise, however, they were not mixed with the men; instead, they had their own group and formation. As they passed us, stomping the ground equally hard, their voice was powerful but extremely pitchy. Since it was still dark, I could only imagine what they looked like or what uniforms they were wearing. After some time, the noise started to fade as the crowd was moving away from where we were resting But it did not grow quiet. Far in the distance, I could still hear the noise of the young trainees.

As I was still pondering over what I had just experienced, to the east of where I was, heavy gunshots started to sound, indicating that there was another group training with guns and battlefield scenarios. This was exactly what I had wanted to experience and was looking forward to when I left home. I wanted to learn how to use guns and be part of these Eritreans who were fighting in Asmara and environs to free Eritrea from the occupation of Ethiopia.

Sitting on the now-cold riverbed, with darkness still commanding the sight, I started to imagine how my involvement in all of this would look like. I never realized how far I was from Asmara at that point, nor did I realize that fighting for Eritrea did not necessarily mean fighting in Asmara. The chance that I would be involved in fighting around my hometown Asmara was very remote, but that was not obvious to me then. I still expected that after I had learned the required military skills, I would be sent to Asmara to fight. I also had no idea how long the training would take – maybe three or five days – it surely couldn't take longer than 10 days. That was my expectation. I wanted these days to go by very fast so that I could start my Rambo-like action against the Ethiopian soldiers in Asmara. As I was dreaming of my assignments, we were told to pack and get moving.

As soon as I got up from where I was sitting in the riverbed, I felt hundreds of insects pouring down my legs and I started jumping up and down screaming in terror. The tear in the back of my pants had allowed sand to enter through while I was tossing and turning at night. It turned out it was the sand pouring down my legs, not insects as I had thought. Relieved, I dusted off the remaining sand and we moved toward the bush at the edge of the river. There we met the remaining of our group that had been lucky to get a truck ride and arrive in Kerkebet a day earlier. They made breakfast and served us tea and *kicha*.

The women who had come with us were told to pack and move to another location. No one knew where. I felt bad that the friendship I had built in the last few days would already be coming to an end. This was my first taste of letting friends go, sometimes forever. We gave each other hugs and they left.

The men were told to join another group of young Eritreans who were waiting for more people to come so that they could form a *Dewra*, a 100-man-strong unit. That morning, the new group gathered and we learned that we were now going to start military training as a team. We were assigned a unit name. Each group in the training camp was named after popular martyrs.

Our first assignment was to learn a song that we as a group could sing every morning. The song lyrics went *"Nwegenom kiblu zchuqunu, nzdelyu tqmom n'merbah ... aytdelin eya Eritrea nay Tsbah"*, which roughly translates to *"Tomorrow's Eritrea has no place for those who oppress others to benefit themselves."* The song reflects the ideals of the fighters and their love for Eritrea. This was a great thing for me because I loved songs and I was part of a youth band in a protestant church back in my hometown. So, singing made me feel at home and kept my morale high.

The tune of the song was sweet. Although it took a lot of effort and rehearsal to sing it nicely as a group, after we mastered the song, the choir was amazing. When I was in Asmara, I only sang with school and church students of my age, which made the songs a bit pitchy. But the voice of these adult men was beautiful and simply overwhelming and made the song so special to me. Even today, if I sing that song or listen to it, I get very emotional. Part of me wants to go back in time and experience selective moments of my life in the jungle.

The first few weeks in the training camp seemed to be fun, learning our environment and some basic military discipline and marching as a group in sync. The food, however, was terrible. We got dry, locally made *kicha* every morning and horrible-tasting local food called Ge'at in the evening. Ge'at was flour and water mixed and cooked to form a pudding-like food. Normally, Ge'at is served with butter and hot chili spices. This was what they would serve when I left home to celebrate the birth of my sister. In the camp, however, they didn't have butter or spices. Besides, the way it was prepared was disgusting food that I passionately hated.

We also got hot water with sugar in the morning. To make it feel like we were getting tea, we would pour sugar into the pan and burn it a little before pouring hot water over it. This gave the drink a dark tea-like color and a distinctive burned-sugar aroma. This menu was a daily meal that never changed. Sometimes the Ge'at smelled like gasoline and it was difficult to eat. This was mainly because gasoline containers were loaded on top of the wheat flour bags in the same truck and the containers sometimes leaked, spoiling the wheat.

So, after a few days of eating the same food, I didn't like the food anymore and my body seemed to agree with my feeling. I started to get sick, mostly because of Ge'at. Every time I ate Ge'at which was served at dinnertime, I would vomit. So, I started skipping dinner to avoid being sick from Ge'at. Unfortunately, not eating dinner made me weak, and every morning, when we would have to run for miles, I started feeling tired and couldn't keep up with the group anymore.

As I got weaker and weaker, one trainee, named Ibrahim, noticed that I needed help. Ibrahim asked the group leader to allow me to eat bread in the evening instead of Ge'at. The request was rejected because there could be no special treatment of one person above the others in the military. So, Ibrahim, a young boy who couldn't communicate with me properly because he was from a different ethnic group "Dankel" and spoke a different language, decided to save half of the bread he got for breakfast for me to eat at dinner. That was an unbelievable act of selflessness and sympathy from Ibrahim, a total stranger who happened to have a big heart. Every evening, I would eat a portion of his breakfast as my dinner. Soon, we became good friends and I started teaching Ibrahim my language.

Despite Ibrahim's efforts, the small portions of food that had no proteins or vitamins, the physically demanding training, and the lack of hygiene pushed my soft and frail body to the limits. I became seriously ill. During training or running in the sun, I would get dizzy and feel like fainting. Physically, I became very weak and could no longer tolerate the training. Inevitably, I had to be admitted to the camp's hospital.

In the hospital, I got to taste a relatively decent meal after weeks of disgusting food. For the first time, I was reminded of what I was missing by leaving home. The delicious food that my mother used to feed me daily was no longer here. I started to feel low and homesick. Unfortunately, the point of no return had been reached as soon as I got admitted to the training camp.

After a few days in the clinic, I felt better and joined my group again. This time, however, the doctor gave written instructions to the group leader to allow me to eat dry bread for lunch and dinner. Finally, Ge'at would be removed from my daily nutrition. I was classified as a weak and sick boy who needed special attention from his fellow fighters. The cooks now had to deal with this exception when they prepared food.

Every evening, just before we headed to our sleeping field, various issues would be discussed in a meeting. After the order to change my diet was communicated formally, someone raised the concern that this special treatment request would cause daily hassle for the cooks. Our unit leader, Alem, told the team that it was an order from the doctor and they would have to respect it and keep making *kicha* for me. Alem was a well-built young man with long, wavy, and silky hair. He was soft-spoken, with good leadership skills, and I looked up to him.

Our trainer sometimes used to come to the meeting to listen to the team getting ready for the night. It was dark and no one knew he was there. After the trainer heard the discussions and complaints about me needing attention, he came out of the darkness and addressed the team. He got really angry that the group couldn't take care of a 13-year-old who was unwell. He told them, if the fix was as simple as making *kicha* for me, they should have taken the responsibility of taking care of it before I got sick. "It was a shame that a doctor had to tell you to care for your fellow fighter who got sick. This is not in line with the spirit of camaraderie." The team got an earful from the trainer.

After the meeting, our trainer pulled me from the crowd and asked me to come the next morning to the staff area to eat breakfast with him. That was very nice of him. He realized that he could not afford to lose a young kid of his unit for the trivial reason of not providing proper food.

I had no idea what the breakfast would be like at the staff kitchen. As instructed, the next morning, instead of joining my team for breakfast, I went to the staff kitchen which was a secluded area under a large tree. Needless to say, the entire staff area was completely off-limits to trainees. I was scared to approach the staff kitchen fearing that I would get chased away by other trainers who did not know about the invitation I had from my trainer. As I managed to get closer to the staff area, my trainer was there, and the moment he saw me, he called my name, giving me a green light to enter the premises unchallenged. I was the only student in the kitchen and I felt like a beggar.

I got presented with a piece of bread that was made from a much better quality of wheat and a cup of sweet tea. This was real tea, not the stuff we made at the camp by burning sugar. By now, weeks had gone by without me getting any real tea or decent food. So, getting tea with decent bread was quite a luxury. Satisfied, I thanked my trainer and went back to my group. This would repeat over the next several days until I felt better physically. After a few days, I felt bad about going to the trainer's kitchen to eat better food while everyone else survived in the camp eating food that would typically be given to animals.

Going to the staff kitchen made me feel guilty and reflected poorly on me. At some point, I needed to show that I was a regular trainee and could survive in my group eating whatever food had been made for us. So, I stopped going to the staff kitchen voluntarily. I also felt physically better so I started tolerating the training routines. Yet, going to the staff kitchen and eating bread with tea was such a luxury that I experienced it as the highlight of my stay in the training camp.

A lot of the training was physically very demanding. It required the students to be coordinated in their moves as they marched. This was a lot more difficult for the older students. But for me and the other young students, this was the fun part. We started to shine and be singled out from the group to show the older guys how high and fast you should move your legs and arms when marching.

We also learned the military orders which were in Arabic much quicker than the older men. There were few seniors and illiterate men amongst us who had real difficulty following and responding to orders. The punishment for not getting things right was severe, and I felt bad when these older men got beaten because their legs didn't move high enough or they couldn't synchronize their moves with the rest of the team. If I had difficulty fitting in with the group because of my age, the older guys must have had it much more difficult. At least I didn't get penalized because I couldn't do basic military maneuvers. In fact, on the contrary, when the group had to be punished because the collective effort was weak, the trainer would take me and the other young boys out of the group and punish only the adults. So, the treatment I received at the camp, given the circumstances, wasn't all too bad.

11. *Nights in Kerkebet*

After a long day of hard work, training, digging wells and trenches, my body would be so exhausted that when it was time to sleep, I would crash on the ground instantly. That was only fair, one would think. But, nighttime in Kerkebet was terrible. Every evening, before we headed to the trenches, the leader would select a team of 5–10 people who were assigned a job for 5 a.m. The team's assignment was to try taking away our weapons at night while we were asleep.

We were trained to sleep with the weapon, or a piece of wood resembling a weapon, firmly between our legs while embracing the barrel of the gun. If anyone at night tried to take it away, we were supposed to wake up and fight to rescue the weapon. Those of us who felt tired and slept deep would wake up the following morning with no weapon. This was a terrifying feeling because the punishment was harsh. In addition, it was embarrassing to be a weak fighter who couldn't protect his weapon at night.

The morning routine was – after we woke up we would assemble in formation. Then the trainer would order those without their weapons to step out of the formation and line up separately. People would then come out one by one, with their heads down and pride hurt, to line up in shame in front of the proud men. Several men were always part of this team of losers and they got ridiculed for that. I experienced this feeling a few times.

So, every day that I woke up and found my weapon between my two legs, I thanked God for that night. But at the same time, I feared that I might fail the next night. If there had been an option, I would have preferred not to sleep at all. Occasionally, the team members told me they were skipping me deliberately since I was too young and they felt sorry for me. After all, at this age I was not supposed to be in the middle of nowhere, sleeping on the ground with my shoes as my pillow and no cover. I was not supposed to be bit by scorpions, snakes, and other insects. I was not supposed to be terrified that one day a hyena might drag me out of my trench while

I was deep asleep. I was a city boy who knew nothing about the outside world, let alone sleeping in the middle of nowhere with no tent or plastic to cover my body when it rained.

The rain was a story of its own. Although it was not normal in Eritrea to rain at night, those few days that it rained, the trench got filled with water while we were asleep. It almost felt like drowning in your bed.

Another terrifying experience I hated was when in the middle of the night one of the trainees woke up screaming and started to sleepwalk. He had this problem almost every night and it was terrifying when I woke up and heard the commotion play out in the darkness. Overall, the nights in Kerkebet were my worst experience.

After making it through the cold nights and the occasional embarrassment of not having your weapon with you, at around 5.30 in the morning, we always headed for our daily run. This was not free-running or jogging. It was a well-coordinated movement of legs and arms with 100 strong men hitting the ground in sync. A unit of 100 men was called a "Dewra". Most of the running took place on the dry riverbed. The riverbed was covered with a deep layer of white sand similar to the pristine beaches of Miami. It was very difficult and exhausting to run on the sand.

The morning hours in Kerkebet were pretty dark. Although we couldn't see each other in the darkness of the morning, there was stiff competition amongst the various units on who would make the most noise and who would hit the ground the hardest. This was true, not only at the individual level but also at a Dewra level. Some of the Dewras were powerful and based on the noise they produced, you could tell which group was approaching or passing by. The same applied to the instructors; their powerful and distinctive voices were a delight to listen to when they led the companies.

If we did not generate the expected level of noise when thumping the ground, severe collective punishment awaited us. One of the actions taken to punish the underperforming group was to order the entire company to march into a water basin that was collected on the side of the riverbed. The mornings in Kerkebet were really cold and so was the water. Marching into the water early in the morning was not a pleasant experience. Most of the time, the kids were spared from being punished along with the older trainees. Only after the company performed well as a collective could we get back to our camp for breakfast. Fortunately, there was a limit to how long we could stay in the open. Even if we performed poorly, we couldn't stay in the dry riverbeds for too long for fear of Ethiopian MiG jet fighters that hunted for anything that moved during the day.

The physical and military training became a daily routine, and we all knew what was expected from each of us. Yet, I had a hard time adapting to this harsh military life. I missed my family, my friends, my school, and above all my Sunday church songs where I enjoyed listening to the piano player. I also missed my friend Lula whom I had a crush on and started innocently baby-dating back in Asmara. When I got a chance to enjoy a lonely moment, I cried my eyes out and contemplated going back home, abandoning all my ideals of becoming a hero in the jungle. At one point, I secretly asked our trainer if there was a chance that I could go back to my home since I was feeling sick. His response was unequivocal. With his threatening big eyes popping out of their sockets, he scolded me and said, "You will never dare to ask this question of anyone anymore." His uncompromising response did magic and I dropped the idea altogether.

Necessities like going to relieve yourself became a painful and miserable experience. You can imagine when you have hundreds of people who are not fed well and have to do their business every day in the open, it does get sickening. Also, the product we dropped everywhere became land mines and dangerous when we walked, ran, and trained throughout the camp. We were not allowed to venture outside the jungle as to not reveal the position of our camp to the jet fighters.

So, a decision was made to dig trench-like holes to serve as massive open-air toilets. For the first few days, it seemed like a good idea. As the trenches started to fill, however, it became a hazardous activity to do our business. Imagine this: carefully walking on two pieces of wood that serve as a bridge on top of the trenches and carefully lowering your body to a squat position while maintaining your balance to not fall into the hazardous waste. As you settle on to the desired position, the humid fume that rises from the trenches makes you feel drowsy, especially during the day when the temperatures soar to over 40°C. To this day, I don't understand why they didn't think to cover the trenches and leave a few holes. Someone must have thought that covering the trenches was just too much work to accomplish – if it ever was contemplated. Regardless, It was quite a challenge for a kid who was used to doing his business on luxurious Italian full-sized toilets in Asmara.

So, life, in general, became unbearable for the 13-year-old boy I was. But, the option of going back home seemed more and more far-fetched by the day. Failure was not an option, and I had to pull myself by the bootstrap to make it through the two months of military training.

At the end of the two months' training, we were trained to perform basic military maneuvers, self-defense, assemble and disassemble weapons, fix and unfix bayonets, as well as target shooting. Since a bullet was very precious and difficult to come by, we were allowed to shoot only five bullets before we qualified as fully trained soldiers. We also learned to march in unison, stand upright, and maintain an assertive and correct posture: chin up, chest out, shoulders back, stomach in. But, above all, we were trained to understand the purpose of our struggle and the sacrifices we would have to make to accomplish our goal. We learned all this while we bonded and lived in harmony with all the different ethnic groups that I never knew existed in Eritrea.

12. Deployment

After two and a half months of training in the camp, we were ready to deploy to the frontline units for combat operations. This had been the dream of every young and old person who underwent the training. Finally, there would be no strict military life confined in a camp. We were ready to move around from hills to hills and from villages to villages to chase the Ethiopian army. Just like those fighters, in places like Adi Shmagle, who had made such a heroic impression on me before I joined. I looked forward to being a full-fledged fighter with curly Afro hair, dressed in khaki shorts, and enjoying my life companion, the AK-47. At least that seemed like a very logical thing to expect at the time. What happened, however, was disappointing.

After a formal inauguration ceremony for more than 500 fighters, the young boys were pulled out and formed into a new platoon. Every person was ready to move out of the camp and all our belongings, which amounted to a single bedsheet and any spare clothes we might have, were packed. As the rest of the graduates marched out of the camp to go to unknown destinations, we were left behind – a bunch of young boys nicely lined up and in kneel/attention position. We started to worry and speculate on what was going to happen to us. We all knew that as long as they didn't return us to the camp for more training and horrible living conditions, we were happy to go anywhere.

Fortunately, after everyone left the camp, we were told to get up and start moving out of the camp as well. No one told us where we were heading and no one dared to ask what was going on. Two fighters were assigned to us who were going to take us to wherever we were heading. In the army, when you were told to move, you were expected to move and not ask questions. So, when the fighters told us to move in line, we simply followed them and headed out of the camp and toward the east.

We were joyful that we were leaving the camp, but at the same time sad that we had been separated from our adult comrades with whom we had spent two long months of hardship and training. The good thing was, because of our similar age, we had a lot in common and were very close to each other. More importantly, Yonas and Ibrahim, the two young boys I had a great friendship with, were with me. So, although I had no idea what the future held, I felt good.

We looked good. We were given brand new military outfits with camouflage patterns, and my red flashy underpants would no longer be an embarrassment. My red underpants were problematic in many ways. They were made from thick material that was fluffy, similar to a towel. With the poor hygiene and humid environment, body lice found a perfect breeding ground in my underpants. They would be parked inside the fluffy material during the day and go on the attack at night to suck blood from the softest tissue of my body. Head lice were very common and easy to deal with, but body lice were terrible. Once a week I would take off my pants and put them on the riverbed and cover them with a layer of sand. After a few hours, the heat from the sun would kill the lice and that would give me a break for a few days. At one point, I seriously considered throwing my underpants away, but the alternative would be going around with a naked butt.

After hours of walking, we were very excited that the direction we were heading in was east, where Asmara city lay. Although we were hundreds of miles away from the city, this could mean that we would be deployed in the Asmara area if not in the area known as Kebesa (highlands), the stronghold of the Ethiopian army.

Before we reached any inhabited area, darkness set in and we were told to make our dinner. Our dinner was the infamous Ge'at. This time there was no exception for me. I had to eat whatever was given. But first, we had to find a way to light a fire using two wooden sticks. Not an easy task if you haven't done it before. Although Ge'at made my stomach sick, the choice between having something in your stomach and not having anything was easy. This time the wheat was clean, not mixed with gasoline like when we were in the training center, and it tasted better.

After dinner, we kept walking in the darkness. I couldn't understand how the fighters were navigating the terrain that had no physical markings or landmarks. Fortunately, the clear skies allowed the moon to shine brightly, allowing us to see the person in front of us in the line. This was a repeat of the long trip we had taken to get to Kerkebet – we were just heading back now toward the east. Soon we were exhausted and the fighters told us to lie down on the ground and take a nap. Before the sun rose, we woke up and started walking again.

Some sections of the fields were torturous. Spread across the fields were small thorny seeds *(Kuakito)*, the size of hardened chickpeas, everywhere on the ground. These thorny seeds penetrated the plastic sandal shoes we wore just enough to poke our feet and make walking very painful. Occasionally, a very strong thorn called Che'a, the size of a large needle, would go right through the plastic sandal and into the bottom of my foot. I remember taking these thorns out of my feet was more painful than when they went in.

After two days of walking, we saw a thick forest in the distance, and for the first time, we came across a dirt road heading west to east. We knew we were still very far from Asmara as it would take another three days of walking to get there. However, we hoped that a truck would pass by and we could take a ride. If that ever happened, I knew I wouldn't repeat the mistake I had made when I missed the truck on the way to Kerkebet.

After following the winding road through the forest, we arrived at a place with a few homes that looked similar to what you would find in Indonesia or some tropical place – built with wood, but good-looking homes. They were inhabited by both civilians and fighters. It was a very strange setting. Many of the civilians seemed to dress in overhauls and some were walking with farming equipment. There were goats and sheep, but more surprisingly, green bananas. We soon learned that the place was very close to the city of Agordat and it was a huge banana farm that had been set up by the Italians and was now run by the fighters.

Kalashnikov

(Photo Credit EPLF)

III

Kalashnikov

January 27, 2011. Delta Flight DL514, Mexico City to Salt Lake City
I had a great time in Mexico City. I will remember the city for one of the best French restaurants I have ever visited. The owner is an amazing person who pays special attention to new visitors. I traveled with two female colleagues and we had a good time chatting about our personal lives. Unlike many of my male colleagues, the part of my story that fascinated them the most was not the jungle life but my love story in Holland, giving me the impression that women are wired differently.

The people at Aero México, the airline I visited on this trip, were very nice. We bonded well and I think we have a great opportunity to close some deals. They are very forward-looking and eager to transform the airline operations utilizing Boeing's technology. Super excited.

13.   *The Prison - Mogoraib*

A fter exchanging greetings with the fighters, we were presented with water. We were very excited that we had reached the vicinity of Agordat which was only 90 miles from Asmara. Late in the afternoon, after hours of relaxing and chatting with the locals, we heard a loud rumbling from a red Italian truck Fiat N3 that was parked under a tree.

We were told to board the truck. Excited, we ran to the truck and tried to find the best spot possible, ideally on top of the cabin to allow us to enjoy an unobstructed view and scenery. I was not fortunate to get that spot. I sat very close to the front on top of the sorghum load that the truck was carrying.

All vehicle movements took place in the darkness for fear of deadly MiG jet fighters that controlled the skies during the day. At dusk, the Fiat N3 started to emerge from the forest and we noticed that the truck was going west and not east as we had hoped. This was a devastating observation because the west was where we had just come from. We knew there was not much action there other than a hot desert, sparsely inhabited villages, and no civilians that spoke Tigrinya. But, we couldn't ask questions, so we each suffered from within, without showing any sign of dissatisfaction, and started our journey toward the fading sun.

After a few hours of a rough drive, we reached a location with only a few huts – it looked like a checkpoint. There, we jumped off the truck and were asked to line up again. By this time, it was pitch black and we were not in the mood to walk. But what we feared was inevitable, and we started walking in line. I remembered Mr. *Teharek* and started to worry. Fortunately, this time the walking was not that long at all and we arrived at a hut where we were greeted by a fighter who was visibly older than any fighter we had met so far. He was cheerful and received us with a smile. A tall female fighter whose hair was cut very short accompanied him. She was beautiful and had a smile that lit up the darkness. Her well-built body and strong posture combined with the tight shorts she wore emphasized the size of her legs. She took charge of our logistical needs. We spent the night outside on the ground spread around the hut.

In the morning, unlike the 5 a.m. wake-up drills, for the first time in three months, I was able to sleep until the sun rose. It was about 8 a.m. and no one seemed to be in a rush. No one told us to line up or run for miles. We noticed more fighters around us. They were eager to meet the young boys they had heard had arrived at the central "office" (the hut).

After we had washed our faces with clean water and looked presentable, we were escorted to a makeshift kitchen where we got breakfast, real tea, and good traditional bread. This was quite a different experience where life seemed a lot relaxed. Everyone was having fun with us and delighted to see the young city boys.

The fighters here hadn't seen young boys from Asmara for a long time and were eager to hear our stories. While we were enjoying the conversations, the older gentleman who was the commander of the units came in and interrupted our discussion. "Boys, it is time that you see your final destination and meet your units," he said. "We are going to split you into two groups. The first group will go right now and the second group will wait here until the escort arrives." I was put in the first group and so was my good friend Ibrahim who had shared his breakfast with me at the training camp in Kerkebet.

The escort of two fighters arrived, but this time, unlike the escort that took us to the training camp, these fighters were very friendly and we weren't told to line up. Instead, we started walking casually without any formal military orders and we separated from the other team. As we left the central office, remarkably, we headed to the open field with no fear for MiG fighters. In the distance, we saw a thick forest the likes of which we typically would camp in, but the area had no mountains or hills. There were a few shrubs, but no trees.

After 15 minutes of pleasant walking, we arrived at a huge makeshift camp that was completely exposed to the sun. As we approached, we noticed a very strange setup where there was a huge compound encircled with smaller huts. This was a very odd setup in that we were constantly being trained to stay out of open areas to avoid the jet fighters from discovering our positions, and here we could see a massive camp in the middle of an open field. Welcome to Mogoraib.

The smaller huts around the facility, about 10 of them, were all made with bundles of palm-tree-like branches. On one side of the compound, about 200 feet away, there was a big tree, the only tree in the area, which was used as the cafeteria for the fighters. We walked to the cafeteria where we were received by a few fighters who were cooking food. The food they cooked was good in comparison to what we had at the training camp, but by no means could it be called great food. It was flatbread mixed with a watery, soup-like sauce made of lentils and onion. The onion and lentils were added as spices, just enough to give the bucket full of boiling water a little aroma and flavor.

After we all had a cup of sweet tea, they took us for a quick tour around the compound. We were introduced to every freedom fighter in each of the huts that surrounded the camp —two fighters in each hut. The fighters and their military gear resembled the fighters I had met in Adi Shmagle: skinny body, bony cheeks, long afro hair, and diverse in ethnicity; except they looked cleaner and well-dressed.

We arrived at the largest prison of the ELF located in Mogoraib. This camp was a prison center. The huts were homes for the guards, the prisoners were locked inside a huge compound. At the entrance of the prison were hundreds of badly damaged pairs of shoes spread around but still placed in order. The prisoners were not allowed to walk with their shoes inside the prison. This was to prevent them from escaping. The shoes were packed in one location outside the compound and the prisoners would just take whichever shoes they got first when they were allowed to step out.

In the center of the compound stood a large wood-framed structure covered with tree branches that could accommodate hundreds of people and which served as a shield from rain and sun. It was surrounded by giant thorny tree branches, cut from Acacia trees, piled on top of each other to form a thick wall of thorny barrier erected 20 feet high and 10 feet thick. Inside the prison, although there were more than 200 prisoners, it was very quiet – almost no sign of life. The few people that moved around were on the outside of the compound, the guards who seemed very relaxed.

The other group was taken to another prison a few miles away. That prison was established in a similar setup but housed civilian prisoners. The prison that I was assigned to, however, was a "military" prison established to incarcerate ELF fighters.

The same day around noon, a tall man who looked very frail and sick came out of the prison. He was escorted by a fighter as he started walking very slowly toward the outskirts of the camp. When he looked at us, he stopped and asked the guards who the young kids were. The guards allowed him to greet us. After exchanging greetings, he said that I looked familiar to him. He asked whose son I am and where I lived in Asmara. I told him my name and my father's name, and he started shaking his head with disbelief. After a long silence and with deep sadness on his face, he politely asked me if he was allowed to hug me. He told me who he was. His name was Andemichael.

After looking deeper at his face, I recognized him, primarily because of his gold tooth and thick eyebrows. He was a wealthy businessman and close family member who was also a good friend of my father. When he had been in Asmara, I remember, he had had a beautiful Opel car and a good family life. I was very shocked to find him in this condition where he was sick, bony, and the weakest person in the prison camp.

Most of the prisoners were Eritrean fighters who had committed various crimes ranging from refusing to obey orders to instigating political movement, corruption, rape, and attempted escape to Sudan. I did not know why Andemichael had been imprisoned, but he surely was paying a hefty price for whatever he had done.

After about 10 minutes of talking, he was escorted away for his daily visit to the fields around the area to relieve himself. The midday break/walk was a privilege given only to the sick. Everyone else was allowed to take a walk only in the morning and afternoon.

After we completed the tour of the compound, a mentor was assigned to each one of us, and our respective mentors took us to the huts that would serve as our home going forward. We never understood what the responsibility of the mentors was at first. But we soon learned that these fighters would act as our custodians to help us with the transition from training to real-world life. My mentor's name was Yehualashet. He was in his forties and had a Taliban-like beard and remarkably light skin. He was very nice and like a fatherly figure to me.

The weather in Mogoraib was hot. During the day we stayed in the huts, but at night it was too warm to sleep in the huts and we simply slept outside on the ground. But during the morning hours, around 5 a.m., the temperature dropped very low to the point where many fighters would get muscle cramps from the cold. Since we didn't have mattresses of any kind, Yehualashet used to share with me his small white canvas, cut from an old tent. He laid the canvas down on the ground not to add cushioning but to protect me from the dirt.

Yehualashet taking care of me was not making me feel like a proud fighter. In reality, I was only a 13-year-old boy who had ended up safely under the control of responsible fighters who did everything possible to make me feel at home. The fighters knew that I didn't deserve to be there and they knew that if my mother would know where I was that she would want them to take care of me as a kid, not as a fighter. To my annoyance, they did just that, treating me like a little boy who needed protection.

With only a thin bedsheet covering my body and a single layer of canvas separating my body from the cold ground, the nights were horrible. To my shock, one morning, I woke up and found out my pants were wet and couldn't believe that I had peed in my sleep. The canvas that belonged to my mentor was also wet. Yehualashet pretended to have seen nothing, saving me from embarrassment. Now, not only did I not like the nights because of the cold but also for fear that I would urinate on the canvas. I was terrified to fall asleep. Unfortunately, it kept happening daily. Apparently, in cold weather, blood rushes to our organs at a higher frequency, forcing our body to filter more blood than normal. This results in us having to pee more often.

The full-fledged fighter that I wanted to be seemed an elusive goal. I was frustrated and losing confidence. Although I was unable to control myself from peeing, I had to come up with a solution. To avoid the morning embarrassment, I made sure I didn't fall asleep before my mentor. As soon as he fell asleep, I would roll off the sheet to sleep on the ground. It was terribly cold, and I would wake up covered with dirt and occasionally mud, but that was better than risking repetitive embarrassing moments.

To make things worse, after a few weeks, they assigned me and another young friend, Maasho (who is currently an engineer living in Canada), a daily job. The job was guarding a farm and protecting it from animals and birds while the prisoners who worked at the farm took a lunch break. With this assignment, being a real fighter remained an unfulfilled dream.

So, every day at noon, Maasho and I would head to the garden/farm at the riverbank where various vegetables like tomatoes, onion, and okra grew. The prisoners were put to work to grow these vegetables. The vegetables were shipped to the front's central hospital in Hawashayt river to help the wounded and sick get better nutrition.

As I matured in our position, I started helping out with various tasks that the guards performed, including escorting prisoners to clinics and restrooms. Mostly I would escort the weak prisoners, including Andemichael.

I felt very sad for the prisoners, especially Andemichael, who was very sick. To help him out, every day I would take a pinch of salt from our supplies and give it to him. Salt was a privilege that only a few lucky prisoners who had connections could get. As small as this seemed, it was the best gift I could give him, short of letting him escape from prison.

The condition of the prison, especially the food, was horrendous. Sometimes, necessities like sorghum flour that were normally trucked from Sudan became scarce. The shortage was exacerbated during winter when the rivers would be flooded routinely and the transportation of supplies would get disrupted. At one point, I remember we ran out of supplies and the prisoners had no food to eat for three days. We ended up collecting Doum fruit from Arkobkobay tree (Palm tree, also known as Gingerbread tree) from the jungles around us, and that was all the prisoners ate.

Most of the fighters were addicted to tobacco, and when the supply was disrupted many of them got sick. The dark brown tobacco powder which could easily be mistaken for roasted coffee powder was widely distributed. To use it, it was moistened with water and a dip placed between the lower lip and the gum. All of the fighters spit constantly to get rid of the excess saliva mixed with tobacco in their mouth. The smell of tobacco waste was horrible. But, for many of the young fighters, using tobacco was a sign of adulthood. Inevitably, I was presented with an opportunity to try it out under peer pressure. After a few minutes, I felt sick and threw up. What was supposed to be a moment to show off my adulthood turned into an embarrassing moment and I never tried it ever again.

Regardless of logistical challenges, the vegetables were meant for the wounded fighters, and neither the prisoners nor the fighters were allowed to take home vegetables from the garden. Nevertheless, Maasho and I had no limitations. The best thing about our part-time job was that we got to eat as many fresh tomatoes as we liked. It was one of the best places to be during the hot weather – where freshwater from the well was available in abundance, a green oasis in the middle of the desert. Compared to the typical work the other guards did, I started to like my part-time job in the garden a lot.

One day, as Maasho and I were doing our daily duty at the garden, we heard MiG jet fighters in the distance. We ignored the MiGs thinking they were too far away. But very soon they started hovering over the area and circling unusually low. Then, before we could even think about what was going on, there was a loud blast. Shocked, Maasho and I ran for cover. The blast was exactly where the prison was located. We started worrying about the poor prisoners packed like sardines in the encampment with no way to get out of the prison and no cover to hide from. Another massive blast followed in less than one minute, hitting the same area. A third blast targeted the huts in the garden area around us. We were terrified and ran away from the garden.

As suddenly as the sound of bombs and screeching of MiGs had come, it stopped, leaving surreal silence hanging in the air. We wondered if it was over or if the planes would come back. Confused, we started running toward the camp. We realized that if the blast had hit the prison, it would be carnage. On the way, we met a fighter who had been sent to check on us. He was relieved to find both of us alive. The three of us started running back to the camp. The camp was on fire and thick smoke filled the sky. When we arrived at the camp, we saw hundreds of people scattered, looking for some shade under the trees near the riverbed. The guards and prisoners were mingled. Surprisingly, not even one person had been killed. The planes had hit some of the fighters' huts but missed the main prison. Thank God, the carnage was avoided.

The scorching heat forced everyone to search for cover under the trees. The hundreds of shoes that were parked at the entrance of the prison had all been burned and the prisoners were walking barefoot. The ground was so hot that no one could walk barefoot for long. So, the prisoners couldn't move away from their surroundings. Hoping that the airplanes would not come back, we all took a temporary shelter in the bushes around the area until the ground cooled off. The prisoners could have used this opportunity to escape, but they all remained, helping each other and cooperating with the guards.

Mogoraib was very far from the frontlines and apparently, no one was bothered about security there. Occasionally, we heard that another group of Eritrean fighters opposing our organization had hijacked our fighters, but it wasn't seen as a serious threat. Also, although the Ethiopian MiG fighters flew low to find targets, the prison camp that was exposed in the middle of an open field didn't look like a suspicious target to them and we never feared an aerial attack.

Having survived an attack that could have been devastating, the front decided to move the prison the same day to another location, about 80 miles away. Barefoot, the poor prisoners started the long walk to the new location. Amazingly, the prisoners didn't attempt to escape during the attack or the long trip to the new location. This was mainly because they were all waiting to finish their term and go back to their units to fight for the country they loved.

14. Jegorba

March 2015. Delta Flight 34 Seattle to Paris. I am heading to Abu Dhabi on a stressful sales campaign. The plane is a Boeing 767 with Wi-Fi connectivity but the interior is so old that I just posted on Facebook a picture of the business class entertainment unit and complained that Delta has to upgrade its fleet to meet today's needs of business travelers. How ironic that I posted the complaints while I am about to write a chapter of my life that contrasts so strongly with what I posted. I guess that is what some may call a "spoiled refugee".

After a long walking with the prisoners, we reached a place called Togorba. Togorba was a historic place. The first battle ever between the Ethiopian army and the liberation fighters took place in Togorba on 15 March 1964 and the fighters captured a few rifles from the Ethiopian soldiers which introduced the signature Eritrean slogan – "Fight the enemy with their weapons."

Our new location was chosen to be along the river, under thick bush covered with huge trees to make the camp invisible to the jet fighters. The initial decision to place the camp in the middle of the desert was primarily to prevent prisoners from escaping unnoticed, but that was no longer a consideration in light of the aerial attack we had sustained. The new prison perimeter was built quickly with the same thorny tree branches as we had in Mogoraib.

We stayed there for a few months during the rainy season when the logistical supplies were routinely interrupted due to flooded rivers blocking the trucks. In addition, the supply capacity was stretched thin due to the worsening military situation at the frontlines, primarily around Barentu. I remember for many days we ate wild vegetables collected from the surroundings. We simply boiled the vegetables in water and added a little salt to them. The taste was bad and our guts were cleansed in the following days. Unlike in Mogoraib, there were no palm trees around Togorba. The prisoners had it worse and some took drastic action to make it clear to us.

On one of the cold and rainy evenings, the prison camp was very silent and dark. Each of us, like we always do, took our positions and got ready for the night. On a rainy night like that, we would hunker down covering our body with whatever piece of plastic sheet we had, and simply try to get some sleep. Night movement around the prison was strictly regulated. Once the night guard schedule was on and the first guard was assigned just before the darkness ruled the night, any movement in and around the prison would raise suspicion and unwanted tension. The prisoners were not allowed to talk once the guard gave a stop sign using a flashlight. Complete silence was demanded.

Our leader, as the only person with a watch, was supposed to kick-start the night guard schedule by notifying the first guard to start his one-hour guard duty. After that, each guard would wake up the next guard according to the schedule. That fateful night, however, our leader fell asleep and the first guard didn't bother to start his duty either and fell asleep. The entire prison camp slept with no guards on duty. The prisoners noticed this easily because it was common for the guards to frequently turn on flashlights to check on them, but that night there was no flashlight.

The prisoners in the camp had diverse backgrounds, representing the nine different ethnic groups that spoke various languages in Eritrea. Three of the prisoners were from the Kunama tribe. The three Kunamas were most of the time living somewhat isolated from the rest of the prisoners because they spoke only the Kunama language. Their isolated life within the camp must have made life difficult for them and that night they saw an opportunity to change that.

Early in the morning, having performed no guard duty and enjoyed a good uninterrupted night sleep for the first time, we woke up refreshed. A refreshed feeling that quickly was smashed by the news that the three Kunamas were nowhere to be found. Panic set in and we frantically started investigating how they were able to escape. We dispatched a search squad and radioed all units in the vicinity to keep an eye for three fugitives.

A quick inspection of the perimeter uncovered the holes they had dug under the wall of thorny branches to make their escape. More shockingly, we found out that no one from our unit had been on guard duty that night. They had escaped while the guards were asleep. We quickly looked for a scapegoat and asked, why were other prisoners not able to hear them and prevent them from escaping?

This peculiar expectation was communicated to the prisoners in a meeting where our leader berated the prisoners and blamed them for failing to meet their patriotic duty. Their excuse was they didn't understand the Kunama language and therefore couldn't possibly know of the escape plan hatched in their presence.

Subsequently, an unwritten rule was enforced to speak only in the commonly spoken Arabic and Tigrinya in the prison, else one would be regarded with suspicion. We the guards also got an earful from the leader and felt ashamed of our perceived dereliction of duty. But, in our hearts, all of us concluded that it was worth the uninterrupted sleep we had enjoyed that night.

By that time, except a few cities, the entire Eritrean land had been liberated from the occupying Ethiopian army. Togorba was close to Barentu, one of the cities that were not liberated despite repeated attempts by the fighters. The mood in Eritrea was very positive and everyone believed that it was only a matter of time before the entire country was liberated and independence declared.

Little did we know that the Ethiopian army, supported by the Russians and Cubans, was preparing the biggest offensive that would start from inside Ethiopia across the border. Once the offensive started, it was obvious to the liberation fronts that it was suicidal to try to hold ground against such overwhelming firepower and hundreds of thousands of soldiers. A strategic withdrawal was declared.

It took the Ethiopians a few months to capture all the towns the ELF and EPLF had liberated in years. However, the front put up enough resistance to allow an orderly and strategic withdrawal of all units from the liberated areas. This meant all the prison facilities had to move to safer locations.

In August 1978, we started a long retreat toward the west, further away from Asmara and closer to the border with Sudan. Once our fighters reached appropriate terrain, we made a last stand. The ground offensive that swept large parts of the country resulted in thousands of displaced civilians. The offensive finally was semi-permanently halted with the EPLF holding the impenetrable Sahel mountains and the ELF occupying the hot and arid land of the Barka region. This meant that our fighters and all the logistical infrastructure were condensed and concentrated in a smaller area in the Barka region, threatening our existence.

Flight S7 1155A. Moscow to Rostov. I arrived in Moscow a few days ago and am now heading to Rostov for a two-day meeting with Donavia Airlines. My daughters have sent me two brand new songs they recorded while I was gone. I am listening to their songs as I write this story. It is one of these days when I am the only person who looks like me, everyone else looks and speaks differently. This is a domestic flight in Russia and you wouldn't find people who speak English. So, it is not a bad idea to continue writing my book at this point. An interesting coincidence is that I am in Russia while I am writing about Russian interference in our struggle for independence.

Under such treacherous circumstances, moving hundreds of prisoners from one location to another was not an easy task, especially when you haven't set up a new place where the prisoners were going to move in. In addition, a lot of prisoners could easily escape during the long trip which mostly took place at night. Nevertheless, although the prevailing conditions called for desperation and escape, no prisoners from our camp attempted to flee. After all, these were Eritreans who had left home voluntarily and joined the fighters to liberate Eritrea. They just happened to have made a mistake and were serving their sentence expecting to return to service soon.

The situation however was very different for the Ethiopian prisoners of war (POWs). We had thousands of POWs located in Keru working on a massive farming project. Moving these POWs at night was going to be a huge challenge. There was a legitimate concern they would all try to escape, especially in light of the advancing Ethiopian army. It was also rumored that the Ethiopians had plans to free these prisoners, which would give a tremendous morale boost to their army.

As we were retreating from Togorba, it wasn't clear to me where we were heading. But I never questioned anything and I thought wherever we were headed would be just fine. We had this odd feeling of invincibility. However, the ever-increasing noise of artillery was a reminder that the front was under severe stress. Some of the fighters in our team had to be sent to the frontline as reinforcement, and we had to manage with fewer guards. The separation from the comrades who were sent to the frontline felt as if a family member was being asked to move out. Some of them might never come out alive, and others we might never see again. It was a very cold feeling that took several days to get used to.

As the youngest member of the group, I was taken care of very well by the older fighters. Mike Eyob, our unit doctor, realized that I was the most vulnerable in the group and he made sure that I was not given difficult jobs. He would give me supplemental vitamins to help me resist the severe shortage of nutritional food. So, thanks to him, I never faced any health issues as we retreated from Togorba through the Hawashayt river to the new location called Alet.

15. *Life in Alet*

Except for the POW prison, the entire prison facility and
security offices settled in a location called Alet. Similar to
Togorba, the prison was set up under a thick forest on the
banks of the Alet river. My life in Alet was not too bad. By this time,
I had adapted pretty well to the life of a guard and knew my routine.
I was considered a full-fledged fighter and was given full
responsibility, like taking prisoners out to visit a doctor or for
interrogations. I was also allowed to stand guard at night which
meant that the entire platoon could go to sleep while I was on guard.
To be safe, two guards were deployed at a time; one would climb on
a makeshift observation post in front of the gate and check the
movement of the prisoners inside while the other walked around the
prison to check for anyone coming from the outside. We carried
powerful lanterns to shed light on anything suspicious.

Of course, this responsibility was gradually introduced. First I
was allowed to stand guard the first hour of the night when everyone
had not yet fallen asleep. Then slowly, I was given more
responsibility. I dreaded waking up in the middle of the night to
stand guard – it was very challenging. My body wanted to shut down
even as I walked around the prison. Especially when I sat at the
observation post, I had to insert a string of grass in my nostril and
rotate it to keep me awake; otherwise, my neck wouldn't hold my
head up.

When not on guard duty, the nights in Alet were enjoyable.
Before we fell asleep, the silence in the camp would be deafening.
Lying in my dedicated spot, every night, the sky opened up wide and
clear to give me a deep view of the universe in its vibrant and yet
darkest colors. The pristine night sky was breathtaking. It was dark
and filled with thousands of stars of different light intensities. I had
my favorite collection of stars that I admired and deeply connected
to. Occasional shooting stars, some with short trails and others with
bright and long streaks of light vaporizing high in the atmosphere,

would add suspense to the daily sky watching routine I practiced. I miss it now.

During the day, I never had any problem with the roles I was assigned, with one exception. There was one daily routine I never liked: taking prisoners to the "restroom". The prisoners were allowed to relieve themselves twice a day, early in the morning and in the evening.

The routine went as follows: when it was time, they put on whatever shoes they could find at the entrance, all of them would get in line and we would take them for a walkabout half a mile in a given direction. Then we would order them to find a spot where they could do their business. It was like taking many dogs for a walk. When one dog feels the need, it circles and sniffs to find a good spot, but the other dogs may not be there yet and pull you in the other direction. The prisoners would do the same. Once they knew we were close to what seemed an appropriate location to do their business, they would all crisscross each other, within the allowable boundary, to try to find a good spot.

Toilet paper or any kind of paper was not heard of. The most suitable location, therefore, was a place where many small brushes would offer privacy and lots of stones that were not too sharp. Sharp stones could damage the outlet as they tried to wipe. This was also true for the guards except that we had the option of going further away to find better wiping tools.

As the prisoners settle to do their business, we have to surround them to keep an eye on them and make sure no one can escape. Once they start producing waste, depending on the direction of the wind, the smell of hundreds of human-induced bio-pollution would make us almost faint. This problem always caused an argument amongst the guards about who should stand where. It was vital to find a strategic location where the wind blew to the opposite of where you stood. This was a job we did twice a day and our senses I am sure were desensitized by the smell. No one looked forward to it.

As you can imagine, going through this process for a long period resulted in all of the stones around the prison, regardless of which direction we went, being contaminated. Thankfully, the hot temperature of the region helped dry the stones quickly, making them ready for reuse in a couple of days.

Occasionally, less pleasant things took place. I remember there were only three female prisoners and were kept on the other side of the river. One of them was named Okba. Okba was a very beautiful girl in her mid-twenties who was accused of providing intelligence to the Ethiopian soldiers resulting in several deaths of our fighters. She was in prison for almost a year and then the judge handed her the death penalty by execution.

She was taken from her prison and was told she was going to "move" to another location. A grave had already been dug for her about a mile away. On the way to her new location, and just before they reached the grave, the two fighters who accompanied her shot her in the back and just like that ended the life of a young and beautiful Eritrean lady. In some ways, compared to a confrontational execution, this was humane since she didn't know that she would be executed on that fateful day and didn't suffer a traumatic experience.

The execution of Okba affected me deeply. I believed that she could have served her term and then been allowed to join the fighters. Unfortunately, in a system that didn't know mercy, the execution was her fate. Similarly, the punishment for gay people, although a very rare occurrence, was ten years to the death penalty which I never liked. At that time, I believed that gay people needed psychiatric help or medical treatment to become normal people, not execution. This for me was one of the darker moments in the history of our struggle in the 1970s.

Another embarrassing activity I participated in was waking up one of the disorderly fighters to do whatever business he had to do while I stood guard. It was one of the disgusting things I have done during my deployment as a guard, which I regret sincerely. When I would take guard and everyone would be asleep, that individual would ask me to wake him up at night to seek sexual encounters with a woman fighter who was the assistant nurse of the platoon. She was the only female member of the unit and she stayed in her small hut that served as a clinic. Facilitating such an encounter was not appropriate, and would have been certainly punishable by law had the leadership known about it. Yet, both of them seemed to be content with what was happening. She could have reported this to her superior and my friend would have been in trouble. I never thought the whole thing through to realize that it was not the right thing to do. If anyone had come to know of it, I would have ended up in the very prison that I was guarding. Much later in life, I understood why my father had always told me "staying away from bad friends is a challenging thing, it is much easier to avoid befriending them."

The winters in Alet were really bad. There were mosquitoes everywhere and malaria was a rampant problem. We had no mosquito nets. At night the only thing that stood between me and the mosquitoes was a thin white sheet that covered my body. Each morning, I would wake up to find my sheet spotted with little red dots of blood. I have been sick multiple times from malaria. Fortunately, the doctor of our unit, Mikel, took care of me as if I were his young brother. He would request my commander if I could be assigned to help him (the doctor) during a visit to the prisoners. The supply of medication was very limited, yet the doctor would give me malaria-prevention tablets as well as a Vitamin B12 injection when available in quantity, just so I could feel strong and not get sick. This was a special privilege that no other fighter was getting.

Mikel felt very sorry for me. For him, I was too fragile and too young to live away from home in such a hostile environment. My appearance and how I looked as a young boy made every fighter that met me feel sympathy for me. I was a typical city boy with soft skin and feminine features. In a place where everyone dressed the same, many fighters would mistake me for a young girl. There is no worse experience for a teenage boy than to be mistaken for a girl. My appearance was made worse particularly by a problem I had with hormonal balance during my puberty years. I developed pointy nipples that I couldn't hide. If you have too much estrogen or too little testosterone, the tissue of the breast swells and forms a breast bud. Right when I thought I was transformed into a seasoned 14-year-old warrior, pointy and painful breast lumps put a dent in my ego. Ibrahim had the same problem but much worse – it generated slimy fluid. But the look of his face and body muscles was so masculine, he had no issue.

Relatively speaking, life in Alet was one of the most luxurious periods of my life in the jungle. We had water wells in the river supplying us with reasonably clean water, a good supply of basic wheat, salt, and sugar. Even those who were addicted to tobacco were served well. Heck, we even were able to purchase a goat and eat meat once a month. This, however, applied to the guards only. It was a different story for the prisoners. Most importantly, we were never detected by the jet fighters that flew low over the riverbanks looking for any sign of life in the jungle.

As for the prisoners, most of them, after serving their term, went back to join the fight, and many lost their lives in the process. Andemichael was also freed and went on to be the first person who was able to relay a message to my parents, through messengers who traveled to Asmara, that I was alive and well.

Leninism & Marxism

IV

Leninism & Marxism

February 4, 2014. United Flight, Los Angeles to Hong Kong. This trip is a special one. For the first time, I was able to take my wife with me to Hong Kong. She is sitting in first class while I am stuck back in business class. United Airlines happened to have great first-class mileage deals. She deserved this. Normally, my trips are never set ahead of time and many times get canceled at the last minute. Therefore, it is always difficult to decide to take someone with me. Hong Kong is one of my favorite cities after Sydney, and enjoying the city with my wife would be an amazing experience. The last time I visited Hong Kong, there was a Category-4 typhoon that shut down the city. No cars were allowed to drive and we were stuck in the hotel the entire day canceling our meeting with Cathay Pacific. I am glad the weather forecast is good this time. In the meantime, we have a long way to go and this is a perfect time to work on my story.

16. *The Vanguards - Merih*

In 1979, at a point when I had just begun to feel accepted as a full-fledged fighter, the ELF leadership noticed that there were too many young kids joining the revolution. They decided that all fighters who were under the age of 16 needed to be brought to a central location and given advanced military and political training in preparation for a long liberation struggle and to develop the next generation of fighters. This was in line with our motto, "Our struggle is long and bitter but our victory is certain." An order was passed to all units to send all young fighters to a newly set-up camp.

It was a very difficult order for me to accept, but there was no choice. About 12 youngsters collected from various units stationed in Alet were sent to this camp. This meant that after more than two years apart, we, the young kids who had come together from the training camp in Kerkebet, would get together for a reunion. We handed over our weapons and headed to the camp for a new and exciting challenge. This time, however, we didn't need an escort – we were expected to navigate our way to the destination on our own.

After a few hours of walking and crossing several rivers, we arrived at the new camp in a place called Lakoyb. Lakoyb is the name of a river that runs parallel to the border with Sudan. At a mere distance of only 25 miles from the border, this was the farthest location I had ever been since I left home.

Once in the camp, we were received by a tall, well-spoken man who was the commissioner of the camp – Mr. Yohannes. He wore civilian attire and looked more like a teacher than a fighter. In his very intellectual-sounding explanation, he briefed us on why we were there. He said, "This camp was established to cultivate a new generation of fighters. The name of the camp is Hayltat Merih, meaning The Vanguards, and the front has high expectations of you."

We joined other youngsters to form a 100-man strong unit (Dewra), a Deja-vu moment that reminded me of Kerkebet, the first military training camp. Except, unlike in Kerkebet, the girls and boys were not segregated. We all lived and trained together. The girls were newbies and still sported the "city girl" look. They were beautiful and sophisticated. I am not sure why they thought it was a good idea to mix teenage boys and girls in the same camp.

There were about 15 girls of about the same age in the camp. This was a new experience for all of us and I knew it was going to be an exciting camp as soon as I realized a beautiful young girl had been assigned to my unit. For the first time since I left my hometown more than two years ago, I saw girls my age who came from the highlands and spoke my language. It was as if I had landed on a different planet where beautiful young girls roamed freely under the shades of gigantic acacia trees. Despite the difficulty of having a private moment with anyone of them, every time I got a chance to command a smile or attention from any of the girls, I felt an immense adrenaline rush. It was a sign that my stay in the camp was going to be exciting, and I embraced the place with a full heart. What a special feeling that was!

At that age, appearance and how you look are everything. It is important for your self-esteem – yes, even in the jungle. Since I was under the good care of my friend and steward Dr. Mikel, I still bore some semblance to a city boy. Arguably, I must have not looked unattractive if people were mistaking me for a girl, not the greatest experience from a man's perspective.

Yet, I never knew how I looked. I had never had a chance to look in a mirror. I desperately needed to know how I looked. The last time I'd seen my face was years before – when I used to borrow a very small mirror from my mentor Yehualashet in Mogoraib. Even then, I was never able to see my entire face. The mirror was not only small but also cracked. I had to scan the mirror around my face, one piece at a time, starting with the left eyebrow moving to the right, going down toward my cheek and down to my lips. My favorite part of my face were my eyebrows, yet I never knew how they contributed to my overall look since I had no way of seeing my entire face. Nevertheless, the glimpse of a few parts of my face gave me hope that I was an okay-looking young boy. My self-confidence was heavily influenced by how I saw myself. Since I had no way of seeing myself, I settled for seeing parts of my face that boosted my ego. Eyebrows did the job for me.

The front was going through very stressful times. A year earlier, a massive Ethiopian offensive forced us to withdraw from all liberated areas. As A result, being in a teenage camp couldn't be considered a bad situation by any standards. Elsewhere, many fighters were falling to defend our bases. But, Lakoyb was safe to the point where, other than a handful of security personnel, no one carried a gun in the camp.

The first serious job we were given upon our arrival was to build a shelter from the tree trunks and leaves. There were also large tents that we had to set up which could sleep 30 people at a time. For safety reasons, these tents and shelters were built deep in the bushes so that no jet fighters could detect them from the skies. Unfortunately, the deeper we went into the bushes, the more dangerous it became due to encounters with wild animals like hyenas, snakes and scorpions. The tents and shelters served as protection from rain and the sun. They were not designed to protect us from gusty wind or cold weather, much less from wild animals. When gusty winds or sandstorms hit the area, we struggled to keep the tents in place.

Those of us who came from Alet and joined the third Dewra, because of our two years of deployment experience, were some of the more respected youngsters. We were politically seasoned and militarily matured. At least, we felt that way. It was obvious to us that all the other kids in the first Dewra were taken straight from the military training camp to this Vanguard camp, with no "real-life" deployment experience. But when it came to physical activity, the first unit was superior since they had received intensive training for more than six months before our arrival. We had a lot of catching up to do to reach their level. So, just like in Kerkebet, there was very healthy competition amongst the units.

Once a week there was a cultural event where we all got together for a dance near the riverbank. The band that played the music during the events consisted entirely of the first unit. In a bid to diversify the talent pool, our unit was asked if we had any kids with talent in music or art in general. During my deployment at the prison, I had learned how to play a traditional guitar called *Kirar*. I became so good at it that I used to frequently entertain our unit (the prison guards) by playing the instrument.

Another fellow from our unit by the name of Wodi Keshi was a great singer. We teamed up to create a band and planned to give a show at the weekly event. We performed one song and the entire camp was in love with the song. It became an instant hit in the camp and every week they wanted us to perform the song and more. The song was catchy and the chorus was about the core asset of Eritrea and why many countries colonized Eritrea – the Red Sea.

Having seen how much talent there was in the camp, the leadership decided to create a single band from various units. The band consisted of about ten boys and girls, with me and another boy named Muktar Saleh being the anchor instrument players. Our drum player was Abdela, who made an improvised drum set using hide from wild pigs.

Being in the band allowed us to mingle with some key players from the other units. We soon became the stars of the camp, and we were privileged to get together outside the regular hours to rehearse. This enhanced our social life and routinely got us out of the military lifestyle to enjoy being teenagers with unlimited creativity. We experimented with various instruments and combinations of sound. Since everything was handmade, we had to make an instrument that would generate a bass sound and make drums from wild pig leather.

As more and more youngsters joined the camp, the importance of the cultural event increased. The band had to play songs in different languages reflecting the culturally diverse population of the camp. Entertainment included not only creating music, but also writing scripts, acting, poetry, and acrobatics.

April 17, 2011. Tupolev 154B, flight from Moscow to Orenburg. This is my first time flying a Russian-made passenger airplane. I have traveled in Russian-made equipment before, specifically an M8 military helicopter, but never a plane. This airplane seems heavy but flies solid through the turbulent air. Two loud Russian men sit in front of me and they sound like they drank too much alcohol. I wish I had noise cancellation headphones.

This part of Russia is very different from the fancy lifestyle of Moscow. Everything is worn out and needs an upgrade, including the dedicated transportation bus provided to us by Orenburg Air. This trip wasn't glamorous at all.

The trainers in the camp were very intelligent and superior military trainers. Since this camp was new and no one had any experience on what to expect with hundreds of teenagers in a single camp, it was somewhat experimental for the organization. The trainers were clearly divided in their objectives. The military trainers wanted to produce the next commando units with advanced military skills and the vanguards that could become commanders in the future. The political cadres on the other wanted to produce a new generation of leaders based on the Leninist–Marxist doctrine, who would eliminate corruption in the army as well as the abuse of power by military commanders. These two objectives were not in sync. Yet, we were getting the best training available in the organization and gained tremendous knowledge on both military and political fronts.

As a result of our training and political upbringing, our theatrical acts and songs started to reflect what we were taught in the camp. Fighting corruption became almost a revolution within the revolution. On every occasion, we would highlight the abuse that took place by military commanders in a very entertaining way. Our young age was a shield that no military leader could penetrate to shut us up, and we got away with statements and songs that others would end up in jail for. Additionally, we were fierce believers in women's rights and wrote poems and songs against the gender and cultural oppression Eritrean women were subjected to. Equal right for women was non-negotiable.

As a prominent member of the cultural band, I ended up playing instruments, singing, acting as well as writing songs and theatre scripts. I enjoyed art and the creative process very much. Together with Muktar, who was the second musician, we started to become the stars within the camp. Muktar was a young Muslim boy born in the city of Keren. Although I am a Christian, our cultural and religious differences were not an obstacle to our close friendship in any way. Our shared interests in music and the social life in the camp allowed us to become best friends. The social experience and friends I made allowed me to become a well-rounded young man with tremendous tolerance and respect for multicultural diversity. I learned to speak several languages like Tigre and Arabic. This allowed me to enjoy other people's cultures and habits even better.

Armed with a friendship that knew no borders, the band became a phenomenal team that amazed everyone. We became the pride of the organization in how young people could be transformed into a powerful fighting force. We would go on tour to various remote places to perform live and show off our athletic and commando skills, like jumping through a ring of fire. Later on, our revolutionary songs started to play on the radio and we became the stars in the jungle.

Our political view was shaped by Mao's *Little Red Book* and the Leninist–Marxist ideology. They became our bible. We were trained to debate and analyze logical arguments to arrive at the truth. We started looking at complex political and social challenges from multiple perspectives to arrive at the most realistic and reasonable reconciliation of ostensibly contradictory information and positions. We were trained to resent materialism and we became idealists striving to achieve justice for the oppressed masses.

We were brainwashed to be a pure communist power and started to hate capitalism and imperialism. Our objective and goal for Eritrea were to embark on a path that would take us from feudalist society straight to socialism, bypassing capitalism. Coupled with the influence of some Arab countries in the region, we also started to list Zionism as one of our enemies. We sympathized deeply with the cause of the Palestinians and we learned about other movements in Africa, Vietnam, and more. In addition, we were brainwashed to hate the second Eritrean organization, the EPLF, depicted as a reactionary organization that, by refusing to unite with the ELF, had prolonged the suffering of our people and the liberation struggle.

We were fed well and walked around the camp top-naked, showing off our upper body strength that was impressive to look at – at least so we thought. After all, appearance is in the eyes of the beholder. Each one of us wanted to be the Rambo of the jungle. Physical appearance and strength were what we all wanted to shine at. Muktar and Ibrahim had incredibly well-developed muscles that we could only dream of. But, unlike my friends, I didn't develop much muscle that I could proudly show off.

To highlight my physical weakness, a family member who used to work as a veterinarian in the area stopped by to visit the camp, and when he saw me, he said, in a very concerned voice: "Mulugheta, you have serious signs of severe protein deficiency – your belly is bloated". He continued to examine me like a doctor by gently pressing my belly and kept mumbling that I was not well. I don't remember how I reacted. If he only knew the damage he caused to my ego and self-confidence that day!

In addition to the "bloating" issue the vet pointed out that I had a serious itching problem under my arms. That was not news to me. I had to constantly hide my irritated skin. If there was any major problem in my jungle life, it was the allergic reaction I had, possibly due to some of the plants in the jungle or the food, which made my life difficult. With the extreme heat of the lowlands and humidity, the itching was sometimes unbearable. Occasionally, the itchy spot would get infected and I would feel the pain for an extended period. With my friend and custodian Dr. Mikel not being there, I was not able to get the medical treatment I used to enjoy earlier.

17. The Hunting Expedition

During wintertime, the front had a serious problem with logistics and supply. The fighters scattered everywhere in Eritrea had to be provisioned with food and ammunition at all times. Our new camp was located on the banks of one of the biggest rivers in Eritrea, the Barka River. We moved there because Lakoyb couldn't accommodate the expansion of the camp.

When it rained in the highlands, the Barka river would be very full, and no person or truck could cross the river to deliver any food to our camp. So, just before the rainy season would start, we were supposed to hoard enough food for the winter. Sometimes, early rain in the highlands brought unpleasant surprises and we would run out of food in the camp. That was when we would go hunting for warthogs. Imagine how many warthogs would be needed to feed more than 500 teenagers for many days.

Hunting warthogs was one of my favorite things. A team of four of us was sent to hunt as many warthogs as possible. Our team leader was my best friend Ibrahim, and we were equipped with a few hundred bullets each and four guns. We walked a long way off the camp to find the warthogs. We were experts on where and when to find the warthogs. It was usually after the heat of the day cooled off, just before it got dark when they would all come out to drink water or graze. We would kill as many of the warthogs as possible and ask the villagers (more like order them) to load the dead warthogs on their camels and transport them to the camp.

As we wandered off too far from the camp, there was no way we could accompany the loaded camels to the camp. Instead, we would simply send the villagers alone to deliver the load to the camp. We stayed roaming in the remote areas for days. We had no place to sleep and no communication with the camp other than through the messengers would deliver warthogs to the camp. With every delivery, we would receive a message requesting us to return to the base, but we would conveniently ignore the orders and keep enjoying the wildlife and the freedom. We were free to shoot at whatever we thought was a good target. With hundreds of bullets at our disposal and our curiosity in the wilderness, we had a lot of fun.

The gun I carried, my favorite Belgium's rifle L1A1.

At one point, I remember coming across hundreds of monkeys, and we were confronted by them. Fearing the leader of the monkeys could launch an attack on us, we targeted the male leader first and shot him dead. The monkeys wouldn't go away without taking the body of their leader so we shot more monkeys. The screaming of all these hundreds of monkeys and jumping from one tree branch to another for us was funny at that time and we never thought that we were inflicting so much pain and misery on the monkeys in their habitat. Looking back on this incident makes me realize that once a person has a gun and feels the power of ruling the jungle, he or she turns off the part of the brain that controls reasonableness and turns into a monster.

The freedom of being able to do whatever we wanted without any sense of accountability was an experience that I will never forget. We did silly things like agreeing to punish the person who sleeps the most and waking him up by shooting a gun at a very close range to that person's ear. What a stupid idea! I have to say we never did that more than once since the first person who was the victim of such a silly deal experienced extreme ear pain for days after the execution of our reckless action. Nevertheless, we experienced it as fun and acted just as we were designed to act – like teenagers.

After we ran out of ammunition, we would go back to the camp. We were received as heroes who fed the camp for days, but at the same time received a lecture from the camp leader that we ignored orders to return on time. If we hadn't run out of ammunition we would have stayed away from the camp for a much longer period. No need to say that the number of bullets we wasted compared to the number of warthogs we killed was not proportional. Yet, we received a certain status that allowed us to brag.

The abundance of meat in the camp however created a problem for us. Wild animals like hyenas and huge pythons were attracted to the camp and started to settle closer and closer to our camp. In the mornings, we would find hyena droppings everywhere in the camp and we started to panic. Fortunately, no incident took place and we lost no one to the hyenas who could be extremely dangerous.

The pythons settled in our camp and mainly in the area where we cooked food. Twice, we found huge pythons who dug a hole in the middle of our camp, and I had the honor of facing them as close as no more than 3 feet before killing the two pythons with an AK-47 while they were still rolled up in their hole. That was by no means bravery considering social media is full of videos showing people catching pythons with their bear hands. Of course, both pythons we killed were a great addition to the list of animals we could get protein from.

The animals that don't provide protein and can't be killed with an AK-47, however, were terrifying to me, especially the big black scorpions. These scorpions with thick tails were highly venomous, unlike the smaller white scorpions. During the first rain of the season, the baby scorpions popped out of the ground in hundreds – a terrifying event! Fortunately, these are not very venomous. I was a victim of these scorpions a few times. One day, I washed my only underwear and placed it on a branch to dry. A small scorpion happily found a home in my underwear. Unsuspecting, I pulled up my underwear and was stung in a very uncomfortable location. Needless to say, I took a life lesson not to just drag your underpants up but shake them off first.

But a real terror came from the skies. Like many other people, I was very terrified when the MiG jet fighters flew low above the ground trying to find our camps. The pilots could see that there was a road that led to the camps in the jungle. However, once the road disappeared into the jungle, they couldn't pinpoint the exact location of the camps due to the thick forest covering the road and the extreme caution we exercised not to be noticed. Most of the time, we could hear the jets ahead of time and we would prepare, but sometimes a terrorizing thunderous roar would fill the air out of nowhere testing our emergency preparedness system.

We never cooked during the day to avoid smoke exposing our location, and we made sure that no items were left in the open that could give away our location. We had dedicated security personnel whose hourly routine was to inspect the entire camp to make sure none of the items were exposed. We also made sure that none of us wore clothes that were not camouflage. Due to the shortage of supplies and uniforms, sometimes we would be given civilian clothes that came from Red Cross or some non-government organizations. We made sure that every civilian dress was soaked in dark green dye to make it camouflaged and less visible to the jet fighters.

Unfortunately, despite the precautions we took, the jets started to fly over more frequently making us believe that they were seriously looking for the camps. One day, they finally noticed what they were looking for. A few kids who had wandered off the forest area were sighted by the MiG jets. They started to circle our camp. Although we could have stationed anti-aircraft guns to try to shoot one down, that would have given our position away and we would have become the target for daily bombardments by the MIGs. Two bombs were dropped across the river, about a mile from where our camp was.

The kids who had wandered off and given their position away belonged to another youth camp called Tsbah, meaning "The

Future" or "Pioneers". Tsbah was a camp of young kids from ages 5 to 16 and they were being trained to become the next educated leaders of the front and eventually our country. Unlike our camp, the youngsters were not intended to get advanced military training. Instead, once they complete middle school, they were sent to Sudan to continue their high school education.

Fortunately, the MiGs did not detect our camp. The training we received to stay put and not venture out during bombing raids paid off. Although the fire that started as a result of the bombing quickly spread across the forest, it was extinguished on time, which saved us huge effort and mobilization. Tsbah camp was fortunate that the MiGs didn't try to carpet-bomb the entire area. The camp got away with only a few kids losing their lives.

We were extremely wary of fires in the camp. During the rainy season, it was common for lightning to strike some of the tall trees, and the forest caught fire. Sometimes, it took us days to fight and extinguish the fire and years for the forest to recover. Fighting fires was probably one of the hardest tasks and most frightening experiences. The sound of fire burning trees and crackers around you was terrifying, not to mention the squeaking sounds of all kinds of animals that get burned alive. Had the MiGs dropped incendiary devices to firebomb our positions, we would have had serious issues to deal with.

18. The Graduation

After the massive Ethiopian ground offensive in the summer of 1978 that forced the ELF and EPLF to retreat to remote areas bordering Sudan, the Ethiopians attempted five massive conventional offensives, primarily against the EPLF's positions in the Sahel mountains. The failure of these offensives in which tens of thousands of Ethiopian soldiers died gave the Eritreans fighters a chance to recover.

In the early 1980s, the tide was turning in our favor. The ELF and EPLF started to launch counter-attacks on Ethiopian government positions. By the summer of 1980, it was obvious that the front had survived the onslaught of the Ethiopians, Russians, and Cubans. It was time to consolidate our forces and get ready for a comeback. Multiple reconciliation attempts to unite the two fronts, however, did not succeed. On the contrary, the ELF and the EPLF grew further apart and the animosity between the two escalated.

In August 1980, after more than a year of training in advanced military tactics and socialist doctrine, our Merih camp produced young fighters who were brainwashed in communist ideology as well as strong individuals who were fearless in voicing their opinions and fighting for justice. We were ready to celebrate our graduation. Our creative minds went wild in creating songs and theatrical acts that depicted who we were and what we stood for. Several high-ranking officials were expected to attend the ceremony. This was our chance to shine.

While the preparation and rehearsals were in full swing, very unpleasant news started to emerge. A major battle had broken out between the ELF and EPLF. Unlike the many skirmishes that had taken place in the past, this time the fighting seemed to have taken a very different nature. It would be up to historians to research and confirm who started the attack and why. We were told by our leaders that the EPLF leadership had started the war to eliminate the ELF to have a single organization lead the liberation front.

All the attempts made to unite the two organizations since 1974 and the numerous joint military coordination exercises that had given our people hope for unity were replaced with a bloody fight amongst brothers. It was clear the attack that was launched was a major undertaking aimed at removing the ELF from Eritrea. Several years earlier, the ELF unsuccessfully tried to eliminate the EPLF claiming that Eritrea cannot tolerate more than one organization. Ever since, the animosity had grown worse.

Over the years, the ELF received significant support from the Arab countries to the point where it lost its independent thinking. The EPLF, however, since its inception in 1970, relied primarily on its resources with full political independence. The result was that ten years later, the EPLF became a powerful and disciplined force that was fiercely independent and militarily more powerful than the ELF.

The timing for the graduation was very unfortunate. Due to the serious nature of the war, the ELF leadership decided that the fresh graduates should immediately head to the battlefront to reinforce the units. In addition, all fighters who were engaged in civil and other non-combat services were instructed to head to the battlefront as well. Sandwiched between the EPLF to the northeast and the Ethiopian army to the southwest, we faced an existential threat.

Hurriedly we completed our graduation ceremony. I marched with the graduates and was excited to finally be released from the camp. We packed whatever belongings we had and readied to leave. The sense of insecurity and excitement was nerve-racking, but we were ready to defend our territory and organization from the EPLF's aggression. Deep within me, however, I resented the idea of fighting against Eritreans and family members who had joined the EPLF. My uncles Solomon and Zekarias had joined the EPLF and so were many of my neighbors. I didn't sign up for this. Silently I hoped, if my Kerkebet experience was any indication, that we would be spread all over Eritrea and I be assigned a job other than fighting my own.

After the graduation ceremony, the day that everyone was expected to be marching out of the camp, nine youngsters and I were called to the administration tent. We were told that we would be staying in the camp to join the staff members to help train another batch of youngsters who had arrived in the camp a few weeks earlier. Envying the fighters who were ready to deploy, we took offense to the decision. We felt that we were not good enough for combat operations. In reality, we were selected because we were considered a special talent that needed to be retained. Some of the group members were my best friends, including Muktar, which made the news bearable.

Other groups of talented students, like my friend Maasho and music band members, were sent to various non-combatant assignments and training programs, but later, they too joined the battlefront to prevent the collapse of the organization. It was clear to me that the reason I was selected to stay in the camp was not because of my superior military skills but primarily because of my musical skills and my ability to connect with the trainers. They must have seen something in me that needed to be preserved. Whatever that was.

Recognizing the achievement of the Merih camp, the ELF leadership decided to increase the budget and supply us with more military hardware. Russian-made B10 rocket launchers and DShK anti-aircraft machine guns arrived in our camp, and we started the trainer program. At the same time, hundreds of new fresh young fighters arrived for training.

Within a few months after our assignment, while we were still assimilating to the transition from student to staff members, the battle between the ELF and the EPLF that was taking place far away in the Sahel mountains moved closer to our base in Barka. The sound of heavy machine guns and rockets was getting louder and louder. We started seeing rocket launchers and mechanized units taking positions in the mountains and hills around our camp. This was a clear indication that our fighters were being pushed back and were constantly withdrawing from their positions.

Rows of camels loaded with food and utensils arrived at our camp. These were units that prepared food for the fighters at the frontline. Things were moving too fast and in the wrong direction. The next thing we saw was medical units started arriving around our camp with wounded fighters. Concerned, we were told to be alert and ready to defend our camp. We were also told to look out for individual fighters who might be trying to escape or were lost during the retreat from the frontlines, a dose of the bitter reality that being a fighter doesn't always mean you are always victorious.

Yitbarek, my uncle who had joined the ELF years before me, was at the scene. I had never heard of his whereabouts. But somehow, he knew that I was in the camp. Soaked with blood all over his military outfit, he showed up in our camp and asked for my name. Things were chaotic and the situation seemed out of control. I ran down to the riverbank to meet him. It was around 5 p.m. and the sun was setting.

We hugged each other and Yitbarek said to me, "Make sure you get the hell out of this camp and never volunteer to go to the frontline," in an alarming tone. Acting as my big brother, he added, "Are you listening? I am dead serious! You need to find a way to get out." His tone and words were subdued but caring at the same time. I knew the front was in deep crisis and told him I would be fine. After spending about 10 minutes with me, he had to leave for his unit and disappeared just as quickly as he had shown up.

It was getting late. Hundreds of fighters descended to the riverbed indicating that our camp was now in danger of being attacked the same night or the following day. A sense of frustration, bewilderment, and shock marked the atmosphere in the camp. How was it possible that for years we had withstood the offensive of the mightiest Ethiopian army while we were outnumbered by at least 10 to 1 and outgunned by a multitude of that, and we now seemed to be chased out of our positions in just a few months by our brothers who were marginally equipped better? No one had an answer. However, our leadership responded to the military setbacks by declaring a "Martial law" that gave unlimited authority to commanders to shoot fighters who were escaping or retreat without permission.

About five trucks came to our camp and we were given instructions to evacuate the camp ASAP. Not to risk being stuck in the sand at that critical moment, the trucks were made to stay across the riverbed. So, as we moved the students across the river, we were joined by the fighters and medics from the frontline, making it look like a confusing withdrawal. We rushed to load every student and accounted for everyone in the camp. Leaving the fighters behind, loaded on Fiat N3 trucks, we made our escape from the area to a safer distance, toward the border of Sudan.

The darkness created a sense of security, but at the same time, I was saddened by what I had heard from my uncle and by what I saw during our withdrawal. The organization that once was known for its bravery and ferocity in battles now was disintegrating in front of my eyes. I started imagining what it must be like to remain behind and fight in and around our camp at night. I kept remembering Yitbarek's blood-soaked appearance again and again with a sense of helplessness. Occasional flashbacks of the time when Yitbarek was a handsome young man riding his red motorcycle in Asmara confused my brain. I didn't want to believe what I was experiencing.

Now that we encountered many fighters from the frontlines, the news started to trickle about the fate of many of my graduated friends. I heard that Yonas Beraki, whom I had made friends with in Meqerka, a village where we registered for the first time to join the fighters, was martyred on his first deployment day to the frontlines. I was left in disbelief and devastated when I heard that Wodi Keshi, who was the first singer I had ever performed with, had also lost his life in the mountains around our camp. Later, many more snippets of similar sad news followed. Many other boys and girls from our camp had lost their lives in a senseless conflict. We were not the invincible fighters that I had always thought we were. I realized how lucky I was not to be sent to the frontlines if it was that easy for my friends to disappear. That was when I started to believe in fate and higher powers guiding life.

Graduation and deployment time (Yonas Beraki who martyred is 2nd from left)

Early morning run and physical training on the river sand

Military dicipline was a fundamental culture in the camp

The fighters in front lines sleep wherever they can
(Photo credit EPLF)

Life in Barka in its most luxurious form (photo credit Muller Zergaber)

My unit: Final military parade before deployment to the front line

Pioneer Camp: Trained to be a disciplined force to serve in the future
(Photo credit Muller Zergaber)

EPLF Trainees (Photo credit EPLF)

Empty Pouch

Kirar (music instrument) was an essential element of daily life
(Photo Credit EPLF)

V

Empty Pouch

August 8, 2014. Flight El AL Amsterdam to Tel Aviv. The check-in counter of El Al at Schiphol looked terrifying. Armed Dutch military was stationed at every corner. Given the history of Israel, I was not surprised to see the tight security. Everyone in the line was speaking Hebrew and there was not even a single black person to be seen in the crowd. After a rigorous security check, I was led to a special office where I was interrogated for more than 45 minutes. I told them I work for Boeing and have a meeting with El Al Airlines. But that was not believable. Eventually, I was asked to turn on my computer and show the presentation I planned to discuss with El Al airlines. They kept me in the office while everyone was boarding the plane. Eventually, they escorted me to the plane and I was free to go. The security protocol I went through was simply insane. I don't blame them. But, as much as I love El Al team in Tel Aviv, this may be my last flight with El Al.

The war between the ELF and the EPLF lasted exactly a year. During that time, the Ethiopian soldiers quietly observed the fighting between the brothers, waiting for one to fall so that they could finish the job of destroying the other easily.

Some ELF units that were stationed deep in Eritrea withdrew for more than 800 miles while putting up resistance, but in the end, they realized there was something wrong with the ELF leadership. Toward the end, they refused to fight anymore, pointing to the mismanagement of our organization and lack of leadership. The senior ELF leadership was in disarray, unable to control the situation. All the fighters did was put up just enough resistance to withdraw to the next line of defense with minimal casualties.

In the meantime, I was transferred from the Merih (Vanguard) camp to the Tsbah (Pioneers) camp where I joined the staff that was depleted because some trainers were simply abandoning their responsibility and escaping the camp. I was 17. During the months that followed, we were forced to relocate several times, toward the border with Sudan. Barka, being one of the most arid regions of Eritrea, once you are forced from your shadows of the thick vegetation, the next shadow was found in the next river you find. Even as we withdrew from one location to another, the training continued in a quickly assembled and improvised camps.

In August 1981, the entire organization, approximately 20,000 strong fighters, including all non-combatant members and our camp, were forced to assemble at the border of Sudan. It was a chaotic scene, with no one in charge and nowhere to go. The EPLF had achieved its goal of driving ELF out of Eritrea within a year, something that the Ethiopian army was unable to do in 20 years. The Sudanese army was concerned and watched our every move. It was obvious they didn't want us to enter the Sudanese territory with all of our arms. We were sandwiched between two armies, the EPLF in front and the Sudanese army in the back.

Eventually, an agreement was reached between the Sudanese government and the ELF leadership to allow us to enter the Sudanese territory, provided we surrendered our weapons. An order was circulated to all the units to disarm and hand over all our weapons to the Sudanese army until further notice. Some fighters quickly buried their weapons and others simply refused to give up their weapons. Those who didn't want to enter Sudan started slipping back into Eritrea or surrendered to the EPLF. Many who couldn't process the loss committed suicide. Others decided to simply stop fighting and go back home, wherever that may be.

A small group of a few hundred fighters managed to squeeze their way out to the north with their arms and somehow managed to stay intact, away from the Sudanese army and EPLF fighters. That group was led by a notoriously anti-EPLF leader named Abdela Idris. The rest of the ELF fighters were assembled in two locations inside Sudanese territory – Korokon and Tehaday – all with empty ammo pouches. I was located in Korokon camp which was close to the city of Kassala in Sudan. The camp was under full control of the Sudanese army and no one could move out without proper paperwork.

The camp was supposed to be a temporary shelter, but gradually it turned into a permanent military camp. We all wore military gear and lived a military lifestyle, but carried no weapons and no bullets. We were still fighters in spirit and purpose. However, with no weapons and no leadership, our numbers started to decline gradually. Every night we would hear of people escaping the camp – they felt that this was the end of the road for the ELF.

All attempts to revive the organization were in vain. On the contrary, there was huge disagreement amongst the leadership and they started assassinating each other. The fighters were split into multiple factions and there was no hope of getting back to Eritrea as a single organization. The armed group that had escaped to the north eventually turned out to be a fraction of the Islamist movement that, to begin with, could be considered the source of all the tension within Eritrean movements. The ELF, the largest and oldest organization that had fought the Ethiopian occupiers from 1961 to 1981 was on the verge of collapse.

Yet, for me and thousands of other fighters, there was nowhere to go. Whatever the situation might be and however long it took, we were determined to stay with the organization with the hope to re-enter Eritrea and continue our struggle against the Ethiopian occupiers. In the meantime, the fighters' morale was badly damaged and the leaders had to do something to improve the morale before they could try to implement any operation aimed at getting us back into Eritrea. What better way to do this than through music and poetry?

Music and poetry are known to invoke strong emotions and were used in the Eritrean struggle for independence as a major instrument to mobilize people. The front assembled quickly whatever musicians and singers they could find and there I was once again finding myself playing the guitar in a new band.

In the middle of the hot, arid, and dissolute landscape of Sudan, we were privileged to have gotten access to some of the most advanced musical instruments you can find. We had top-quality lead guitars, bass guitars, drums, keyboards, trumpets, and saxophones.

Massive PA systems and a dedicated generator to power the instruments were made available to us.

Most of us were very young, between the ages of 16 and 18, but we were trusted with expensive equipment. It had come to this because the advanced and best of the best musicians that Eritrea had to offer had left the organization and escaped to Sudan. That was why the trumpets and saxophones are not in the picture. They were in storage since no one could play them.

I had the honor of playing the guitar that used to be carried by the best Eritrean guitarist, Tewolde Reda, before he left the ELF cultural band.

The ELF Cultural band in Korokon camp 1981. From left: Me, Tesfaldet, Mimta and Akuay. This photo was taken after ELF was defeated and we were waiting to regroup hoping to return to Eritrea, which never materialized.

Our bass guitarist, Tesfaldet whose last name I have now forgotten made it out alive. However, he wasn't as lucky as we are, unfortunately. I met him in Khartoum in 1993, 12 years after we separated, roaming the streets of Khartoum. Despite my attempt to remind him that he was a great bass guitar player, he didn't recognize me and couldn't remember anything of his previous life. I have no idea what happened to him, but I was sad to see him in that state. I hope that he has now recovered and in a better place.

The young drummer Tsehaie (known by his nick name *Akuay)* inherited the drums that used to be played by the famous musician, Wedi Awalom. Akuay eventually joined the EPLF and fought for over 10 years until the war was over. He could write his story to tell what happened to him after we separated. Fortunately, he made it out alive and I met him when he came to Bologna in 1991 to perform with EPLF music band.

The young kid to the right is Mimta (Kidane Ghebresilasie), holding a guitar that Yusuf Ibrahim used to play

Mimta is currently living in Sweden and is a formidable guitar player. He has two sons and he is enjoying life and music. As seen on the photo, he is younger than I but his obsession with Gym and workouts these days makes him look even younger. I see him post his photos of his fit body on Facebook rubbing the noses of his friends who are not as fit.

Most of the band members and other Merih and Tsbah camp members who made it alive now reside scattered around the globe. The experience we shared as young boys and girls was so strong we consider each other as brothers and sisters. Thanks to social media, we do keep track of each other. Although, I haven't been to one yet, there is also a retreat that gets organized annually to reunite everyone and keep the connection alive.

This was my favorite spot where I sit and immerse in my music world

19. The Escape

After we entered Sudanese territory, I met a lady who used to be my neighbor in Asmara – Abrehet. Abrehet was well connected with the ELF leadership. She told me that she could help me send a letter to my parents by mail to let them know that I was alive and well. She said I could use a return address of one of her connections in the city of Kassala, in Sudan.

I don't recall what I wrote in the first letter I sent to my family five years after I left home. I had no idea if the letter would ever make it to my parents, and as such, I didn't give it much importance. I gave her the letter and simply forgot about it. Several months later, I received a letter, a foldable aerogram with a blue background, with the very familiar handwriting of my father, addressed directly to Mulugheta Abraha, care of … I remember unfolding the letter carefully so as to not tear it. Sitting alone in my favorite location where I escaped the heat, under the shade of a small Gaba tree located on the river edge, I read the letter with intense fondness. If there was anything that made a tremendous impact on how my life turned out to be, it was that single letter I got from my father.

My father was careful not to write anything about the ELF, the fighting, or anything related to our struggle for fear of the letter being intercepted by the Ethiopian security apparatus. After a standard greeting, an opening paragraph, and confirmation that everyone was okay, one by one he listed my sister's names and their current levels of education. Bottom line, all my younger sisters were attending high school. My oldest sister had immigrated to Italy. A few of my close family members had ended up in Sweden and Saudi Arabia. My father concluded the letter by encouraging me to stay strong and that if I could find a way to go to Kassala city in Sudan, I would receive financial support from the various family members. He had even arranged a place for me to stay in Kassala. There was a lot of information in the letter and it was difficult to process. I felt overjoyed and overwhelmed with emotion. Over the next few days,

I read the letter repeatedly to reaffirm my understanding and to make sure I didn't miss any messages relayed in between the lines.

My father's intent was obviously to encourage me to save my life. The main message I took from his letter, however, was not a desire to escape. Instead, I ingested a dose of devastating news that made me realize that my world had remained stagnant for several years while that of others was moving fast and progressing. The fact that my younger sisters were now more educated than me while I burned five years in the jungle was very painful to digest. Devastated and emotionally scarred, I resorted to the only thing I knew would keep me going – playing music.

The feeling of being left behind was a motivation for me to open my eyes and to dream not about escaping but about becoming an educated person. To do that, I would have to escape first if I wanted to be in a position where I could get a shot at education. So, I started to explore and accept the idea of escaping from the front. After all, I had been in Korokon for a full year waiting for our incompetent leaders to get us back to Eritrea. But escaping was not acceptable to me. Leaving my post would make me a traitor, I felt. After five years of being brainwashed to be a hardened fighter, I couldn't afford to get the label "traitor". So, I had to think of other ways to get to Sudan.

I decided to apply for a five-day "family visit" to Sudan, falsely claiming that my family was coming to the city of Kassala to see me. At that time, the state of the liberation front was in chaos. The internal power struggle was so bad that no one trusted anyone. The morale of the fighters was at its lowest. So, in this kind of situation, there was no reason for my leader to deny my request to "visit" my family. It was extremely brave of me as a young boy to even ask permission while everyone else was escaping at night. As expected, I secured two-week permission to go to Kassala, Sudan.

Given that my dream was to pursue my education, I started to worry about any logistical challenges I might encounter if I ever made it to Sweden. In my naïve thinking, I imagined that I would somehow end up in Stockholm. I thought entering Sweden was easy because the father of my uncle Yitbarek lived in Sweden and I assumed he would magically take me to Sweden. When I was in Asmara, I knew Sweden was funding many of the protestant churches I used to go to. So, I had a good feeling about the Swedish people. Moreover, a year before, I had crossed to another country and didn't see a huge obstacle there. All this gave me the fallacious confidence that Sweden would be my future home. The one question that started to bother me was not how to get from Sudan to Sweden but how I would be admitted to a high school in Sweden if I couldn't even show a certificate proving that I had finished middle school somewhere.

At that time, I was working as a teacher in Pioneer camp while playing music with the cultural band. The simplest solution I came up with was that I could try to take a blank certificate from the school and issue myself a certificate. But this could be very risky. If I got caught, it would jeopardize my entire plan of lawfully entering Kassala city. Fearing the consequences, I decided to talk to the school supervisor, Mr. Adem, and share my dream with him and see if he could write me a certificate showing I had finished middle school in the ELF. I told Mr. Adem that I wanted this certificate in case our liberation front got completely dissolved and we all ended up becoming refugees. I would then have a sporting chance to be admitted to a high school in Sudan.

Surprisingly, the plan worked. He admired my desire to study and agreed to give me a certificate signed by him. Granted that we had to negotiate on the actual scores for each of the subjects. After obtaining the certificate, I felt as if Mr. Adem had issued me a new passport with an entry visa to Sweden.

Armed with an invaluable middle school completion certificate, I felt I had a fair shot and access to life outside the jungle. A few days later, it was time to formally say goodbye to Mr. Adem and all my friends. I boarded a Toyota Land Cruiser and headed out of the camp and my five-year jungle life ended for good.

20. *Kassala*

After years in the jungle, I was thrilled to see the city of Kassala, a Sudanese city on the border that we considered as our logistical hub. All supplies intended for ELF-controlled territory came through Kassala, ranging from Red Cross assistance to displaced civilians to weapons and supplies for us, mostly sent by Arab countries.

The drive was uneventful. This was my first time riding a Toyota Land Cruiser, which typically was reserved for the top ELF commanders. We passed the customs with no problem. As soon as the car entered the city of Kassala, I felt the car was going to crash at any time or we were going to kill someone on the road. As we were cruising through the roads, the car's speed in proximity to objects, people, animals, and other cars felt so fast that I was terrified and held on for my life. I experienced the authentic feelings of a jungle-man entering a city, an experience I can recall to this day.

Although I had spent a long time planning my escape to Kassala, I had not planned what to do when I got there. I had to take it a day at a time and hoped that my father's statement regarding financial assistance was true. If not, I always had the option of going back to my familiar life in the jungle. Regardless, I was not worried.

Finally, we arrived at the office of the ELF in Kassala. To my surprise, many of the fighters who had escaped from the camp in Korokon were regular visitors of the office. In just a few hours after I arrived, I met multiple fighters whom I knew from Korokon, including my friends Maasho and Ibrahim. They took me under their protection. The feeling of belonging and friendship was so incredible that I felt secure and in good hands immediately. I arrived in the city without a penny. Everyone I met there was willing to share whatever they had with each other. Unless you experience it, it is hard to imagine – humanity is at its best when it has little. I have seen Eritreans be at their best when they needed each other. The mentoring and coaching I received from people I met there and the sharing of resources from people who had so little were heartwarming.

Within days of entering the city, my family members, as my father had promised in his letter, sent me money from Sweden, Italy, and Saudi Arabia. It was a mystery how people who got the message were able to find me. In a few days, I went from being broke to having 600 US dollars in my pocket. This money in local standards was worth a year's salary. Since I did not have a home and couldn't afford to keep this much money in my pocket for security reasons, I asked a friend who had rented a home to keep the $500 in his home for me while I used the first $100 to refresh my look. I bought myself a new shirt, pants, shoes, and a Casio watch, and had plenty still left for daily expenses.

Five days after arriving in Kassala, my uncle Yitbarek arrived in Kassala to pick me up. Yitbarek was the fighter I had met at the riverbed in my camp during the withdrawal and who had told me to make sure I stayed safe. This time, he instantly took control of my life. He told me we were going to depart the next day for his place about five hours' drive from Kassala. We had to rush to my friend's house to collect my $500. The next morning, without a chance to say goodbye to many of my friends, we boarded a bus and off we headed to the west, to a town called Gedaref.

Ironically, while I was heading west, the same day, my comrades whom I had left in the Korokon camp headed east. They returned to Eritrea in a massive operation that enabled them to join the EPLF fighters in Eritrea. After a long negotiation, the EPLF and a fraction of the ELF leaders agreed to allow the fighters stuck in Korokon to join the EPLF. This would allow Eritreans to jointly fight the common enemy Ethiopia – which should have been done in the first place. Had I stayed a few days more in Korokon, I would have returned to Eritrea, and who knows how my life would have turned out. One thing is for sure, though – I would have not been in a position to write this book.

Mikel, the nurse of our unit and the prisoners.

Mikel was one of the thousands of young men and women who grew up in Addis Ababa and made a 750 miles trip to join the liberation movement. He gave me this picture when I met him in Kassala, Sudan.

Ibrahim Ali (Dankali) and I met in Kassala (Sudan)

*With my Merih camp friends
(Aug 1982, Kassala Sudan).*

*Standing from right to left: Maasho
Solomon & Isaak Gebretnsae,
sitting me and Ali Jahor*

*The certificate I issued myself in the hope that this would allow me to be admitted to middle
school in Sweden.*

Transit

VI

Transit

April 18, 2019. Air Austral flight from Reunion Island to Chennai. I boarded the plane somewhat disappointed because my itinerary showed that I was flying premium economy. For a nearly six-hour flight, Boeing should have given me a seat in business class. To my surprise, what Air Austral calls premium economy is business class, but because the seats don't convert to a flatbed, the seats are classified as premium economy. So, I am happy and excited to spend time writing my book.

21. *The Privileged Poor - Tenedba*

After a couple of hours on a bus, my uncle Yitbarek and I entered the city of Gedaref. Yitbarek had entered Sudan months before me and had found a well-paying job. He worked as a nurse in one of the refugee camps for the International Committee of the Red Cross (ICRC), which is a humanitarian institution based in Geneva, Switzerland. Our destination in Gedaref was the office of the ICRC. The primary goal of going there was to check if transportation was available to the remote village of Tenedba where Yitbarek lived.

Tenedba was a refugee camp inhabited primarily by Ethiopians of Tigray origin. There was no asphalt road connecting Tenedba to Gedaref. The only way to get there was with the ICRC Land Rover that visited the town once a week to bring medical supplies. Yitbarek and I occupied the two empty seats available in the Land Rover heading to Tenedba.

At that moment, I had no idea what to expect at the destination. However, before boarding the Land Rover in Gedaref, my uncle bought a tape player and radio. He also bought a few cassette tapes of mainly Ethiopian and Sudanese music. This could have been a bad sign, hinting that I was moving to a virtually empty house where there was nothing. Or, conversely, a great sign that I would be getting my bedroom in his villa. I opted to assume the latter and came to a temporary conclusion: he was just buying me my tape recorder to live in one of the rooms in his villa. After all, back in Asmara, Yitbarek used to live in a nice villa and had a good life. I remember him as one of the coolest young men as he rode his motorcycle cruising through the main streets of Asmara.

As we went off-road and started negotiating our way to Tenedba, the Land Rover kept skidding in all directions. The rainy season converted the road into one giant mud field. By comparison, I felt that the roads we had built in the jungle were better. Fortunately, the Rover did what it was designed to do and after many long and torturous hours, it got us to Tenedba safely.

Once we had entered the town, I couldn't believe my eyes. I must have been so shocked that I don't remember how I reacted to what I saw. Tenedba was by far the poorest town I had ever seen. Hundreds of the same-looking huts were spread over a flat muddy field with no roads or infrastructure to speak of. A few donkeys were sprinkled across the sea of huts, tied and standing lonely in the cold.

We rolled up our pants and started walking on the muddy ground toward what would be my home. After 20 minutes of walking in the mud, avoiding puddles of brown water, we came across my uncle's hut. I had no clue how he was able to identify his hut from the rest. It was just another hut indistinguishable from the rest in my eyes. The door was made from wobbly corrugated metal and was locked with a chain and a locker. My uncle pulled out a tiny key and unlocked the locker. He opened the door outward, which required considerable force as there was no clearance between the door and the muddy ground. The height of the door was insufficient to allow us to walk into the hut upright. Lowering our heads, we carefully entered his windowless, dark hut.

Inside, there were two beds, one on each side, equipped with mosquito nets, a large water container with no cover, and a kerosene lamp (lantern) on a small wobbly metal table between the two beds. The floor was spared from turning into mud thanks to an improvised water barrier dug around the hut. My uncle unpacked our newly acquired tape recorder. He provisioned the tape with four large *EverReady* batteries and carefully placed it on the small table next to the lantern. He inserted a tape and pressed the play button. Great-sounding Ethiopian music heralded the new chapter of my life in the hut. Needless to say, this was not the villa I had thought my uncle might be living in.

While enjoying the music, I struggled to understand how I could have ended up in a practically empty hut when I had just had a chance to enjoy city life in Kassala with so many of my friends. My brain started to think at full capacity and tried to envision how I would spend my days ahead in a village where there was nothing to do. I would be stuck virtually the entire day in a small room surrounded by muddy fields, for God knows how long.

After a few days of acclimation in the muddy village, one morning my uncle took me to his clinic. The clinic consisted of a couple of huts and was the only medical center serving the village. Two Eritrean medical personnel were operating it. In addition, two other surveyors shared the same facility. It was a small group of people who seemed to share a very good relationship with each other and a happy work life. My addition to the group brought joy to the team. I was welcomed warmly. After two days of being locked in a dark hut surrounded by a sea of mud, the visit to the clinic was a good and uplifting change.

In the weeks to come, I learned that life and the essence of happiness are determined by your closest circle of friends and social life. It is not luxury and money that define happiness. Every day, during lunch and after work, the social life and friendship of these four men made a huge impression on me. All four men were ex-fighters who now found a relatively luxurious position with relatively decent salaries. It was through these relationships that I started enjoying life in the village.

Every day at noon, we would walk to this one hut to be served an exclusive lunch. Later, I learned that the lady who lived there was contracted monthly to feed the four men. The food was very good and packed with plenty of protein. The walk from the clinic to the hut was an interesting experience. As we walked past the sea of huts, the old men and women who lived in them would come out to greet these four men and show their respect for the work they were doing in the village. The villagers would refer to these four men as "doctors". It was such a genuine greeting filled with respect, I realized that the less you have in life, the more you appreciate seemingly small things. I felt privileged to walk alongside these four men who made a significant difference in the community every day – a very rewarding job.

Yitbarek, in particular, was very popular with the women in the village. Not only was Yitbarek a handsome young man but he was also the best person to deliver babies with incredible ease. Virtually every pregnant woman in the village would have been elated to have him assigned to deliver their baby. Many women pleaded for him. I was very proud of him. I was also amazed that NGOs like the ICRC, who funded the clinic and employed the staff, made such a huge difference in the lives of poor and neglected people in the villages and refugee camps. Little did I know that, later on, the same organization would play a huge role in my life as well.

Locked in the hut and with so much time on my hands, I had to find ways to kill time while Yitbarek and the team were at work. I asked Yitbarek if he could get me books to read or to work on, ideally a math book. I also asked him if he could get me some blank papers and a canvas so I could spend time drawing. I used to love drawing when I was in Asmara. He ordered pencils and blank papers from Gedaref and the next week our reliable Land Rover delivered it to our hut.

My artistic abilities impressed the team. Excited, Yitbarek ordered more materials and water paint. Our empty hut was now decorated with multiple pieces of artwork I had created, and become the museum of the town. After a couple of months, Yitbarek talked to the ICRC manager who used to visit the village occasionally and asked him if they could offer me employment opportunities in some kind of artwork or vocational development program.

The charity work that the ICRC did extend to more than providing food and medical assistance. It also offered opportunities to refugees to become self-employed. The manager was open to the idea and allowed me to apply for a job in Gedaref. The ICRC had a large facility in Gedaref where artwork was produced by refugees. This was exciting in many ways. First, to know that I had a skill that could potentially land me a job was humbling. Then, the job would be in a large city away from the muddy village which was another plus. Excited, I reserved a spot in the Land Rover to visit Gedaref for an interview with the manager.

A week later, I found myself back in Gedaref meeting a middle-aged white man at the ICRC office. I vaguely remember how I was able to communicate with him since my English was very bad. After a short discussion, he drove me to the workshop and had me try out some of the work they did there. The workshop was manned by about 15 people and each person had a distinct skill that contributed to a collective production of colorful t-shirts and other artwork.

An Eritrean refugee was given the task of testing my artistic abilities. He gave me a project – to draw and paint a vase with flowers and use stencils to transfer my work onto a bedsheet. This method of stencil transfer was new to me. He was gracious enough to allow me to shadow the transfer technique of artwork onto a t-shirt to give me an idea.

I completed the drawing and painted the vase with bright colors. It looked good. Then, I laid the stencils on top of the drawing and carefully cut out the stencils – one stencil for each color. After this was done, I transferred paint onto the bedsheet using the stencils I created, one stencil at a time. Each stencil had to be aligned properly before pressing the paint onto the cloth using sponges. This was an eye-opening technique for me. I had never seen a stencil-based transfer of artwork before, and I was fascinated. Surprisingly, I managed to pull it off and the artwork was presented to the British manager for evaluation.

After a discussion with his team, the manager decided that my skills were good enough to open a new branch in the village of Tenedba. He suggested that I receive all supplies necessary to start a business in the village and start selling my artwork in "my" village. "My village"? A deflation! This was not the outcome I had expected. I didn't want to live in the remote village of Tenedba. That was not "my village"! On the positive end of things, I was excited that my skills were valued and trusted enough to start up a new business.

I returned to my village with mixed feelings. A few weeks later, I received all kinds of supplies. Interestingly, one of the boxes I received was full of X-ray film images. I was supposed to wash off the x-ray images and make a transparent sheet that I would use as a stencil; not a fun job but the cheapest way to recycle these films. So I started my own business that would keep me busy for almost eight months. I produced many t-shirt designs and pillow covers decorated with flowers. One of my favorite pieces was a man walking back toward the mountains of Eritrea, with the title "Country Roads Take Me Home". Yes, John Denver was popular in that part of the world. Another one was two ballistic missiles carrying the flags of the USSR and US, flying at each other, with the title "Public Enemy Number One!"

Yitbarek and I also experimented with raising chickens, which was fascinating. It went well for a while. Unfortunately, our investment in the chicken business ended disastrously. They caught a contagious disease and all my chickens ended up dead in a matter of a few weeks.

My t-shirt printing business however was going well. The social life in the village of Tenedba was so rich that I consider it to be one of the happiest moments in my life. They were good people with an incredible sense of humor and humility. To top it off, the addition of a female medical staff member enriched our team.

While I was perfectly happy enjoying the daytime activities, the nightlife and going out to local "bars" where homemade alcoholic drinks *"katikala"* were served was not my thing. I was very uncomfortable drinking alcohol, let alone getting drunk. I have to admit there were some fun parts to that. When my friends got drunk, they became even funnier and more humorous.

Even though I didn't enjoy drinking, I could understand why these men wanted to drink and go out at night as frequently as they did. After all, they had spent a good portion of their young lives in the jungle as freedom fighters. The very skill they were practicing to help the villagers were acquired during the struggle for independence of Eritrea. The front needed nurses and doctors to deal with the war casualties. Therefore, they trained hundreds of men and women to be nurses and trauma doctors to treat fighters with bone fractures, cuts, internal injuries, burns, and shock. Their job often required them to operate on critical injuries under stressful circumstances in order to save the person's life. Yitbarek was one of them. The bedtime stories he told me about his time on the battlefields were so depressing and horrible, looking back, I don't know why there was no such thing called post-traumatic stress disorder back then. But again, maybe there was, we just didn't recognize it. For more than seven years Yitbarek fought, first as a regular fighter and later as a medic, at the frontlines. If writing a book was for everyone, his life story would have been incredibly fascinating.

22. *Exit from Jenedba*

R outinely, the Land Rover would deliver mail from many of our family members. Sometimes the mail contained a few hundred dollars inside. Life in the village couldn't be any better. In the meantime, the US offered Eritrean fighters a repatriation program that allowed them to immigrate to the US. The program was called the American Resettlement Program wherein the fighters could register and, if accepted, would make their way to the US within a year. The Canadians also had a similar program, but it was mostly for high-school graduates, and with my seventh-grade level, I wouldn't have qualified. These programs were only available in the major cities. Therefore, Yitbarek and I had to travel back to Gedaref to register for the American Resettlement Program. A couple of months later, Yitbarek was called for a final interview in Khartoum, the capital city of Sudan, which meant that if everything went well, he would be ready to depart to the US a few weeks after his interview.

Incidentally, around the same time, I received a message from another uncle, Zekarias, who was fighting with the EPLF and at that point lived in Khartoum after sustaining a head injury during the battle with the ELF. My family members from abroad had managed to send Zekarias travel documents that would hopefully get me and him to Europe. He asked me to travel to Khartoum ASAP to receive these documents and start the exit process.

My interview for the American Resettlement Program, although one could never be sure, was probably two to three months away. So, with Yitbarek getting ready to depart to the US, I had to find a way to survive for two months in Khartoum (the capital city of Sudan). Staying with my uncle Zekarias made sense.

At the same time, I had to assess what these travel documents Zekarias was talking about were, and how realistic the chance of going to Europe was using these documents. Europe didn't have a refugee resettlement program for Eritreans the way the US and

Canada did. However, if you somehow managed to get to Europe, they were gracious in helping you find a settlement.

With two life-changing opportunities ahead, it was time to say goodbye to Tenedba and move to Khartoum. Yitbarek and I arranged a travel permit to Khartoum and we boarded the ICRC Land Rover to Gedaref. From Gedaref we took a bus to Khartoum. The six-hour bus trip on a freshly built highway was smooth and uneventful.

Life in Khartoum was hectic and very different from that in Tenedba. In Khartoum, there were thousands of Eritreans living under constant fear of being arrested by the police and deported to refugee camps like Tenedba. It was routine practice for Eritreans to be hunted on the streets of Khartoum, loaded onto trucks, and deported to refugee camps, only to find their way back to the city a few weeks later. Normally, they lived in groups of sometimes more than 10 people in one room. The camaraderie they had practiced in the jungle during the fight against Ethiopians was elevated to a whole different level in Sudan. If you were Eritrean and arrived in Khartoum, the first Eritrean you met would take full responsibility for making sure you had food to eat and a place to stay. The level of care amongst Eritreans was unbelievable and only those who lived it can understand it. That being the case, our arrival in Khartoum was somewhat easier. We had some money, family members, and a place to stay in the city.

The first good news came through a few days after we arrived. Yitbarek's departure date to the US was set in a couple of weeks. A new chapter in his life awaited him on the other side of the planet. I was happy for him but I also knew I was going to miss him. He was a caring, humorous, and genuine individual. If everything went well, my departure to the US should also be in a few months, so there were potentially exciting times ahead. At the same time, my uncle Zekarias told us the details of why he had called me to Khartoum. It was interesting and perplexing news to say the least.

The travel documentation he had received from my family consisted of two tickets, two passports, and about 800 dollars in cash. These two passports were meant for me and him. One was a Somalian passport with a picture of a man in his thirties. I forget which country the other passport was from, but it was for a female. So, my uncle decided, in a very caring gesture, that I would get the Somalian passport and he would take the other one. My uncle had two choices. He could dress up as a lady and travel with that passport to Europe or hopefully exchange it for another one. Somehow, he would have to find a way to get out of Khartoum and make it to Europe. Given that Eritreans at that time were stateless and carried no identification of any kind, it was up to the creativity and network of individuals to get an ID from one of the friendly countries. It was rumored the State of Somalia used to be one that provided travel documents and IDs for many Eritreans, including the leaders of the ELF and the EPLF.

After doing some research on how to get out of Khartoum to Europe, it was obvious to my uncle that we would need a lot more money to bribe officials to let us board the plane. More importantly, there was no way we could do this on our own, not knowing the intricacies of how the business works could easily make us lose our money or even land us in jail. My uncle didn't want to take the risk of me being stopped at the airport immigration before even making it to the airplane.

We needed expert brokers who could navigate the web of networked officers on our behalf to make sure no officer in the chain of command was skipped or offended. The Sudanese officials were notorious for receiving bribes to provide any service, let alone a "lucrative deal" like traveling to Europe, which involved a coveted hard currency.

Before we could start the immigration process, however, the passports would require entry and exit visas. So, we needed to find people who could stamp a visa on our passports – which required a different skill. Eventually, my uncle found a well-known broker who provided an all-in-one service.

After assessing our situation, the broker told us that the cash we had would not cut it to get even one of us out of Khartoum, let alone both of us. After looking at all the available options, he offered to sell the second travel document and ticket that was meant for my uncle and the money generated would cover the expenses to get me out. That was the only way to get me safely out of Khartoum. As I write this, I am realizing how selfless my uncle was to allow me to get out of Khartoum first, essentially taking a huge risk for himself.

Compared to Tenedba, Khartoum was a fast-paced city, and I was not able to follow what exactly was being done by whom to arrange such a complex operation to get me out of Khartoum. The idea of bribing corrupt Sudanese officers and hustling with smugglers that sucked out your entire savings or that of your family to get you to Europe would have qualified as a movie story in Tenedba. But, without a premeditated plan and with no control of my destiny, I found myself in a dangerous reality where invisible powers were shaping my future.

I was worried and unsure whether going to Europe on such a risky undertaking was better than waiting two months for my US Resettlement Program interview. The problem was that the interview did not guarantee access to the US. Often, if one bungled a simple thing during the interview, one could end up languishing in Sudan for the rest of one's life. So, I blindly followed my uncle's recommendation to trust the smugglers and go to Europe. The calculation was – if for some reason I got deported to Khartoum, my other option of going to the US was still available to me.

Realizing that I was about to enter a new chapter in my life, I decided to give all the art stencils that I had brought from Tenedba to my uncle who would stay behind in Khartoum. I showed him how to use them, and he was excited. He was somewhat confident that he would be able to make money to sustain him after I left Khartoum. In the meantime, Yitbarek was ready to go to the airport on his way to the US, a dream come true. He took off to the land of opportunity and the final destination for many ELF fighters. My departure to a whole different destination was set to take place three days later. All documents were finalized and I was told I was in good hands. Oddly enough, I had no idea what my destination was and what it meant to be in "good hands". At age 18, fresh from the jungle and the muddy hut village, I simply couldn't follow the complex process of the smuggling operations about to unfold.

The night before my departure, it was time to take a photo with those who would stay in Khartoum. After all, we would be separating, and no one knew what the future would hold for both of us, so a picture felt like a good idea. With my passport firmly in the hands of my family members, camouflaged by the *Times* magazine, we took the last photo in Khartoum.

Just so it is clear, the US wasn't taking Eritrean fighters for humanitarian reasons. It was a well-calculated political move to lure fighters out of Eritrea and deprive the liberation movement of critical resources. This move was expected to effectively kill the liberation movement in favor of big Ethiopia and was offered only to Eritreans who were fighters.

23. *Khartoum Airport*

O n the morning of September 20, 1983, with my belongings firmly packed in a piece of bright light-blue luggage with two leather straps securing it, we headed to the airport. One of my cherished belongings was an album that contained pictures I was able to collect while in Sudan. Unlike today, where selfies and instant video shots are common, in those days, getting a picture was a process of several days and was quite an event. Most of my pictures, therefore, were taken in a photo studio with my friends and family members, with photoshopped backgrounds depicting a luxurious life that we could only dream of. Sometimes I collected headshots of the friends and people I met in Sudan. When separating from people, not knowing when we'd meet again, it was very common to exchange passport size photos as a way to remember each other.

As we were driving to the airport in a taxi, my uncle would reinforce and recap to me, several times, what I needed to do to make it through the airport security safely. If I made one mistake, a single customs agent could make it impossible for me to pass security without paying him a bribe, especially if the agent knew I was Eritrean. The repetitive warnings and instructions from my uncle made me nervous. Especially stories of Eritreans who were returned to Khartoum from various airports in Europe sent shockwaves through my spine. How unfortunate one must be after spending all the money and going through hell to get to Europe to then be returned to square one.

Once in the departure hall, the sheer number of people who travel and who came to say goodbye was overwhelming for me. I don't remember saying goodbye to my uncle and his friends, but in the middle of all the chaotic airport activities, casually I found myself handed over to a young man who was dressed in uniform, and I was told to simply follow him. This was an experience where invisible smugglers and higher powers orchestrated the activities in the airport and I just had to trust the system and follow instructions.

The person whom I was following ran me through the check-in process, the security steps, and passport control. I don't remember doing anything other than following him. Once I was in the waiting room at the gate, he disappeared without any further communication. Throughout the entire process, he didn't say a word to me. I never talked to him and he never said goodbye. Just like that, I changed my status from a potentially criminal person who was illegally crossing customs to a free traveler mingling with legitimate European and Sudanese business travelers lined up to enter a huge airplane operated by Air France.

I have no recollection of how I was transported from the airport terminal to the airplane seat. Next to me sat a middle-aged white man. To him, I was just another traveler and he had no idea that I had paid lots of money to seek a peaceful life in an undisclosed foreign country. I wonder how many of "me" were on board the plane.

The doors closed and the airplane started taxiing to the runway. In the distance, I could see hundreds of people on the terminal balcony waving goodbye to their loved ones. As we disappeared further away to the start of the runway, I gave up on trying to identify my uncle in the crowd. Then, the sheer thrust of the engines propelling the plane forward on the runway forced my head backward. I vividly remember how I struggled to keep my head straight, a feeling I had never experienced in my life before. As I was admiring the acceleration effect on my body, we floated in the air and all was peaceful. The airport terminal with people waving goodbye gradually zoomed out and eventually disappeared in the sea of brown sand.

My seat was next to the window overlooking the airplane's right-hand wing, at an angle slightly behind me. Every air disturbance that caused the wing to vibrate and slightly bend was an event I would wait to admire throughout the flight. It was soon time for lunch, and the flight attendants started serving food. After I received my plate, I reached in my pocket and took out a $100 bill. I stretched my hand to give it to the flight attendant, apologizing in broken

English that I didn't have a smaller change. She struggled to understand what I was saying. My fellow passenger, who seemed to understand what was going on, interfered. He told me the food was free and I didn't need to pay. It took me a while to understand what he was saying. Confused, I obeyed the new rule of free lunch but struggled for a while to process it. I am not sure what these two people who witnessed this thought of me at that moment. I ate my free lunch, the taste of which was not good enough to remember. However, I was amazed at how delicious the orange juice was.

After an uneventful flight, we landed at the airport of our destination and it was time to follow the crowd toward the exit. Once I stepped out of the airplane, I felt a shocking temperature drop. It was September. Coming from one of the hottest cities in the world, it had never crossed my mind to dress warmly. I only had a simple shirt on while most of the passengers were dressed appropriately. Fortunately, it was a short exposure and we quickly entered the terminal. I had no clue what to expect at the airport. I started wondering if I was on my own or if I should expect from the higher powers that another uniformed person would be waiting for me to help me navigate airport security again.

With no available options, I just followed the crowd and soon found myself lined up in front of passport control agents. Surprised by how long the queue of travelers was, I looked for alternatives. I noticed there was a lonely customs agent who seemed to have just opened his kiosk. There was no queue in front of him and I decided to go straight to him. The only thing I was carrying was my passport, a wallet, and my tickets. I had no carry-on bag. I handed my passport and ticket to the agent. My passport was not forged, it was a legitimate passport, but neither the photo nor the name was mine. I remember my uncle worrying about the picture because the person on the picture had a somewhat recessed hairline while my hairline almost intersected with my eyebrows. The visa must have also been legit although it was common to obtain a forged visa on travel documents.

The agent placed the passport under ultraviolet light to check for forgery. After a few tense minutes, he stamped my passport. Just like that, I passed the immigration control and I was a free man in Paris at the Charles De Gaulle (CDG) airport. I assumed the airport agent at CDG, just like the agents in Sudan who got paid to smuggle refugees, to be part of the smuggling team. How else would a customs agent let an 18-year-old boy pass for a middle-aged man who was half-bald? "Money rules the world" was my conclusion. I struggled to understand the news I had heard in Khartoum about Eritreans being returned to Sudan after reaching Europe. Did they not pay enough bribes to the Paris agents or did they make mistakes that I was told not to make? Puzzled but still realizing that my journey was not done, I continued walking with the hundreds of travelers to the arrival area of the airport. Logically, I assumed that someone was following me or someone was waiting for me.

The last photo we took with my family members in Khartoum (Sudan),
the day before my departure.

The Flight

VII

The Flight

June 14, 2019. Emirates Flight EK from Mauritius to Dubai. I am coming from a long trip to Mauritius where I had the opportunity to meet the former president of Mauritius, a renowned biodiversity scientist Dr. Ameenah Gurib-Fakim. I was introduced to her by Kedisti, my sister-in-law who works for the Bill Gates Foundation in Seattle.

Dr. Ameenah was a gracious lady and she invited me for lunch. We had a great conversation about the various challenges Africa is facing, including the Chinese taking over. We also talked about what it meant to be the first Muslim female president. She is a bright communicator. My primary goal that day was to sell services and products to Air Mauritius, an all-Airbus fleet customer. But the conversation was great nonetheless.

As I write this note, Dr. Ameenah is sitting on the upper deck of the A380 next to me. We happened to board the same flight and sit one row apart, which was quite a surprise. The A380 airplane, as bulky as it looks, its business class cabin is one of the best. The entire upper deck is provisioned with business class seats and there is a nice lounge bar. It is a great experience.

Today, I am heading to Istanbul through Dubai and I am excited. My daughter Salina will join me in Istanbul and I am looking forward to spending some time with her. She is working at the UN office in Bonn, Germany, and I haven't seen her for some time.

24. A Jungle Man in Paris

I was a free man at the airport, but I had no clue where to head to next. I knew I needed to get my blue luggage but where would I find it? The logic of checking my flight number to find the right baggage carousel escaped me entirely. The idea of multiple airplanes landing at the same time and the logistical complexity of baggage handling simply was too much for me to comprehend.

I waited in the first luggage area I found for a long time and no light blue luggage was visible in the area. After an extended time of waiting, I started walking with no sense of where I wanted to go next. Then, I realized that there were multiple locations where luggage could be delivered. Hallelujah! There it was! At a distance, unmistakable bright-blue luggage was still rotating on an empty carousel waiting for its rightful owner.

Miraculously, I managed to get to the exit where taxis and cars were picking up passengers. One taxi after another was loading travelers and disappearing as quickly as they showed up. Every person that came behind me jumped into a taxi and disappeared. In my case, I had several issues I had to resolve before I could take off in a taxi. I had no answer to several fundamental questions like: Where was I heading? Why was there no one to receive me? Whom should I contact next and how?

I had 200 dollars in my pocket. One hundred had been given to me by my uncle and the other by the lady who joined our team in the Tenedba refugee camp, Zayed. When Zayed had learned that I was leaving the camp for Khartoum, she had given me, from what little she had, 100 dollars. That shows how Eritreans, strangers who met in Sudan, took care of each other selflessly. Armed with 200 dollars, my guess was I could survive for about 30 days in Paris. After all, 200 dollars in Sudan would have lasted me for four months, with no alcohol, of course.

Confidently, I decided to look for a hotel somewhere in the city, taking a risk that I would be paying 5–10 dollars a night. I lined up for a taxi and asked the first taxi driver to take me to a cheap hotel. As broken as our communication was, the lowest price I heard was 50 dollars for a night and another 40–50 for the taxi ride. That meant half of my wealth would be burned in just one night and I started to panic. I thanked him and retreated. I stood at the taxi stand for a long time, completely lost and not knowing what to do next. Suddenly, a Sudanese man came up to me and asked if I was waiting in line for a taxi. We started talking in Arabic and I volunteered to inform him of my problem of not finding a cheap taxi and a hotel.

He told me he could take me to a cheap location if I went with him. The two of us, African brothers but strangers to each other, entered a taxi and headed to the city in what seemed endless driving. For a moment I asked myself, "Could he be part of the smugglers' network who is playing an angel? What are the odds of meeting a Sudanese man in Paris while I am still in an unfinished smuggling operation?" My brain worked hard to remember instructions I had gotten from my uncle that would match the situation I had found myself in.

During the taxi ride, as my companion learned more about my story, he understood the seriousness of my situation. Suddenly, he realized he had met a homeless person that he wanted to find shelter for. He ended up making decisions on my behalf and chose a logical destination. He told me he would take me to the UNESCO hostel where they had affordable beds. He was very familiar with Paris – he must have been a businessman or a frequent traveler. He was a God sent angel who had arrived at the right time and the right place to do the right thing.

After what seemed endless driving, we reached the UNESCO office. He asked the taxi driver to wait for him, and we entered the office. After speaking to the officer in French, he turned to me. "Bad news," he said. "They don't have any beds available." They recommended that we go to a place called "Office De Tourisme" in the heart of the city, Champs Elysée Boulevard. He told me that this place is a tourist information center, but that we were very far away from the recommended location and the best way to get there was for me to take the underground metro and disembark next to the office. Never in my life had I heard the word "underground metro," let alone ride in one. Realizing that I had only dollars in my pocket, he gave me a couple of francs to purchase a metro ticket and he pointed out the metro station that I needed to depart from. He reassured me that this would be a simple ride with only one metro line involved.

April 25, 2018. Flight from Dubai to Amsterdam. It is a redeye and everyone is sound asleep. Uneventful flight. I am torn between writing my book and preparing to support a meeting with a minister of transportation from Ghana for an ongoing airplane sales campaign. This work seems to be nonstop and people expect you to work anytime from wherever you are. It is very demanding and leaves little room for life. Yet, it is a blessing to have this opportunity.

After thanking him for his generosity and support, with extreme anxiety, with my blue bag firmly in my hand, I started walking toward the metro station. By then, it had been more than five hours since I had landed, and darkness had set in. The temperature had dropped significantly, and after a five-minute walk, I felt like I was freezing to death. As I walked to the metro station, the lights and the meticulously lit streets of Paris were a source of bewilderment to me.

I arrived at the metro station but struggled to find the entrance. Soon I realized many people were going through what looked like a gate. I got closer to the gates to understand how they were getting in. They were passing one person at a time. I noticed that after they inserted a coin, up came a ticket, and the gates opened. I waited until there was no one before trying to insert a coin into the machine that supposedly opened the gates. I took out one of the coins I had received from the Sudanese man and tried to insert it in the slot. The coin didn't fit in the slot and I figured the coin was too large. The obvious next step was to get a smaller change.

I went to a small magazine stand that was next to the station and asked for change. To this day, I don't recall how I was able to communicate and make myself clear to a Frenchman way back in 1983. Even in 2019, the French are not known for their linguistic skills. Somehow, I got my change and headed back to the gate. After several attempts, I realized that inserting smaller coins was not working either.

My technical skills and ability to analyze the issue reached their limits quickly. I couldn't come up with any other solution. Then, I saw three boys close by. The boys were very young, not older than 12 or 13. I approached them and asked if they could help me to get into the station. Surprisingly, they recognized my dilemma and they took me back to the magazine stand and helped me purchase a ticket. They walked back with me to the gate and showed me how to insert the ticket in the slot. It was the ticket that was being inserted into the machine and not coins. The ticket would then be stamped and comes out to be picked up while the gate would open at the same time. That was an eye-opener technology.

I entered the metro station and waved goodbye to the boys. Once in the station, I took the escalators and found myself next to many people waiting for the metro to arrive. The Sudanese man had warned me not to forget the name of the metro destination/direction I needed to take. Standing on the edges of the metro platform, as I was processing the information flowing through my eyes, I noticed the name of the destination was displayed on the other side across the rails. Interestingly, I was smart enough to realize that I needed to be on the opposite side to catch the right metro train. My brain worked hard to find a way to get there. I promptly ruled out the idea of jumping down off the platform and walking across the rails to the other side. I confidently concluded that I would have to go out and enter the station from the other side of the building. I grabbed my blue bag and went down the escalator heading for the exit.

I exited through the same entrance area where I had found the three boys. Surprised, the boys asked, "What happened?" I told them, "I need to be on the other side of the railway." Shocked, they told me I didn't have to get out, I could have just gone down through the tunnel under the railway to cross to the other side. My ticket was already stamped and invalid for re-entry. Now that I was out, I needed to buy another ticket to get back in. The only francs I had got from the Sudanese man were spent, and I had no French money to buy additional tickets. Now what?

Concerned, the three kids got together, and after a quick deliberation in French, they came up with a solution. They managed to collect money and pay for a new ticket for me. I headed to the magazine stand again for the third time. Incredible! With their clear instructions and help, I entered the station and walked to the right side of the metro platform. Those boys were the next angels I met in Paris, after the Sudanese man. They were at the right time in the right place to do the right thing.

When the metro arrived, a wall of people poured out through the door. I was not ready for that and got pushed back rudely. I managed to push my way back and hopped into the metro just before the doors closed. The distinctive chime heralding the doors closing or opening is engraved in my mind. There was no seating available in the metro, it was crowded, and there were many things that could distract me, but my brain power was completely consumed with processing how to track where the metro was at all times so as to not miss my destination. I couldn't afford to make a mistake again.

After passing several stations, I somehow knew I had reached my destination and got out of the metro. I followed the crowd that exited the metro and ended up emerging from the ground onto a busy street. The fancy shops, the elegantly dressed people, and the beautiful cars driving back and forth on the wide boulevard left no doubt in my mind that this was the heart of Paris. On the other side of the street, I saw lit up in large letters: OFFICE DE TOURISME. I was very proud that in the jungle of Paris, I had successfully found my target. I almost felt that I had reached my final destination.

The *office de Tourisme* helps tourists find affordable hotels. After realizing my budget, a woman at the counter told me that the cheapest hotel she could find was in the suburbs of the city for 30 dollars a night. Left with no other option, I accepted the offer. To get to the hotel, she told me, I would have to take multiple metros. She gave me a map that showed the metro network in different colors. The office also gave me a metro ticket. As challenging and overwhelming as the metro ride ahead of me might be, I was not worried about that. My worry was how long I could survive in Paris at 30 dollars a night. I had only 200 dollars – covering a maximum of six nights.

It was very late in the evening and the metro ride took a long time. Surprisingly, without any issue, I managed to transfer from one metro line to another and found my way to the exact station I was supposed to disembark at. The instructions and colored map of Paris metro lines must have been clear enough for a jungle man like me to navigate properly. I reported to the hotel receptionist like a young pro-traveler. Upon arrival, I was told that my room had two beds and was a shared room with another person. I don't remember having any issue with that.

25. Agonizing Three Days

The last meal I had eaten was on the airplane. Hungry, physically and mentally exhausted, I collapsed as soon as I lay on my bed. The next morning, I woke up and noticed that my roommate was gone. Soon, there was a knock on the door and I was told to leave the room because they had to clean. I left my room and went to the small lobby and started to strategize what I needed to do next.

My uncle in Sudan had given me the phone number of my family member in Italy. After getting some help from the receptionist on how to make a call, I was able to get a hold of someone who spoke my language, but it was not my family. A man told me to stay put where I was and that someone would come to pick me up in the days ahead. Disappointed that I couldn't talk to my family, I took comfort with anyone who could help me. The higher powers were back in action and I felt safer.

Not knowing how long that might take, I was careful not to spend all my money. I bought French bread and every day I ate French bread with water. Given the budget constraint, I couldn't afford to pay for coffee or tea. At one point, I remember stealing an apple from my roommate and taking it out to the streets to eat. Three days passed, and no one came or called to ask about me. I started to get nervous.

Even though it was very cold, I remember going to the city to test my metro navigation skills a few more times. I walked into different malls and I remember feeling puzzled when I saw French couples kissing on the escalators. That is a NO-NO in Eritrea. In Eritrea, romance and showing affection was a private matter in those days and was not for display in public. Even holding hands was not considered socially acceptable if it was between lovers. In Sudan, it was even worse.

The days felt longer in Paris. With no end in sight, I started to wonder what the next adventure would be. Calling the man again would cost me money. On the fourth day, late in the evening, the receptionist called me to come down to the lobby because someone had asked for me. Excited, I went down. A middle-aged man, light-skinned and soft-spoken, was waiting for me. He hugged me and told me that he had come to pick me up. His name was Tommy. He said I needed to get my luggage to depart as soon as possible, the bus left in two hours and we had to go immediately. I paid my four-night bill, at 30 dollars a night. I grabbed my blue bag and started a new journey with yet another stranger to an unknown destination.

As we were walking to the bus station, Tommy asked me to hand over my Somalian passport to him. He gave me another passport that I would use for the next travel segment which would be entirely by bus and at night. He told me to remember my new name on my passport and to just relax. Tommy's calm demeanor and confidence in the smuggling process were very reassuring and I never bothered to consider if I was committing a crime or was in any danger.

At this point, I had no clue where I was headed, but I had complete trust in the higher powers and the smuggling operations. Yet, I had no idea if what I was doing was risky or against the law. That was just the way every Eritrean mined his or her luck in life and I was fortunate enough to be part of it. After all, many Eritreans were stuck in the muddy villages in Sudan or, even worse, in the war-torn country back home. The fact that I was experiencing the smuggling operations in the way I did was a blessing reserved to a few.

Once the bus left the city, I saw what seemed to be an endless row of yellowish lights in the distance. Not knowing the concept of highways, the lighting of the highway was very impressive, almost out of this world. I kept staring at the row of lights as we negotiated the hundreds of miles of road ahead of us. After a few hours, we reached the first border checkpoint. My partner in crime asked me to pretend to sleep. When the border agents came on the bus to check, Tommy spoke to them in their language and he handed them our passports. Without any issue, we passed the border checkpoint. Hours later, we passed the second checkpoint in the same manner.

Early in the morning, we reached our destination and my bus journey ended there.

Tommy took me to his home by metro. We were greeted by his wife and two kids. For the first time in my life, I got to see how people in Europe lived. His apartment was on the second floor. All I remember of Tommy's home was how small and packed the rooms were. Although I felt like I was home and had reached my destination, for Tommy the work was not done yet. He started educating me on how the UN refugee protection and asylum system works and how I could apply for asylum in Europe. He told me the earlier we do this the better. He asked me to give him the passport back and whatever money I had left. He interviewed me to understand my story and highlighted areas that might increase my chances of being accepted as a refugee in the Netherlands. The Netherlands, a country I had never known it existed on the map, seemed to be my final destination. Tommy was confident that my life story was such that it didn't need any polishing or highlighting of key facts that the authorities look for. My journey embodied a story of a typical Eritrean fighter turned refugee.

The Shock

Korokon 1982, just before I entered Kassala, Sudan

VIII

The Shock

26. *Singel Straat*

It was a cold morning in September 1983. The streets of
Amsterdam were packed with activities. The trams ruled the
streets with their distinctive ringing noise alerting pedestrians to
stay away, while other trams made even louder sounds when making
turns as the friction between the rails and the wheels produced a
terrifyingly shrill noise. Thousands of people ran back and forth, like
an aggressive ant colony racing against time, riding their bicycles in
an orderly fashion on both sides of the streets, while others walked
on foot. The city buses, taxis, and cars all competed for the narrow
streets and precious real estate.

Blending with the crowd, Tommy and I were walking on foot,
crossing multiple canals to a destination only known to Tommy. As
we approached a street called Single Straat, Tommy said, "We have
come to a point where I can no longer walk next to you." He showed
me the office from a distance and said, "Just walk in there and tell
them you came from Eritrea and explain the rest of your story." The
only redaction he reminded me to make was what had happened on
the last day as I could not expose his name or the name of the
smuggler and his description. "By the way, the age thing is up to
you," he added, referring to a few administrative options he had told
me about the night before. I could choose to be 23 years old or I
could tell them my real age, which was 18 years old. "That is all
discretionary information that may be adjusted to suit your short-
term or long-term needs," he said. In my case, I agreed to the
redaction of the last day's story, but I chose to be honest about
everything else, including my age.

We hugged and said goodbye to each other and he disappeared into the crowd. With no money in my pockets and no ID of any kind, I picked up my blue luggage and made my way across the canal to get to the office located at Single Straat. I rang the bell and the door opened. In the office, there were several immigrants, two of whom were Eritrean girls. I was instructed to take a seat and wait until I was called. *Verenigde VluchtingenWerk Nederland* (VVN), loosely translated as United Refugee Support in the Netherlands, was an organization that helped refugees apply for asylum, find a home, and supported them as they settled in the Netherlands.

I filled out a form and my application was processed. After an hour or two, the two Eritrean girls and I were given a reference letter and told to walk to an address nearby. We easily found the address. It was a lodging place where we would stay temporarily. We had no idea what all this meant, but clearly, the induction process worked like a well-oiled machine. Just like the smugglers in Sudan, the VVN created miracles by navigating the complex system, finding lodging, and assigning us a volunteer who guided us through the process of establishing ourselves as refugees. A major difference was that, unlike the smugglers, we never paid for the service that VVN provided.

The lodging area must have been run by a religious institution. Similar to a hostel, it offered many bunk beds in one room. They served us food daily and taught us prayers, which was optional. On the second day, realizing that I was not dressed for the weather, the VVN referred me to a store where I could pick up a jacket to keep me warm. The store was a second-hand store where used outfits were sold, but I don't remember paying. I selected a few jackets that I thought were fashionable and was ready to roam the streets of Amsterdam. During the day, wearing my warm new jacket, I explored the city on foot. I felt like a tourist, not a refugee. Amsterdam was a city full of character and there was no shortage of things that challenged our African attitude and mentality.

After a few days, it was time to say goodbye to my two new friends. The VVN found a home for them in the town of Hilversum.

I was told to move to another location in the heart of the city, called De Wallen, the famous Red Light District in Amsterdam. While my Eritrean friends were upgraded from a hostel to a home of their own in Hilversum, the Hollywood of the Netherlands, my accommodation went down drastically in comfort and dignity.

The place I was told to stay at opened its doors at 9 p.m. and closed at 9 a.m. It served as a night shelter only. The people who stayed in the shelter were not the average Europeans I had expected to see. Many were people who had lost everything they had. They would beg for money during the day and come to this shelter to sleep at night. Like them, I practically had nothing in life, and as such, I was categorized as a homeless person. The difference was that my dreams and aspirations seemed very different than those of the average homeless person staying in the place.

Every night before we went to bed, they served us soup to keep us warm. I sat alone and enjoyed my soup. In the morning, we were served breakfast, and by nine o'clock we were sent off to roam the streets of De Wallen.

As shocked as I was regarding the degradation of the comfort level and the fact that I was staying in a homeless shelter, roaming the Red Light District in Amsterdam by far was the most shocking experience. For me, considering my strict upbringing in a culture where women's sexuality is extremely respected, the women behind the glasses could easily have been mannequins without any moral or cultural value whatsoever. How could they pose in front of everyone, almost naked, and dare to ask men to have sex with them? In my mind, this was insane!. There was no way I could reconcile what I saw in the red light district with anything resembling normalcy to my standards.

What shocked me the most was that there were buses full of Asian tourists, primarily elderly men, who were dropped off at the entrance of the Red Light District to admire the prostitution business. They were standing at every shop and scanning the different sex toys and pornography displayed in public. I have no words to describe how insane this felt to me at that time.

Touring my way from one sub-district to another, I realized the place was segregated somewhat geographically and ethnically. There were East Europeans and Caucasians on one side, Latinas on the other, and African women surrounded the oldest church in Amsterdam, Oude Kerk. This is the only place I have ever seen where religion and prostitution face each other. The church was surrounded by window brothels, bars, cannabis shops, and pretty much anything that offends Christians. There was even a sex museum! I had no idea of what it displayed since I wasn't able to afford the entrance fee. The multitude of experiences I was subjected to in such a short time was an overdose in culture shock.

After a few days of staying in the district, I started to acclimate and get the hang of the district's concept and appeal. My 18-year-old hormones were activated, overpowering the sense of dignity and respect I had carried with me from a different continent. I started to think just like the young men walking down the Red Light District streets, fantasizing about beautiful girls. Fantasizing alone would, however, not cut it in the Red Light District – you had to pony up some cash to make your fantasy come true. Good or bad, there was no cash I could use in the Red Light District. Tommy had taken whatever money I had. Despite my young age and the desires that were invoked to partake in the red light business, I was as incapable as the elderly Asian men touring the district.

Back at my lodging place, I was experiencing another culture shock. After every homeless person was in bed, most of them would start loudly farting left and right. In my culture, farting in public is a "NO-NO". It is considered very disrespectful of your environment. In my lonely thoughts, I was trying to make sense of why these men would fart in public. There was nothing I could do other than be shocked and occasionally giggle silently at some of the sounds generated. I stayed there for two weeks in isolation and with no one to talk to, processing what I was experiencing to my fullest capacity.

27. Janet

June 18, 2019. Flight from Istanbul to Antalya. It is only a one-hour flight. I have plenty of legroom since I am sitting in the emergency exit row. The flight is packed with children and it is pretty noisy here. Fortunately, my kids gave me Bose headphones with noise cancellation as a gift and I am super happy with them.

My daughter, Salina, stayed with me in Istanbul for a few days and has just departed back to her home in Germany. We had an amazing time. We stayed at the Hilton Hotel in the heart and the top of the massive city. Istanbul is by far the largest city I have ever seen and so culturally vibrant. We visited the largest mosque in the area, which was magnificent. We also went to the local bazaar. Unfortunately, some of the shop owners take tourists for granted. The prices they start at for bargaining feels like robbery, which didn't sit well with me. Overall, though, a must-visit city.

After two weeks, the VVN found a home for me. They handed me a train ticket for a place "just three train stops away from Amsterdam," I was told. I was excited and happy that I was finally relieved from living with homeless people with whom I had nothing in common. At this point, I felt like I had survived life on a strange planet.

My train ride was expected to be short. But the first stop was 30 minutes later, the second 60 minutes later, and the third and final stop 90 minutes later. The train was moving fast and so was the scenery. The flat landscape, dotted with identical cows and sheep grazing in lush greenery, zoomed past in what felt like a short video clip replaying nonstop. I was immersed in deep fearful thoughts that I was again traveling to the unknown. Since I had left Sudan, the extent of brain-twisting experiences I had been subjected to felt like drinking from a firehose. I had no idea what to expect next, but I had to focus and make sure I got off at the third station – "Meppel Station". Compared to the Paris subway system, the three-stop train ride to Meppel was easy-peasy.

Finally, the train slowed and stopped at a small station. It wasn't difficult to spot the name "Meppel," and I got off the train. The station was almost deserted. Only a few people were waiting to board. I was not sure where I was going and what I would do after I got off the train. By then, I had gotten used to a familiar pattern of strangers popping up to lead my life. "Just trust the system," I assured myself.

I started walking toward the exit carrying my blue bag in my hand. A young white lady, dressed in an oversized dark brown sweater, approached me and asked, "Are you Abraha?" Abraha is my father's name, but I quickly realized she was looking for me. After all, I was the only black person at the station. I reluctantly confirmed I was Abraha. Surprised, I mumbled, "My name is not Abraha. I am Mulugheta." She asked me politely to follow her.

Her name was Janet. She was a soft-spoken village girl who was equally perplexed and unsure about what she was supposed to do with me. Her face was dotted with a few freckles and she had short brown hair. She pulled out her bicycle from the hundreds of bicycles that were parked and she started strategizing how she would carry me and my luggage on her bicycle. She took my blue bag and put it on the center of the front handle and asked me to sit on the back of the bicycle.

Firmly grabbing her waist, with my cheeks slightly leaning on her back, I held tight as she started pedaling. I was amazed at how strong she was. Mind you, back home, I had never seen a woman ride a bicycle, let alone carry a man in the back. After zigzagging through the nearly deserted streets of the small village, we arrived at a home.

The door opened and a gigantic white man with heavy eyeglasses and a full-grown golden colored beard greeted us. A very friendly woman named Patricia quickly followed him. Patricia was clearly the lead and she took charge of the refugee induction process. They seemed happy and super-nice people. We sat at the dinner table and they started asking me questions while taking notes. My English, as broken as it was, must have been good enough to answer all their basic questions in the two hours I stayed there.

Janet was one of the VVN volunteers, a young woman who helped refugees settle in Meppel. She guided them through the initial process and formality they needed to go through to settle. This time, however, she was also providing transportation. After the interview was completed, zigzagging through more empty streets, with me sitting in the back of the bicycle, Janet and I arrived at a huge apartment complex. It was getting dark. She took me to an apartment located on the fourth floor. She opened the apartment door and turned on the lights. There was no one in the fully furnished apartment.

She gave me a tour of the three bedrooms, a large living room, a bathroom, and a kitchen. She suggested that I sleep in the smallest of the three bedrooms. She said she would be back the next day at 9 a.m., but assured me that this apartment was my final destination. Three weeks after a journey that had started in the sandy and hot city of Khartoum, I had reached my destination. Finally, I was home. Home – in a strange country, remote village, with unfamiliar people, foreign culture, a language I couldn't understand, and an alien lifestyle. Nevertheless, home sweet home!

I turned off the lights and crashed in my assigned bedroom. That was the first night in so many days that I could sleep alone and with no farting or snoring noises. I rested well and woke up to a beautiful apartment, experiencing extreme loneliness. I started exploring the rooms in a somewhat dreamy state. Out of necessity, I paid more attention to the kitchen. I was hungry and needed to make breakfast and tea.

Going into the kitchen reminded me of a lesson I had learned in the army. "Your first mistake is your last," we were told during training on how to secure unexploded landmines and plant landmines. I had never seen a refrigerator in my life and never used a gas stove before. The buzzing sound of the refrigerator was intimidating. What if I made a mistake and the stove exploded? I feared. I decided to pull out and avoid the kitchen altogether until Janet came back. Having no breakfast was a safer option.

Janet came at 9 a.m. sharp. I was glad but somewhat surprised. In Eritrea, when you have an appointment, no one was expected to come on time. Arriving one hour later than the agreed time was considered punctual. Janet had a packed plan for the day. She said, "We are going to visit the police to register you and get you a temporary ID, then we go to the bank to open a bank account for you, later we will go to the social services office to apply for assistance, and lastly we are going to do some shopping for food." I didn't follow her fully; I only understood the two tasks she planned to complete – buying food and getting an identity card.

Off we went again, sitting at the back of the bicycle with my arms firmly around Janet's waist, to accomplish her plans. We first went to the police station. There, I was asked my name and personal information. For the first time, I was asked what my last name was and I had no idea what that meant. I told the police officer, "I only have a name, no first or last." They tried to help me understand what a "last name" meant. They said, "The last name is like your father's name." Well, *that* I knew. "My father's name is Abraha." So "Abraha" was registered as my last name. In Eritrea, we do not have the concept of first or last name – everyone simply has a name. Abraha, therefore, is the first name of my father. Napoleon would be very disappointed that Africa didn't implement his rules.

I also was not able to tell them exactly what my birth date was. We used a different calendar in Eritrea, one that had been imposed on us by Ethiopia. The Ethiopian calendar is completely different from the Gregorian calendar. They have 13 months. Even the clock is read differently in Ethiopia. When the hour hand points at 6, they will tell you it is 12 o'clock. So, I was not able to translate my birth date as per the Gregorian calendar. The police were fine as long as I gave them a date. To make it easy to remember, I gave them January 1st as my birth date, which I later discovered was off by two months from my actual birth date. Interestingly, January 1 was a popular birth date chosen by many Eritrean refugees. I found out later that a good number of Eritrean refugees had been assigned the famous birth date, making it sound like if you were born on that lucky day somehow you would make it to Europe.

The worst was to come when they asked about my nationality. I told them I was Eritrean. Eritrea, however, was not a nation at that time as it had been annexed by Ethiopia. They said they'd never heard of such a country and it was not on the list of countries. Based on my birthplace, they assigned Ethiopian as my nationality. I was upset. After spending five years in the jungle and paying a tremendous price as people to restore our rightful Eritrean identity, they forced me to carry an Ethiopian identity even in Europe. It would have been fair and more proper to assign me a stateless status than Ethiopian. It was a painful experience, but there was nothing I could do about it.

The police instructed me to report to the station every Thursday before noon to get a stamp on my card. Failing to report weekly would jeopardize my asylum process. I agreed, and we went off to the next office that Janet had planned – the bank. The bank visit was short and uneventful. Jannet spoke to the bank managers in Dutch and an account was opened for me in no time. We then proceeded to the office for Social Services.

At the Social Services office, the workers were nice and helpful. We filled out a few forms and, in addition to the monthly financial assistance that would be deposited in my newly opened bank account, Janet negotiated for me to get money specifically for a jacket to survive the winter. I signed the welfare acceptance letter, and at the bottom, I read a statement: "If you do not agree with the assistance and amount provided to you, you can write an objection letter to appeal." What? That was such a weird concept. How in the world would I have the right to complain when someone was helping me and giving me financial assistance? If anything, I should write a letter to thank them for any assistance they gave me! It was such an odd concept for us as refugees, we would joke about it for years to come.

For my age, I got the lowest amount of financial support one could get, which was 710 guilders (about $500 US dollars) a month. In Sudan, getting $200 as a monthly salary was a big deal. By that standard, I was filthy rich, I thought. Little did I know what Janet had in store for me. She suggested I stay in the smaller bedroom because the rent was cheaper. I had to pay 250 guilders for the smaller room compared to 350 guilders for the bigger rooms. The option of raising my age to 23 to receive a higher amount of monthly support would have been very helpful from that perspective. Nevertheless, I could not have been any happier with all the pampering I received that day.

A few days later, the VVN brought two more Eritreans to the apartment. They were older than me and more sophisticated. Both were freedom fighters and one of them had been a commander who had led 1,000 ELF fighters. My social life was enjoyable. It started to resemble that of Tenedba in Sudan – exclusive and privileged friends who enjoy each other but have little to do with the world around them.

Over the next few days, the VVN volunteers started visiting us one by one. These were dedicated individuals with big hearts. They did everything possible to make our stay pleasant and stress-free. They organized free language tutorials and took us on tours of the city and surroundings. They connected us to other Eritreans who had come before us and were already settled in the village. They helped us socialize with locals by taking us to bars and coffee shops. In the process, we made many local friends. They even took us to some farmers around the village. I'll never forget an elderly lady we met on one of the farms. Noticing that I was the youngest, she sent me a handmade pair of socks to make my winter experience warm and pleasant.

Regardless of how much help we received, though, shopping and feeding ourselves was our responsibility. Finding the right things to buy at the supermarkets was a challenge since everything was written in Dutch. So, we depended on visuals and pictures a lot. We heard stories of other refugees buying cat food because delicious-looking chunks of meat were displayed on the label. We made a few mistakes and bought fine sugar instead of salt, but nothing embarrassing like cat food.

A young Dutchman befriended us and started coming to our apartment. In the evenings, he would come home with marijuana and the joint would pass from one person to another. I never was a smoker and was adamant that I wouldn't try it. During my entire stay in Holland, I never tried to smoke anything. I'd always thought that was a slippery slope where I could go wrong and never recover. So, against all kinds of pressure, I stood my ground and never smoked, upholding the "Just Say No" advice of Nancy Reagan.

The nightlife brought its own set of challenges. Strangers approached us with various intentions. I remember one older gentleman wanting a relationship with me. It took me a while to understand what he was after. Homosexuality was a serious offense and a culturally repulsive undertaking in Eritrea. When I was a guard at the prison in Alet, I knew two people who had received 10 years of jail time for being gay. Naturally, my view on homosexuality was very different then. I was terrified once I realized the guy was after me in that way. Every time I saw that person in the shopping area or on the streets of downtown Meppel, I would make sure I disappeared from his sight.

As I learned to interact more and more with Janet and the locals, my desire to learn the language grew. Dutch was a very difficult language to learn. The fact that the English alphabets are pronounced differently made it even more difficult. The middle school certificate I had fabricated when I was in the ELF was of no help. I had to start learning the alphabet from scratch. During my stay in Meppel, I spent most of my time learning words and grammar. There was no language school for immigrants in Meppel. A few VVN volunteers offered to help us out twice a week.

Although I didn't end up in Sweden as I was hoping to when I was in Eritrea, I started making plans for my education in Holland. The many aerogram letters I wrote to my father, who was still in Eritrea, primarily discussed my education plans. My father became my mentor and adviser through his letters. Every week I received a letter from him, mostly a blue post-office aerogram, and I would promptly respond to him, describing my situation in detail. Even before I managed to construct basic sentences in Dutch, we were discussing what I should study in college, setting expectations very high.

My dream had always been to study music and be a music conductor. My father, on the other hand, had different ideas. He gave me a few options in order of priority: aeronautical engineering, electrical engineering, and mechanical engineering. Becoming a music conductor was not on his list. I had never cared much for airplanes, but I respected my father's advice very much and vowed to put the goal of becoming an aeronautical engineer at the center of my life.

I made a ten-year plan and shared with my father how I would get there. I reported my progress to him every week from Meppel. I felt like my father was living with me and knew everything I had in my mind. After all, he was not only my role model but also the person who had remotely sparked my desire for education while I was still in the jungle. I knew then that I was starting a very long journey that might require much more perseverance than the five years I had spent in the jungle. But I was determined, and nothing would get in the way of my aspirations. I never questioned the eventual outcome; I focused on the day-to-day grind.

Also, each person I met in Meppel inspired me in some way. Tewolde, an Eritrean who lived in Meppel for many years and was married to a Dutch woman, took me for swimming lessons twice a week in his shiny Toyota Celica. The first-ever diploma I received in Holland was a swimming diploma, just three months after I arrived in Meppel.

Elias, an Ethiopian refugee who was also married to a Dutch woman and was a boxing champion in Meppel, inspired me to run daily, teaching me that achieving anything in life requires hard work. Elias, who was known for his boxing and karate skills, was working at the Lord Nelson discotheque as a bodyguard and was well respected in the village.

Yohannes, who miraculously survived a sickness against every doctor's prediction and lived an impeccable lifestyle, made me look at the world in a different light. Despite his health challenges, he saw the glass always as half-full. He was always clean and well-dressed. His home was so clean that it could pass for a model home. He loved going out and socializing with the locals with a big smile on his face, making me realize that life requires a positive attitude.

Other refugees gave me a firsthand example of how wrong life could go if you were not careful. I learned from them what not to do, which is the best lesson one can get. I learned to avoid peer pressure and denounce a lifestyle that might sound cool but wouldn't get me far. Every person I met during the first year somehow shaped my perspective of life in Holland. The absence of one of those people I met may have resulted in a different outcome for me.

2013, Flight DL 3300, Los Angeles to Sydney. This was a fun weekend. My kids were invited to perform at the Steve Harvey Disney Dreamers Academy event at the Walt Disney World Resort. This trip gave me a taste of living life as a celebrity. We had a dedicated escort, VIP pass to get priority on any ride, and unlimited access to all the restaurants. It was a blessing to see my girls sharing a stage with music legends like Jordan Sparks, Yolanda Adams, ESSENCE magazine editor-at-large Mikki Taylor, education advocate Dr. Steve Perry, The Sister Accord founder and author Sonia Jackson Myles, award-winning motivational speaker Jonathan Sprinkles, and more. I didn't want to miss the event, so I had to fly to Florida to only come back to Seattle and head on a business trip the next day.

We had a great weekend in Orlando with my family, enjoying the many perks of being the father of three talented singers. I took a flight from Seattle to LA and then on to Sydney. After a 14-hour flight, I will arrive early in the morning in Sydney and will be heading straight to a meeting that will take a full day. It will be exhausting, but for some reason, I am not in the mood to sleep. I prepared for the meeting last week so I can afford to spend time on my book.

28. *Lord Nelson*

Thursday night was ladies' night at the Lord Nelson Discotheque. Each Thursday, the club would be packed with girls who couldn't afford to pay the weekend fees, mostly young teens. One night, my friend Yohannes invited me to join him to visit the club. Not knowing much about clubs and dance floors, I reluctantly agreed to join him.

After entering the Lord Nelson and making our way to the dance floor, the flashing disco lights, the thunderous music, the video projected on a massive screen, and the vibe of the place, in general, was an incredible experience for me. Except for some of my Red Light District experiences, this was by far the most dramatic for someone who had come straight from the jungle and ended up in a sophisticated club where MJ's *Thriller* music video was projected on the walls. The place was packed. Many young girls were lined up at the bar and others were trying to move from the bar to the dance floor while rubbing their bodies unreservedly against anyone in the way. The warm colorful lights reflecting on the exposed white skin of these beautiful girls, who otherwise would be fully covered in the winter, was a stunningly pleasant experience.

After I had recovered from the initial shock, Yohannes told me to enjoy myself and take it easy. He said it wouldn't take long before I would get snatched. "Snatched?" I didn't know what he was talking about because I was still in the process of taking in what was going on in that place. Mind you, this was the first time in my life I had ever gone to a dance club and was confronted by so many beautiful white ladies enjoying the music. Yohannes and I, being the only two young black men in the entire dance club, it was not difficult to be noticed. But more importantly, I was the new black boy who had never been seen before in this place. Since the town was small, everyone knew everyone and I was the surprise guest of the night.

Yohannes was a very popular man. He drove a red Toyota Celica. Wherever he went, everyone in the village received him with a hug and excitement. He was also a charming womanizer who always walked with a big smile on his face. As I was coping with the situation in the club and frozen in one location, Yohannes left me alone and kept dancing with one girl after another. I was puzzled how Yohannes managed to integrate so well with the society in Holland. I couldn't help but admire his every dance move.

While my attention was consumed with what Yohannes was doing on the dance floor, a young woman next to me made a tactical move. She grabbed my glass of Pepsi and took a sip. She apologized immediately for mistaking the glass, opening the door for a chat. Struggling with my English and the loud music, I managed to communicate briefly and told her to never mind about the glass. She followed with a request to dance.

Feeling overwhelmed, I agreed, and we made our way to the dance floor. I don't remember what song it was nor do I remember how well I danced, but I remember I stopped right after the song ended. She asked me to stay on the dance floor for the next song, but I politely declined and headed back straight to my corner. I must have been sweating from nervousness.

She followed me to my spot where we had left our drinks and introduced herself as Alea. By then, Yohannes had noticed that I was in "good" hands and started to wander further away. Before I knew it, he had disappeared from the scene and I was left with Alea. Alea and I were not talking a lot but we went back to the dance floor a few times. Toward the end of the night, Alea asked me if I wanted to go home with her. With Yohannes gone, I accepted the offer, and we headed out of the dance club. Like most of the people there, we headed to the parking rack for bicycles. Out of hundreds of black bicycles that looked the same, Alea magically recognized her bicycle. At that point, I knew exactly what was expected from me as I was not a stranger to getting a bicycle ride on the back seat.

Alea was a very skinny and petite young lady. Sitting on the back of her bicycle, hugging her tiny waist, we headed to her home in the middle of the night. Pedaling hard against the headwind through the tiny streets of the town, she told me that she was 22 years old, a few years older than I was. She was surprised to find out that I was only 18, but didn't take it as bad news.

We arrived at her home and were greeted by a barking puppy. We sat on the sofa for some time while we played with the puppy. As I chatted more and more with her, I learned that Alea was a fun girl and she knew a lot about Eritrea. So, I started asking her if she knew some of the Eritrean men who lived in the town. She said, "I know most of them," and excitedly I started mentioning some names. Her answer shocked me to the core. Every time I asked if she knew a person, she would answer, "Yes, I know him, I f***ed him." When I gave her another name, she would say, "I f***ed him too." All the names I mentioned invoked the same response from Alea. At that point, I started to worry a lot for two major reasons that have significant cultural relevance.

The first reason was that I started imagining how she would tell other Eritreans that she had "f***ed Mulu" as easily as she was saying it to me, which was a taboo in our culture. The second reason, and the funniest thing, was that in my language and the Eritrean "men's world," a lady never f***ed a man – it was always the man that f***ed a lady. So, the sentence she used just didn't make sense to me and I worried that the fun I was expecting that night might not be what I thought it was. Alea might not be a SHE, after all. A scary notion that fortunately wasn't correct as I discovered later that night.

Alea and I dated for a few weeks and things were going well. One day, I went to her home without telling her that I was coming, as I always did. I knocked at the door. Alea opened the door partly and said, "I cannot let you in. I have visitors in the house." Noticing my expression, she added in a serious tone, "You should have called first." It was an obvious cultural conflict. Where I come from, you don't call someone to ask if you could come to visit that person, let alone be denied entry after you arrived at their front door. You just show up at the house, regardless of the "inconvenience" to the host, or you run the risk of the person not being at home. In any case, if someone opens the door, you are guaranteed maximum hospitality.

The excuse she gave me – "I have visitors" – sounded even more insulting in that it implied I wasn't allowed to get to know her guests. What she did was socially very off, according to my social norms and culture. I just didn't get the concept of not welcoming a friend after he arrives at your home.

Poor Alea must have had enough of tolerating my "sophisticated" social expectations for a few weeks. After I not only showed up unannounced but insisted that I come in to her home, she had enough and told me to never come back again. That was a very clear message. Humiliated, I never returned to Alea's house and that was the end of our relationship.

29. *The Guests*

Aug 2014, Delta flight DL33, Seattle to Amsterdam. Today I am heading to two contrasting places on earth – Tel Aviv and Abu Dhabi. Traveling to Israel and then to an Arab country is not a good idea. Knowing this, the Israelis do not record an entry stamp on your passport. Instead, they stamp the entry visa on a separate card.

I am flying with my boss and expect this to be another trip where we firm up a business deal. I have already been to Tel Aviv three times, and the hard work has been done. This is the time to wine and dine to celebrate the hard work.

The Israelis are interesting people. They are difficult to negotiate with but at the same time very straightforward. They work hard and long hours. The oldest group of aviation workers I ever met was at El Al airlines. They are passionate, dedicated, and demanding.

Often, while I am presenting, one person starts speaking in Hebrew, and instantly the situation escalates. The meeting room turns into animated shouting match. I quietly wait until all is over and we go back to the presentation as if nothing happened. This repeats multiple times. Apparently, debating loudly seems so normal that a gavel is placed on the table for the leader to call participants to order when needed. Very peculiar. Yet, the employees at El Al airlines were the best people I met in the airline industry, I enjoyed working with them a lot and made great friends.

Most of the refugees and immigrants were to be found in major cities like Amsterdam or Rotterdam. At that time, the total number of Eritrean refugees in Holland was no more than 700, spread across the country. Meppel had a population of about 20,000. Despite its small size, the place offered a great opportunity for refugees to settle.

One day, we got news from the VVN volunteers that a few more refugees were coming to live in Meppel and that we would have to prepare to greet them. By then, we were seasoned immigrants compared to the newcomers, so we decided to prepare food and drinks and invite them for dinner. For the first time, we decided to prepare a cultural dish called Ingera. The complexity of the job necessitated that we all contribute to making the food the best it could be. We prepared the sauce as best as we could, but the dish was pathetic by any standard. The effort we put in however was significant, and assuming that the newcomers had not had good Eritrean food for a while, we were confident they would appreciate the food we had prepared.

The doorbell rang and I rushed to welcome the guests. There were two men and two ladies at the door. The way they dressed looked very chic – not the type of immigrants that we had expected. The men had been living in Holland for a couple of years, but the ladies were new to the country. As they came into our living room where there was better lighting, I couldn't help but notice how gorgeous the ladies were. We introduced each other and we quickly found out that the two ladies spoke Amharic indicating that they were from Ethiopia or Eritreans who had grown up in Ethiopia.

Traditionally, Eritrean girls from Addis looked down on Eritreans. They called us Tgres, which we thought was referring to a less developed tribe in Ethiopia. Because we were aware of this "demonizing" attitude, the atmosphere in the evening became quite tense. As we inevitably noticed and kept admiring their beauty, they reciprocally appreciated the effort we had put to make Ingera and invite them for dinner.

Once the guests left the house, we couldn't wait to talk about how gorgeous these girls were. We despised the fact that they had come with those men. Without knowing whether the two men were their boyfriends or family members, we started to fantasize about who the luckiest person would be to have the privilege of being a boyfriend of one of these girls, especially the shorter one. She had a small body but a killer smile and incredibly beautiful hair. Although she didn't look straight into your eyes, the few brief glances she offered would force any man to want more of her. Her name was Tiblets, meaning "Be the best." Judging by her beauty, she did justice to her name – she was the best.

Unfortunately, it was a week before she could return to Meppel. She had family members living in Amsterdam and there was no reason for her to spend time in this remote village. If she came back, we thought, it would probably be just to report to the local police that she was still in town. She wouldn't want to live in the village, unfortunately.

To our surprise, however, we found out that Tiblets had moved to Meppel, while the other girl had decided to live in Zwolle with her boyfriend. This meant that all of us would now have a chance to meet the beautiful woman daily. Each one of us planned to try to win her trust. This resulted somewhat in a competition amongst the three of us – at least that was what I felt.

Tiblets shared an apartment with an older Eritrean lady and a couple from Turkey. Since we all had no school or work, we had plenty of time to socialize and make time for each other. Making time for her was not an issue for any one of us. Sometimes as a team and other times individually, we kept visiting her apartment routinely. Fortunately for her, since there was always someone in the apartment, she didn't feel threatened by us, and the encounters were strictly social and familial.

However, for me, I was genuinely in love with her, and every moment I spent with her, regardless of whether there were ten people around or just three, I was very happy that I got to see her, enjoy her beauty, and admire her incredibly pleasant character. I, being the youngest of the men in the village and having an attitude that was not threatening, she felt more comfortable with me. My Amharic was good enough to communicate with her. I demonstrated care and respect for her whenever we met, but I never gave her any hint that I was deeply in love with her. My respect and love were so genuine that she felt I could be a true friend she could trust. Occasionally, she allowed me to go out with her for a walk to the city. A special bond was developing, but no one knew where it would lead.

The more I saw Tiblets, the more I fell in love with her. The more I talked to her, the sweeter she became. Unlike other girls, she didn't try to show off or highlight her beauty by putting on a lot of make-up or by dressing sexy. She was the most humble and proper girl I had ever met. However, for a girl this young and coming from Addis, her calm character was very unusual. Something was off about her behavior, but I never doubted her genuine friendship. Not once did she flirt with me or allow me to flirt with her. She was like a sister, and she considered me a true friend and younger brother in a village where we both were strangers. I went to her apartment so often it almost became my second home. I would stay until late at night and would go home wondering when I would ever get a chance to express what my heart was telling me. For all this, the reward I got from her was not much. At most, she would clip my fingernails and touch my hands in the gentlest sisterly way.

I was not planning to sign up for this brotherly "nail-clipping" relationship. I was deeply in love and had to somehow show her the true intent of my heart. But I didn't know how and when to tell her that I loved her differently than the way she loved me. She was accompanied by the older lady who shared her apartment all hours of the day. Inviting her to my apartment was not an option as I was living with two men in a pretty disgusting home that, by the smell of it, could pass for a marijuana coffee shop. The waiting was grueling, but I couldn't give up. If there was anyone who had a chance at getting to date Tiblets, it was me. As time progressed, the other men gave up, I was the only one who stuck with her, offering my brotherly friendship as a disguise to the burning love raging in my heart.

The older lady in her apartment had by now clearly noticed that I was up to no good. She started teasing me that I came often because I wanted to date the beautiful girl in her apartment. At the same time, she knew she had to give me a chance to have "private" moment with Tiblets. Unfortunately, during the harsh winter in Meppel, the lady had nowhere to go. The only thing she could do, which she did often, was to go to bed early so that Tiblets and I could stay in the living room watching TV and get a chance to be alone. This was a very welcome proposition because it allowed me to experience Tiblets' personality without any external considerations.

Despite the countless evenings that Tiblets and I stayed together watching TV, it was very difficult for me to tell her what I felt deep in my heart. I was showing her all the affections I could, but saying "I love you" was an impossible task. This was mainly because Tiblets was cutting every avenue that could lead to that kind of reaction or initiative from my side. I felt that all her actions were delicately intended to deny me any opportunity in thinking that she was open to the kind of relationship I was interested in. She was sweet and affectionate to me, but very careful not to cross the line that might be construed as an indication that she was interested in anything but a brotherly relationship.

The lonely evenings we spent together watching TV made us very close friends. As days passed, we sometimes crossed the line from friendship to lovers in a very subtle way. Every time I got closer to telling her that I loved her, my heart rate would go up and so would my fear of being refused. As a 19-year-old boy who had little love experience, it was a difficult task for me to read the signs that men look for in a woman to know if she is interested or not. This particularly was very relevant in the Eritrean culture where women would never take the first step in starting a relationship. If a woman was the first to openly pursue a man, she would typically be seen as aggressive and considered a "man-hunter". In the old days, men would shy away from engaging in serious relationships with "aggressive" girls. If only this had applied to Tiblets, my life would have been a lot easier.

I concluded that one day I would have to be a man and tell her that I love her. If that didn't work, I could use one of the intimate evening TV moments to try to give her a gentle kiss before saying good night and heading back to my apartment. Three months had passed and I hadn't got the chance or the guts to confess my love to her.

One day, her roommate, the old lady, received guests from another town and she decided to go with them to spend a few days at their home. This was a God-sent opportunity for me and I knew I had to make use of it. If nothing, I could stay on the sofa the whole night without going to my apartment claiming that she needed protection. My mind was going crazy about how I could capitalize on this opportunity.

Finally, the moment of truth arrived. The older lady left with her relatives. Tiblets and I were left behind in the apartment. My evening would be full of heart-racing and full of cat and mouse games. But with just the two of us, she would know where I stood with Tiblets. As usual, after dinner, we sat on the sofa and the long TV evening started. After several hesitations, I finally broke the news and told her that I had special feelings for her and that I loved her. I held her hands, the hands that she used to clip my nails so often, and leaned in to kiss her. But the kiss was just to confirm the special feelings, not one that could be escalated into uncontrolled intimacy. Surprisingly, I didn't get the resistance I was afraid of. Nevertheless, Tiblets didn't use any words that indicated that she loved me too. No, none of that.

Instead, she tried to tell me that I was too young and that our relationship couldn't work at all. She said, "I love you as my younger brother, but not more." Although my age was the only official excuse she gave, I could tell there was more behind her refusal. I just had no way to guess what it was. It could be that she was thinking that I was uneducated, unemployed, and simply not ready for a serious relationship. Those were all true reasons and I had no way to defend them, but she was not saying it.

After a while, I realized that I couldn't discuss with her the idea of a serious relationship. Instead, the evening should be about romance, romance that she didn't resist. We kissed and hugged each other the entire evening while I told her how much I loved her every minute of it. She would not reciprocate in words. But she kissed back reservedly and hugged back reluctantly as if she felt sympathy for my situation.

As it was getting very late, it was clear that we both were okay for me to stay. She agreed that I could stay and that it was okay for me to sleep in her one-person bed in her small bedroom. The bedroom was very cold and having a warm body in your bed would be mutually beneficial. After we went to bed, we kissed more and talked a lot more. My apparent attempt to escalate this opportunity into a full-blown intimate encounter was adamantly rejected. Hugs and holding her tight were all she allowed.

I respected her decision and refrained from making any moves that would be considered forceful. I acted as the friend she wanted me to be and simply gave her only the love she could bear but not more. It was the longest night ever, but one that opened a new chapter in my relationship with Tiblets. I entered this exciting new chapter where I could look into her beautiful eyes and kiss her at my leisure, consider her my girlfriend, and dare to dream of a long-lasting relationship.

For three days, I was locked in with her in the apartment, and we spent the time enjoying each other's company. At the end of the three days, I was the happiest person, having been able to admire her beauty intimately and without reservation. I was not sure I understood her reservation to intimacy, but at that time I had received enough attention from her to keep me going for months to come. She was like a fresh flower that I was able to smell any time I needed her.

After a few days of my hormonal and emotional rollercoaster ride, the older lady returned. Before I left the apartment, however, Tiblets had to place one more surprising and severe limitation on me, known as "What happens in Vegas stays in Vegas." She said, "I count on you that you will not talk to anyone about the days we spent together. What happened in the apartment stays in the apartment." If we ever wanted to continue the relationship we had built, the rule of secrecy was a prerequisite. As strong as these limitations sounded, she said it in a way that made me love her even more. I promised her that I would never disappoint her and that I respected her desire to keep everything between the two of us. I was hooked to a woman who was so beautiful on the outside but had so much to hide on the inside.

Deep in my heart, I did not understand the reasons for her secrecy and her strong reservation. This bothered me a lot and I wanted to uncover the mystery badly. I wanted to know who she was. Until then, however, I remained blindly in love. Love that became stronger with every second I spent with her.

At this point, I had a special relationship with Tiblets, but was unable to show it or talk to anyone about it. It became suffocating and difficult for me. When I visited her apartment, I had to act as if nothing had happened. The older lady, as much as she suspected that something had happened while she was gone, didn't see any change in our behavior. When she got a chance to talk to me alone, she would tease me saying that I must have chickened out to make a move on Tiblets. I wanted to tell her, "You are so wrong," but I couldn't say that. I kept my promise and behaved like the young brother Tiblets wanted me to be.

With the lady in the house, I couldn't spend more nights with Tiblets. Creativity was needed. One evening, I told Tiblets that I would love to stay the night with her even if I had to jump in through the window of her bedroom. Apparently, as crazy as the idea was, Tiblets smiled and said, "That would be crazy." I translated this to mean "You are approved to come in through the window." Her room faced the walkway and I could easily jump in without anyone noticing.

Every evening from then on, after watching TV with them, I would go out through the door saying goodbye to only come in through the window to say hello. These secret visits through the window made our relationship even more exciting and made my love even stronger and mysteriously rewarding. My home was deserted and I found a new secret home.

The Fight

Comfortably reading a book at one of the lounging rock-sofas around our camp in Barka (Photo credit Muller Zergaber)

(Pictured, Esayas who was one of the instructors in the Pioneers camp (Tsbah) that I looked up to. He later joined the ELF radio broadcast crew and became a recognizable voice. After ELF was defeated, he returned to Eritrea to join the EPLF in 1982 and fought until Eritrea's liberation in May 1991.)

IX

The Fight

Sep 2014, Lufthansa flight from Seattle to Frankfurt. I am on a rescue mission to Jeddah, Saudi Arabia. The Saudis bought a bunch of services from Boeing and now want to renegotiate. These kinds of discussions are not pleasant and require delicate handling. This is a case where I learned that selling is one thing, but delivering on what you committed to is another.

I have to admit, Saudi is not my favorite destination. They expect you to eat heavy meat-based meals with no wine to help digest the food. A suggestion I got from a retired Saudi captain was, after eating a heavy meal, to sit on your side with a few pillows supporting you and let the system do its thing. Essentially, let the entire body's energy focus on digesting the foreign object ingested. That is exactly what I do after a late-night dinner; jetlagged, I head to my hotel, turn on the TV, sit on my bed leaning on the headboard like a pregnant woman, with pillows stuffed around my waist, and just crash in seconds. It works, but it is always with wine.

As is always the case, in any flight departing from Seattle to Europe, you will find a few Boeing employees. At the business lounge in the airport, I met a Boeing sales director who suggested nicely that we would hopefully find time to chat on the airplane. No, we didn't. He was in another business class cabin. That was not a bad thing because I have a lot to do during the 23-hour travel time. Not only do I want to continue writing my book, I also have to prepare my presentation to Saudi Arabian Airlines.

30. The Moeder MAVO

A few months later, Tiblets decided to move to Zwolle to be closer to her friends and family members. That was bad news for me. The secret love life in Meppel ended and presented a more challenging reality.

After meeting many Eritreans who lived in other cities, I too was convinced that Meppel was too small and too far removed from the large cities. Exacerbated by the departure of Tiblets to Zwolle, I started to dislike Meppel. My two former roommates had already left for larger cities. If it had not been for Tiblets, I would have joined them a long time ago. I had nothing to look forward to in Meppel. The only education I was getting was language lessons twice a week by volunteers.

I decided to move to the city of Utrecht where one of my former roommates lived. He encouraged me to move to Utrecht because it offered more education opportunities for refugees. However, Utrecht was very far away from Zwolle. It takes about an hour by train. This meant seeing Tiblets was going to be cost-prohibitive.

Moving out of Meppel was as simple as packing the same blue bag I had bought in Sudan. I took a train and headed to Utrecht. In a way, nothing seemed to change from how we had lived in Sudan. Moving to another city was as simple as making a decision and finding a friend to receive you in the new city. After that, the host and the guest would figure out together the next steps, no complicated planning involved.

Finding a room in Utrecht was very difficult. Individual families who had extra rooms offered them in the market for rent. The government also provided an option where you applied for housing or rental of student living quarters. The latter, however, could take years. So, my job was to read newspaper advertisements daily and visit the various places that were offered by individual families for rental. It didn't matter how fast I showed up at a place that was advertised for rental, the answer I got was "Sorry, the room has already been rented out." After a few weeks, I noticed that this was not true. The same rooms that I was told were "already rented" were still being advertised for rent over the following days. This was my first encounter with what I would later know to be called racism. At the time, I accepted this as an implied reality that my background, color, and appearance could sometimes work to my disadvantage. After all, I was a stranger in someone else's country and it was to be expected. This was not new to me as I had been in Sudan where I was not welcome on many occasions because of being an immigrant. Having experienced the selflessness and generosity of VVN (Refugee Foundation) volunteers in Holland, however, I paid little attention to the "racism" of other folks and did not allow it to be a source of discomfort in my life.

After a long search for a room, I finally found a small room upstairs in a house owned by a Turkish family. It was perfectly located on Amsterdamse-Straatweg, not far away from the Central Train Station. I bought a bed, a desk, and a used bicycle. My next important goal was to find a school. But my skill in Dutch was still inadequate, and my educational background was so low that I would have to start seventh grade at age 20.

In every middle school I visited to register, they would tell me that I needed to find an adult school as I was too old to join the schools with 13-year-old kids. Now, not only did my appearance work against me, but my age was also not helping. All the adult schools were evening schools, offering adults who worked during the day an opportunity to study in the evening.

I also needed to register at the police station as a new refugee in Utrecht and report once a week, every Thursday, until my asylum request received final status. So far, I had been going to the police station weekly for over nine months. In Meppel, this process was easy because there were only a handful of refugees. In Utrecht, it was a different story. What used to be a simple visit to the Meppel police office became a visit to a massive police station in Utrecht, which required waiting in line with many immigrants from different countries. This weekly ritual wasted two to three hours of my time just to confirm that I loved Holland more than any other country in the world.

In the Netherlands, MAVO (Middlebar Algemeen Voortgezet Onderwijs) was a medium-level applied education. It was a four-year low-intensity high school program intended for those kids who were educationally "challenged" and wanted to pursue vocational school (MBO). HAVO (Hoger Algemeen Voortgezet Onderwijs) was a five-year high school program intended for those who had a shot at getting a Bachelor's degree (HBO). VWO (Voorbereidend Wetenschappelijk Onderwijs) was a high school path reserved for the brightest kids who would go straight for their Master's but could also settle for Bachelor's if need be. In our eyes, VWO was for nerds.

In this complex ladder of the education system, although I was 20 years old at the time, based on my education level, I was supposed to join the 12-year-old kids who had finished elementary school. Having studied the system, I planned to take the shortest route. I wanted to join HAVO and hopefully get accepted at engineering school per my father's instruction and priorities. If everything went smoothly, this would require 10-year dedication and focus.

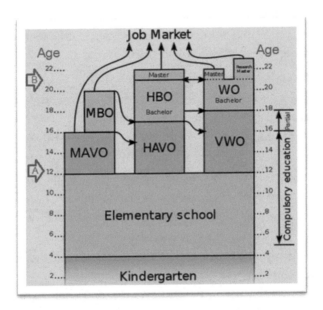

The Dutch education system

The problem with this plan was that I couldn't join HAVO since I did not have any Dutch certificate showing that I had completed elementary school with good grades. So, the best possible option was to start MAVO which didn't lead to a Bachelor's degree directly. It was, however, possible to transfer to HAVO after finishing MAVO, which is a much longer path. So, my educational plan got stretched to at least 13 years. For some reason, however, time didn't scare me and I shared my education plan with my father.

The Dutch are interesting people. They like going to school at a late age or even after they retire. They do this for various reasons. Some mothers and grandmothers who didn't get a chance to complete their high school before they got married want to study certain subjects to help their kids/grandkids with homework or to re-enter the workforce. These people go to schools called *Volwassenen onderwijs*, translating to adult education. In the city of Utrecht, they even had a school called Moeder MAVO, which specifically catered to mothers and grandmothers.

Ten months after I arrived in Holland, thanks to the VVN volunteers in Meppel, I was able to communicate in Dutch with some difficulty. I could understand Dutch a lot more than I could speak it, and I didn't need a translator to go about my life. But, with all the available options and a complex school system, it was difficult for me to figure out what I should be studying. The fact that there were courses for adults made life a lot easier for me. At least, I did not have to go to school with 12-year-old kids. With nowhere to turn for advice, I decided to try out Moeder MAVO. I registered to start the first year, which would be equivalent to seventh grade.

My first day in school was not that bad. I sat next to about 15 older ladies. For each subject, I would have different classmates. During the lunch break, I met two Eritreans who went to the same school – Dawit and Michael. They were second-year MAVO students, a year ahead of me. This gave me a chance to ask them and learn more about what they had gone through in the first year.

Versneld Cursus

A few days into my school year, I learned that there was another type of course available in the same school. Individuals who had completed MAVO in the past but needed to study an additional subject, which may have not been included in their original MAVO package, could attend an intensive course, "Versneld Cursus". For this particular scenario, the school system allowed individuals to take a one-year intensive course where the entire MAVO high school program was compressed into one year for a given subject. Individuals were allowed to take a maximum of two high school subjects per year. This was because the short course covered four years of material and it would be too much for anyone to take more than two subjects per year. These intensive courses were given in the evenings, while the regular Moeder MAVO courses were given during the day.

I didn't give myself time to seriously contemplate taking the intensive course. If I succeeded, this would allow me to save three years. The limitation to two subjects, however, was an issue. I needed at least four subjects to be able to apply to any vocational school or transfer to HAVO. One night, a crazy idea floated in my head. *What if there was another MAVO school in Utrecht that also provided the same intensive course?* I could go to one school to take two subjects and go to another school to take two more subjects. This would allow me to complete a four-year MAVO program in one year, which would mean that I could transfer to HAVO in one year. In theory, this was a fantastic plan.

The next day, I went to another MAVO school on the opposite side of the city and asked if they offered Versneld Cursus. To my surprise, the school did offer the course with the same restriction of a maximum of two subjects per year. Bingo! My plan was possible to accomplish. Whether I could handle four years of content for four subjects in one year, however, was a big question mark. To make things even harder, the subjects that my father "forced" me to take were the difficult ones: math, physics, chemistry, and English. With no hesitation and an extremely positive mindset, I registered to two schools for four intensive classes, two subjects in each school. Thank God there were no computers back then – the schools had no idea that I was violating the limitation of two subjects per year by registering at two schools at once.

Feb 2015, Amsterdam to Dubai. I just had a fantastic interaction with the person sitting next to me. A Dutchman in his late forties, heading to Dubai on a business trip, likes to chat with passengers. I surprised him when I switched from speaking English to Dutch. Now that I connected to his culture, we engaged in a deeper conversation. We talked about the economy, politics, and immigrants in The Netherlands. The stories he told me about how Dutch people see immigrants these days, especially the negative view on immigrants from Eritrea, struck a wrong chord. He was eager to hear how my stay in Holland had been and how I had ended up where I am today. The contrast between the story I told him and what he heard from his fellow citizens was so much that he urged me to contact the media in Netherlands. He hoped they would write and broadcast stories that highlight the positive aspect of refugees. His fascination with my story and the positive impact it had on his perception inspired me further to continue writing my book.

Double Rejection

In the meantime, I received some bad news from the immigration office. My asylum application was rejected by the state. They cited that I should have stayed in Sudan and sought asylum there, never mind that there was no such a thing as "seeking asylum" in Sudan. The ramifications of the decision were devastating to my educational plans. If I was not recognized as a refugee in Holland, I wouldn't be allowed to attend college. I started to worry. So, in preparation for the worst-case scenario, I started searching for options. Back then, there was no Internet, and all the research had to be done in the library or through face-to-face discussions with VVN members.

I learned that an organization called UAF (University Assistance Fund) offered scholarships to selected refugees with "potential", regardless of their asylum status. Armed with my burning desire and energy to complete the MAVO program in one year, in February 1984, I applied for scholarship assistance from UAF. A formal interview at their office in Utrecht followed and I got excited about a positive response. UAF, however, didn't see potential in me and they rejected my application. The rejection letter stated that my educational level was too low. Their advice was that I do what my friends Michael and Dawit were doing: start seventh grade or wait until I got my residence permit and take a vocational course with the help of the labor office.

referentie: 216/vdh/infb.   utrecht, March 29, 1984

Dear Mulugeta,

In reply to your letter dated February 28, 1984
I must inform you that UAF cannot assist you in
the present circumstances.

Due to your insufficient educational background
(which, I readily admit, is not your fault), UAF
cannot realistically offer you help to reach the
level of Dutch MAVO or HAVO in one year.

As I advised you , there are two possibilities open
to you now: either go to a secondary school for
adults and obtain within a few years the MAVO or
HAVO certificates in the most important subjects;
or wait for the positive decision from the Ministry
and then follow a short professional training
course with the help of the Labour Office.

Yours sincerely,

University Assistance Fund
UAF

Klaas Keuning
director

A letter from the UAF in response to my application

I can't blame whoever reviewed my application at the UAF.
After all, I had arrived only four months earlier straight from Africa,
with only an elementary school education. Who in his right mind
would think to discuss university admission and scholarships when
I hadn't even finished middle school, not to mention that I hadn't
taken any formal language courses yet. Things didn't look good and
I hit a brick wall. With no funding from UAF and rejection by the
state, there was no way I could access the higher education system
in Holland. My only option was to complete the MAVO intensive
course on my own and see if I could prove the UAF wrong.

The hard work started. My two other Eritrean friends, Michael
and Dawit, who went to the same school, thought I was crazy for

trying to take four subjects in one year, that normally were completed in four years. They were right. The amount of studying and homework ahead of me was insanely daunting. My life was consumed with studying and keeping up with school. I had little contact with friends and socializing was kept to a minimum.

At that time, all Eritreans were intensely following what was going on back home. The EPLF was under constant assault by a massive Ethiopian military machine. Now that the ELF had disintegrated, the Ethiopians set their goal at resolving the Eritrean case once and for all by eliminating the remaining organization holding their ground in the rugged mountains of Sahel. Eritreans all over the world kept pouring money and anything of value to support the EPLF. Eritreans in Holland were giving 15 percent of their income to the EPLF every month. Those of us who were with the ELF and had been kicked out of Eritrea by the EPLF, however, resented the idea of helping the EPLF. While many X-ELF fighters actively sabotaged the EPLF, I stayed out of Eritrean politics and focused on my education. The only grudge I held was, "I joined the struggle putting my life on the line and the EPLF kicked me out then. Why would they ask me for help now?" In addition, the fighting between the ELF and the EPLF made me lose hope and I took it as a foregone conclusion that the Eritrean revolution was virtually dead.

In the meantime, now that Tiblets and I were separated physically, it became difficult to meet. My love for Tiblets didn't diminish. But the train ticket was too expensive for me to go to see her in Zwolle or for her to come to see me, not that she would do it. For her, my immobility was a good thing. She wanted the relationship to be secret anyway. Although it was expensive to have a telephone line of my own, I figured that was an investment I'd have to make to keep in touch with Tiblets. I had the telecommunication office install a flashy red phone in my tiny room with the sole purpose of calling one number only, that of Tiblets.

The phone bill put a strain on my finances. Purchasing a train ticket to Zwolle was beyond my reach. One day, I decided to take a train to Zwolle without paying for a ticket, risking being caught. Surprisingly, it was not difficult. Back in the day, multiple standalone train units were connected to form one long train. The ticket controller could only be in one of these units at a time. So, one simply needed to play hide and seek. Soon, out of necessity, I mastered how to cheat the train ticket-control mechanism and traveled weekly to see Tiblets. My romantic life was kept alive as long as the train company didn't figure out how to prevent free riders.

Despite the weekly travel and distraction, my school work was surprisingly going well. I could perfectly understand the subjects in Dutch and complete my homework assignments. However, I struggled with class assignments where the teacher asked us to respond to questions verbally. I couldn't do that; my spoken language was very bad. If a teacher walked by me or made eye contact, I would get very nervous fearing he might ask me a question. Despite these difficulties, the result of my first exam was implausibly good. I knew then, even though my love affair was taking a toll on me, I had got the MAVO rhythm right.

It was a normal weekend in Zwolle. Often, on evenings like this, Tiblets and I would talk about where our relationship was heading. But, on this night, the conversation would take a new turn. Nearly a year into our relationship, Tiblets finally decided to share why our relationship could never work. With visible hesitation and pain in her face, she told me the worst news that I had never imagined to hear.

Another man was already in her life long before she had come to Europe. They had met at a young age in Ethiopia, where he remained while she started a new life in Holland. The distance had made their relationship difficult, but Tiblets had left him with a promise; no matter how long it took, she would find a way to bring him to Europe for them to continue their love. She was deeply in love with the young man from Addis.

I struggled to process the confession but could see Tiblets was uncompromising. No one from her family knew about this and she wanted to keep it that way. The mystery of all the hesitation and secrecy I had to deal with was finally explained. The devastating revelation shook me to my core. At the same time, I comforted myself thinking she was not being realistic. You can't just bring anyone you want from Africa to Europe. Recalling the difficulty of my journey to Europe, I figured the odds of "her true love" making it to Holland were almost zero. So, I said to her confidently, "If God wills it to be, he will come and I will disappear from your life. I promise the secret will remain a secret. But if he doesn't come, then promise you will be with me." She was reluctant to agree and said, while softly massaging my hair, "A promise is a promise. I will have to get him here somehow, however long it takes." She had a way of saying hurtful things with so much perceived love and compassion that I wasn't offended at anything she said.

Her dedication and commitment to keep her promise to her lover amazed me and made me love her even more. I convinced myself that I would do everything I could to be her partner in crime, deciding to help her out with the process of getting her lover to Holland. Listening to her words of commitment, I was convinced she was not mine, but I loved her so much "her happiness would be my happiness" – a typical broken-hearted person's attitude.

While Tiblets worked hard to get him to The Netherlands, our secret life continued. Fortunately, my school performance was not affected and I completed my first year of MAVO middle school successfully. This was a turning point and monumental milestone in my life where I proved to myself that if I worked hard I could achieve something in life, something as big as finishing a four-year high school program in one year.

My education level when I had arrived in Holland was so low that I remember being fascinated when I learned that a negative number multiplied by a negative gives you a positive number. I may have learned it when I started seventh grade in Asmara, but with the five years I wasted roaming the jungle, I might have slid back to below elementary school level. Despite all of that, after a few months of informal language tutoring in Meppel, I inexplicably managed to finish MAVO within one year. That was my proudest achievement.

My two friends Dawit and Mike started to rethink their educational plan. After all, they were still in the second year of MAVO while I was done with it in one year. The MAVO certificate could have allowed me to attend vocational schools to become an electrical or airplane technician. But my ten-year education plan that was blessed by my father was to be an engineer, not a technician.

The minimum prerequisite for attending engineering college was a HAVO diploma. Similar to MAVO, I learned some schools provided intensive courses for the HAVO level. If I managed to do what I had done in MAVO, complete the HAVO intensive courses in one year, I would be eligible to attend an engineering college. This would mean I would go from elementary level to college entrance in just two years. Given that the classes were taught in Dutch, this would be nearly impossible for an immigrant who struggled with the basics of the language. But, if I succeed, the UAF should have no excuse to reject my scholarship application. They would have to see potential in me.

Armed with ambitious hope, I set out a plan to complete the HAVO intensive courses with the same rigor and dedication as my MAVO year. I joined two HAVO schools to avoid the restrictions of taking a maximum of two subjects. I was laser-focused on my education and there was no other option for me. I mastered the ability to manage time and stay focused for extended periods. Every day, I would jump on my bike and cross the city to go to two HAVO schools, bypassing the system that limits two subjects per school per year. Winters in Holland were very harsh and the schools were on the other side of the town. I remember I was the only student who always had a tie on and dressed neatly. Everyone else was dressed casually, including my teachers. My Dutch had improved drastically and I felt confident in my ability to communicate. Yet, I was always lonely, inconspicuous, and somewhat isolated. My focus and hard work allowed me to excel in class and my grades were very good.

Toward the end of the class year, my chemistry teacher, Mr. Karthaus, saw me in the cafeteria and approached me gently. With a mild curiosity, he asked me where I came from. Instead of just answering his question, I told him a lot more. He couldn't believe I had been in The Netherlands for just two and a half years, yet I was sitting in his intensive class and taking one of the most difficult subjects offered. He was so impressed with my story, he offered to write me a reference letter right then. That was the first endorsement and recognition of my hard work. It was a huge boost to my morale. Loosely translated, his recommendation letter reads:

Dear reader,

I would like to draw your attention to the special capacities of Mulugheta Abraha. Mulugheta has been in the Netherlands since 1984 and has not only seen an opportunity to master the Dutch language in a relatively short time, but he has proved to be a striking student in the exact (STEM) subjects. It is rare to see a non-Dutch person able to take mathematics, chemistry, and physics lessons with such good results. Moreover, Mulugheta has not only manifested as a very good student at our adult school but also as a very pleasant, well-behaved, and diligent student. That is why the undersigned is happy to recommend Mr. Abraha.

Dr. F.W.J. Karthous
Signed June 4, 1986

UTRECHTSE DAG/AVONDSCHOOL VOOR VWO EN HAVO

Fockema Andreaelaan 7   Rector Drs Th. W. Kok
3582 KA Utrecht
Tel. 030-51 27 97

                                              Utrecht,   4 juni   19

Dag afdeling:
Rubenslaan 91
3582 JH Utrecht
Tel. 030-52 35 22

                        Aanbevelingsbrief.

        Geachte Lezer,

        Bij deze wil ik U wijzen op de bijzondere capaciteiten van
        Mulugheta Abraha.
        Mulugheta is sinds 1984 in Nederland en heeft niet alleen
        kans gezien zich, in betrekkelijk korte tijd, de Nederlandse
        taal eigen te maken, maar juist in de exacte vakken toonde
        hij zich een opvallende leerling.
        Zelden komt het voor dat een Niet-Nederlander in staat is
        de lessen wiskunde, natuurkunde en scheikunde met zo'n goed
        resultaat te volgen.
        Bovendien heeft Mulugheta zich niet alleen als een zeer goede leerling
        gemanifesteerd op onze dag/avondschool voor volwassenen, maar
        ook als een bijzonder prettige, wel gemanierde en ijverige leerling.

        Vandaar dat ondergetekende U graag
        de Heer Abraha aanbeveelt!

        Vriendelijke groeten,

        drs F W J Karthaus
        docent Chemie
        Utrechtse Dag/Avondschool

The recommendation letter from Dr. Karthaus

While my HAVO year was progressing well, my love story with Tiblets slowly reached a critically decisive moment. I kept my word to keep our relationship a secret and, except for some people who were close enough to suspect, I didn't tell anyone. Her sister lived in Utrecht, and every time Tiblets came to visit her sister, she would visit me secretly. Sometimes she visited me with her sister, giving the impression that we had a sisterly/brotherly relationship.

One Saturday evening, we went to an underground dance club in the heart of Utrecht. Since the Eritrean community was small, everyone knew each other, and if there was an event, we all attended.

That night, the dance floor was full of every Eritrean who lived in Utrecht and a few Ethiopians as well. As the night progressed, a drunk Ethiopian man started to bother Tiblets and her sister. Since the sisters were born in Addis, he felt a special bond with them, but he took it a little too far. Tiblets' sister's boyfriend felt that the Ethiopian had crossed a line, and before we knew it, a fight started.

The drunk man, while taking hits from whoever was punching him, grabbed Tiblets and pulled her to the ground. The fight escalated and the dance floor turned into a boxing ring. I tried to help my girl and joined the fighting. In the chaos and confusion that followed, Tiblets didn't think about the secret we were supposed to keep. She hugged me tight and felt safe under my arms.

The music stopped, and while assessing the damage, the eyes of many Eritreans, including my closest friends, widely open, focused on the closely hugged couple standing on the sidelines comforting each other. The secret was out in the open for everyone to see, the genie was out of the bottle. No damage control acting would be able to erase what everyone had seen. The beautiful girl who was known to have no boyfriend in Holland had now been seen nestled intimately in my arms.

The next day, rumors about the event spread. Tiblets' sister was shocked to discover that there might be a romantic relationship between me and Tiblets. Despite all of this, we never publicly admitted a romantic relationship existed, and so our status remained unknown, albeit an open secret.

31. *Amersfoort*

February 2013, flight from Frankfurt to Seattle. I am tired and I want to collapse, but watching the movie The Words inspired me to write my book. So, gathering all the energy I have, while listening to the snoring of two really big guys next to me, here I go. My memory at 38000 ft continues.

E arly in the morning, after a sleepless and devastating night in Zwolle, I woke up tired. I lay half-asleep in Tiblets' small, old bed. I stretched my arms to hug Tiblets but couldn't reach her. Confused, I opened my eyes and saw she was not in the room. It was Monday morning but Tiblets had no school that day. I started wondering where she could have gone. As sometimes the case was, Tiblets didn't tell me everything, so I figured she would be back. Relaxed, I went back to sleep.

She came back from a visit to her doctor and we ate lunch. We reflected on our short love life and how it was now about to come to an end. After a depressing and emotional conversation, we headed to the train station. As we walked to the station, both of us were puzzled that our love story was about to end. Tiblets was unusually quiet and somewhat absent. Yet, both of us took it bravely that day. All the crying of the night was over. It was now back to the business of continuing another adventure in the last chapter of our love story. Secrets seemed to chase my love life. As intense as it was, secret love was probably one of the most incredible experiences in life. But this one was coming to a painful end.

We boarded the train and sat next to each other. While admiring the flat landscape of Holland with the cows grazing on the endless grass fields crisscrossed with manmade creeks, we looked back at the incredible journey only known to the two of us. Yet, we kept asking, "Why is it ending this way?" Why did God end it this way while we loved each other so much?

For the first time, Tiblets told me that she had not only gotten used to me as her boyfriend but that I had made her love me. For a woman that was so strongly committed to her boyfriend, these words were not easy to say. I took comfort in knowing that I was not loving a woman who has no feeling for me. Yes, I had known deep in my heart that she loved me very much. She would have not allowed herself to be this vulnerable had she not been in love with me. Unfortunately, she had to deal with her self-imposed moral boundaries and censorship that put us on a dead-end.

She was heartbroken, but she took it as her fate to love and live with another man. As painful as it was, so did I. Despite my burning and unconditional love, I was not meant for her. Although I wasn't involved in bringing her boyfriend to Amsterdam, my acting as her advisor without any reservation meant a lot to her. As for me, I didn't know any better. I loved her so much that I couldn't hurt her feelings in any way. I could not manipulate the situation to have her for me. I was too innocent and too blindly in love.

As we counted our remaining minutes, the train arrived in Amersfoort city. Amersfoort was where we both had to change trains to reach our separate destinations. Tiblets would be heading to Amsterdam to welcome her lover and I would be heading to Utrecht to my tiny room that would have to serve as my refuge for however long it may take to recover from this devastating drama.

It was a cold day, and after we got off the train, we kept hugging each other tightly. We kissed with tears streaming down our cheeks. There wasn't much time. Both trains with different destinations would depart at the same time and we had to go. We separated for a moment heading in the opposite direction and looked back toward each other. We couldn't help but come back for more hugs and kisses. But time was not on our side and we said goodbye to each other and ran to our respective trains. I didn't give up fully and I shouted asking her to call me to let me know how she was doing. It was a moment that I had never imagined would happen to me in real life. This felt like a movie story that you would watch from a distance on a big screen.

We boarded our separate trains, but refused to go into the cabin. Instead, we stood at the door looking at each other from a distance.

Then moments later, a deafening whistle heralded the new chapter for us and an end to our love story. Both doors closed and I went to the closest cabin and sat at the window to see her. She did the same and the trains pulled out of the station simultaneously in parallel and in the same direction. At one point, the trains came so close to each other that it looked as if we were going to collide. But the trains seemed to be part of our story and did their best to dramatize and accentuate our separation.

After half a mile or so, the trains slowly drifted apart and Tiblets' light blue shirt disappeared in the bright yellow paint of the train. I am not sure how long she had stared at me, but I looked at the train with soaked cheeks until it fully disappeared toward Amsterdam.

Softly, I started humming a Phil Collins song, *Against All Odds*, that I loved so much but never knew the lyrics to. At that moment, I knew the chorus was just perfect for the situation. As I hummed and tried to remember the lyrics, I slowly understood the meaning of the song and how it applied to the situation I was in. The lyrics in the verses were meant for sad boys like me. The song was so powerful it tore me apart emotionally, and I began to silently cry. Afraid that my fellow passengers would see my tears, I turned my face away toward the window and kept looking at the landscape with no focus, a blurry scene that seemed to replay again and again. The song goes something like *"How could I just let you walk away, just let you leave without a trace, when I stand here taking every breath with you. How could you just walk away from me when all I could do was watch you leave You're the only one who really knew me at all, take a look at me now 'Cause there's just an empty space And there's nothing left here to remind me just the memory of your face."* It continues to highlight my situation exactly *"Coming back to me is against all odds and that's what I've got to face but to wait is all I can do, I wish I could just make you turn around, and see me cry. There's so much I need to say to you so many reasons why.."* To this day, when I hear this song it gives me shivers to my bones.

After this unimaginable separation, I lost Tiblets to a man whom she considered her true love. It was devastating emotionally, especially since I couldn't talk about it with anyone. No one knew the secrets I held. The things I told to my few friends were carefully filtered as to not break the promise I had made to Tiblets. Yet the pain was so much that I was afraid it would affect my school and concentration. After all, next to Tiblets, my biggest commitment in life and a promise to my dad was to do well in school and catch up on the years I had lost in the jungle. I couldn't afford to screw that up.

July 13, 2015. Flight from New York to Tel Aviv.
"Have you made your choice for the main meal?" asked the flight attendant as I edited this part of the story. I was so upset and emotional I didn't want to lift my head and show my face. I quickly said, "Not yet". As I struggled to wipe my tears, I asked myself why thirty years later I am still struggling to read this story without being emotional. I wonder if Tiblets will react in the same way when she reads this story, assuming she allows me to publish it.

Days passed without a single phone call from Tiblets, and soon, weeks. I had no way of reaching her. Her sister Mihret, who lived in the same town as I did, knew nothing formally about our relationship other than that we were good friends. I wouldn't know in what light to ask her about Tiblets. I was feeling suffocated and defeated. I lost a dream that had almost become a reality. But I knew I must be strong to not lose my second dream of completing my education. Of all the advice I had received from my father on what I needed to do to succeed with my studies, there was nothing that had prepared me for this.

As depressing as the situation was, I never felt any anger or jealousy. The memories of our love were beautiful, and what I felt for her never diminished. But I just kept asking myself: Why did God take Tiblets away from me in a way that was so painful? Was I so stubborn that I had made her do things she never wanted to do in the first place? Was this a punishment for abusing her soft heart and for attempting to take her away from someone she not only loved but had committed to a life with? Was this what is called love in its most dramatic way? Regardless of the answer, I was faced with a breakup that could affect my education and life plans badly.

Despite the emotional toll Tiblets' departure took on me, I couldn't afford to be weak and was able to focus on my education. Tiblets was gone and there were not many Eritrean women in Utrecht. The ratio was about one Eritrean woman to 15 men. Given that I was so consumed with my education, I could not go out to bars and clubs where I could find other girls from Holland either. So, the chance of moving on and finding a new lover was almost nil. But, finding another girlfriend was my last worry at that point.

Also, having been hurt so deeply by Tiblets' departure, I was reluctant to fall in love again. I was still in love truly with only one person and that was Tiblets. No person could replace her in my heart and no amount of beauty or kindness could come close to how I experienced my first and only love with Tiblets. But, in reality, Tiblets was not mine and she was gone for good. I had no way of connecting to her nor did I dare to dream of connecting to her again. After all, she was with another man now. That was the hard reality and all I could do was lick my wound and hope for a quick recovery. Tiblets was just a special person.

We are now flying at 39000 ft to the right of Iceland and the cabin light is dim. Most of the travelers are asleep except for a few watching movies. I am sobbing softly remembering those painful moments of my life. If I don't stop writing this, I will soon be dehydrated. So, I will call it a day for now and see if I can take a nap.

32. "Oma" - Mrs. Nederstigt

Sept 20, 2015. Flight 134 from Amsterdam to Seattle. I am very tired, really tired. I spent three days at a user conference in Amsterdam where 110 airline engineers had gathered, and I had to give presentations for at least nine hours during the conference. The stress of preparing for this conference was probably the worst part of the whole event. All of our presentations had to be reviewed by multiple people and we had to dry-run our presentation numerous times. If there is one thing I don't like about my job, it is when I am asked to dry-run my presentation. As important as dry runs are, they are not my favorite thing to do, and I always end up disappointing my boss. Fortunately, during the actual action, I tend to do much better, which tells me I could never be an actor.

This conference was filled with so much activity. In addition, right after the conference, I had to fly out to Zurich to attend another two days of detailed technical discussions. In short, I am looking forward to sleeping well on this flight and might not write a lot.

Miraculously, despite the distractions caused by Tiblets, mission impossible was accomplished. I passed the HAVO state exam with excellent grades. Armed with my HAVO certificate, I went back to UAF and asked if they would consider me this time as someone who had the potential to complete college. The UAF officers couldn't believe that I had finished MAVO and HAVO in just two years on my own. The advice they had given me two years before, to settle for a short vocational training and visit the labor office, was misplaced. But, this time, not only did they see potential in me, they also wanted to make sure I succeeded. They offered me a two-month college preparatory language course. Although I didn't need language lessons, I joined a group of immigrants and took what would be my first official Dutch language training course. UAF accepted my application and I received a full scholarship to attend any engineering college of my choice.

In my "ten-year education plan," studying aeronautical engineering was on top of the list, not because I wanted to, but because my father had said so. During an admission interview, the director of the Haarlem Institute of Technology, Mr. Sanders, was shocked to meet this young African refugee who had only lived less than three years in Holland and managed to complete the prerequisites to enroll for aeronautical engineering with darn good grades.

After realizing that I had completed MAVO and HAVO in two years, he sarcastically asked, "So, you are telling me you are a genius?" I told him, "I would never consider myself a genius or gifted, but I know that I am a very hard-working, disciplined, and a determined young immigrant with an unmatched level of perseverance, for sure." To that, Mr. Sanders said, "We normally start with 160 students, and only about 45 students make it to graduation. I am willing to give you a chance, I hope you make it." It was official. I became the first Eritrean, if not the first African, man to be accepted into the college of Aeronautics in Haarlem, The Netherlands.

I was happy to have been accepted at the college that my father wanted me to attend. For many others it wasn't easy. A good friend, Berhane, was struggling to complete HAVO successfully. This was mainly because of the language issue. Knowing that he was equally hard-working, dedicated, and determined, I was convinced that if we found a way to get him into one of the universities, he would make it.

We started brainstorming what we could do to get him accepted. We cooked up an outrageous plan and applied to a university that he was interested in. We requested an interview with the head of Admissions citing a special circumstance. We pretended to have never gone to school in Holland. Instead, we told the admission officer, "We were university students in Eritrea and we spent the last few years in Holland relearning and translating the subjects we had learned in Eritrea from English to Dutch." Assertively, we added, "At this point, we are very confident that we can start college in Dutch. If you have any doubt, we are ready to take a high-school-level test in any of the major subjects." To make our story believable and impressive, we dropped heavy jargons of the major subjects we had learned in Dutch left and right.

If they accepted our story, great. However, if they asked us to take an exam, the plan was that since I had better grades, I would use Berhane's name on my exam and he would write my name on his. Since I had already been accepted at another college, I was not worried about not being accepted. The goal was for Berhane to get admission. Although this was technically a fraud, we thought we were doing the right thing at that point. We needed to bypass the high threshold that kept refugees dependent on the welfare system which was exacerbated by the language issue.

The plan worked like a charm. The Admission officer was so impressed with our confidence and knowledge about the major subjects, he said, "I have no doubt you will do well; we would be honored to have you join our university." We were incredibly happy. Berhane accepted the offer, and I eventually declined.

The educational system in The Netherlands had not been designed keeping immigrants in mind. Unless you were creative in overcoming the initial obstacles at the bottom of the ladder, it was difficult to climb the ladder. In our case, we rigorously applied the idea of "the goal justifies the means" to be in a position where we'd have a shot at getting college access.

My friend Michael, after going through a similar experience, was successfully admitted to a college in Utrecht to study food technology. He continued his college studies for three years. Very sadly, a year before graduation, he passed away due to kidney complications at age 23. That was when I realized, life was not all about hard work, but more often than not, you work hard to find your luck. Unfortunately, Michael worked hard but had not found his luck.

On the other hand, Dawit, who studied MAVO with Michael, decided to attend a vocational school to study computers. He realized, computer technicians would be in high demand as the advent of computers accelerated tremendously in the early 90th. He graduated successfully and landed a good job as a computer technician.

June 22, 2018. Flight from Frankfurt to Seattle. I feel very tired today. I slept only three hours last night. I spent time with my family in Holland and we talked the entire night. I want to sleep, but I read the news that two generals were killed in Ethiopia. Anything that happens in the Horn of Africa region that might affect Eritrea makes me nervous. We just made peace with Ethiopia after 20 years of animosity and I want the peace to last. The people have suffered for over half a century, fighting, and I hope the coming generation doesn't have to go through what my generation went through.

Senait was a young Eritrean refugee who had been adopted by a Dutch family in a village called Zeist, close to Utrecht. She happened to be the sister of my sister's best friend, and as such she was considered a distant family member – I regarded her as my sister too. One day, she invited me to visit her home to meet her Dutch family. At this point, although I was still struggling with the Dutch language, I felt reasonably confident, especially since I had been accepted at a prestigious university to study aeronautics. As a young refugee, I had accomplished something that many believed someone like me couldn't.

Because of this, I became hyper-aware of my impact, always trying to behave in a way that would highlight the positive image of an immigrant. Conversely, I almost wanted to hide from the surface of the earth if I saw immigrants conduct themselves in a way that I considered damaging to immigrants' image. Even speaking loudly in front of Dutch people, which many Eritreans did, was considered damaging to an immigrant's image, according to my sensitive criteria and guidelines. So, I felt, meeting the Dutch family would be a good thing since I was a living testament to the support the Dutch people provided to refugees which were making a difference in our lives.

After eating dinner with the family, during coffee, we started talking about my plans, and I told them that I planned to move to the city of Haarlem to attend college. Senait's father immediately got excited and he offered to help me find a home since his mother lived in Haarlem. He said, "My mother is 77 years old and lives alone in a big house. She might be interested in renting you one of the rooms." This was good news that I had never expected. He called her right away and his mother suggested that we meet for an interview first before she could commit. Given that her son was adopting an Eritrean girl, I figured his mother couldn't have an issue with immigrants unless I screwed up the interview.

A few days later, I drove to Haarlem and went to her house for an interview. Mrs. Nederstigt was a short lady, physically very strong for her age, and surprisingly open to chatting with a young black man from Africa. This was her first time speaking with a black person in her own home for such an extended time. She offered me coffee and we chatted for about an hour about everything in life. One of the most hilarious questions she asked me was if I was the son of King Haile Selassie. She had read a book about the king and there were pictures of the king's family in the book which reminded her of me. I am sure she had also seen the movie *Coming to America* and thought any young African who makes it to Europe or the US must be rich or a prince.

At the end of our discussion, she said, "You are welcome to live in the master bedroom." "The big room with a balcony," she added. With an expression of pain and shame on her face, she added, "I would ask you to pay me 150 guilders to cover food and things like that." I couldn't believe what I was hearing. 150 guilders was almost half of what I was paying just for rent of my tiny room in Utrecht or my first ever room in Meppel! She was not doing this for money. She just needed someone to be in the house so she wouldn't feel lonely. She told me a few house rules like how she did not appreciate people who put their feet on the table when they watched TV. Neither did I. It was a match made in heaven.

We both agreed on terms and conditions and set a date to move in. In a matter of a few days, I was promoted from a cockroach-infested student complex to a beautiful home in one of the best cities in Holland. So began a journey that would allow me to learn the Dutch culture and the language from within. "You will learn the best Dutch language here; the original and pure Dutch is spoken by the people who live in Haarlem," Mrs. Nederstigt told me.

I started my first college class with 165 students at HTS college in Haarlem. The age difference between the other students and me was significant, but it was visually not that obvious. I was able to blend in age reasonably well. Social blending, however, was a different story – nonexistent. I made few friends at school, but had no social life outside school. The language barrier, which had been manageable during my MAVO and HAVO years, clearly put me at a huge disadvantage during my college years. The number of subjects, a total of 22 classes a year, and the diversity of the topics, were overwhelming. The tempo was unforgiving. I spent at least twice as much time as the average student. For every topic we learned, I had to learn the new technical language and the subject, while other students had to learn just the subject. I constantly juggled three books – the subject book, and two other dictionaries to support translation, one dictionary from Dutch to English and another from English to Amharic (an Ethiopian language). This was time-consuming and frustrating.

I remember in my Aero-Engines course, our teacher Mr. Van Bodegom was teaching the various types of bearings in an engine – *lager* in Dutch. Prior to joining college, I had learned the word *lager* to mean simply "lower". However, Mr. Bodegom spent the entire hour on *lager*, representing it with a special symbol on the blackboard. I had no clue what the heck the second meaning of the word *lager* was! Hence, I got nothing out of this one-hour lecture. As soon as I got home, I looked up the word *lager* in my Dutch to English dictionary and I arrived at the word "bearing," which I also was unfamiliar with.

"That is okay," I figured as usual, "I will use my backup translator, my English to Amharic Dictionary." But, I ended up with an Amharic word that I also didn't know. Frustrated, I yelled my favorite anger-relieving swear word – *Godverdomme* – and threw the Amharic dictionary book against the wall, damaging it badly.

The next day, I went to the library to find books on "bearing" hoping to see a picture, and there it was. I couldn't believe my eyes, again screamed *Godverdommeaaaa!* silently, and mumbled angrily,

"This is a *cuscinetto*!" A *cuscinetto* was the word for bearing or lager, something I had been familiar with since the age of 10 but had spent two days researching. If only the Internet had been available then!

I was faced with similar issues daily during my first college year. Computer Science was another topic where I struggled. I had never heard of a computer and had never seen one before joining the class. After a half-hour introduction, we were taken to a computer lab and got a user-id and password to "log in." Every other student was excited and way beyond "logging in," while I was struggling to understand what the heck "log in" meant. With 165 students in a single class, no one could give me attention. My grades in computer science suffered tremendously the first year. I had to borrow money to buy a computer so I could get a passing grade in Pascal Programming. I ended up buying a Philips MSX-2 computer, which was discontinued right after I purchased it. That says a lot about how savvy I was in computers.

Even a few years into college, the language issues kept haunting me. During our final exam of the Dutch language class, I was faced with a dilemma. One of the questions in the exam read, "Using the methodology you learned in the class, describe the *lessenaar* in front of you." I had never heard the word *lessenaar*. I knew what the words *les* (class) and *lerar* (teacher) meant. So, I guessed *lessenaar* must be the combination of these two, which would mean Class Teacher. Six teachers were supervising the exam I described the teacher who was in front of me the best way possible. I finished perfectly on time.

After the exam, I headed to the cafeteria where my classmates were discussing how they described the *lessenaar*. They kept using the phrase "four-legged." Confused, I didn't give any comment to save me the embarrassment because my object only had two legs. After I got home, I grabbed the dictionary and found out what a *lessenaar* meant. It was not a class teacher but a lectern (a reading stand that was standing on the podium)! Surprisingly, I got some points for my work, just barely enough to pass the test. I must have applied the right techniques in describing the teacher well enough to earn points.

However, I never dared to talk about this with either the teacher or my classmates.

While school was going tough, things were going well on the home front. I considered Mrs. Nederstigt as my grandmother and called her *Oma*, just like her grandkids did. Early in the morning, every day, a loud alarm clock woke me up at 7:00 a.m. Sometimes Oma's dog Ricky would wake me up earlier. As I shaved and got ready for school, I would hear Oma squeezing fresh orange juice downstairs. Breakfast was served at exactly 7:30 a.m. By the time I came downstairs, the table was provisioned with a beautiful table cover, fresh orange juice, a boiled egg sitting perfectly on a holder, a glass of milk, cheese, and ham, with a fresh loft of wholewheat bread, ready for me. After a prayer, Oma and I would enjoy breakfast while we chatted. After breakfast, I would get on my bicycle and head to school. This was my routine every morning. It was expected that I show up on time at the breakfast table without my name being called. I never disappointed Oma.

After returning from school at exactly 5:15 p.m., a hot soup would be waiting for me as a warm gesture of a welcoming mother. After eating my soup, I go up to my room and start studying. Around 6:30 p.m., I would hear Oma call, "Muluuuuuu!!!", followed by the stomping sound of the dog running upstairs to remind me to come down for dinner, as if the dog knew I would be in trouble if I didn't come down right away. One thing I learned about Oma, and the Dutch people in general, is that they are always on time and they do not like others being late.

Dinner was the time to enjoy each other's company. The daily chat with Oma improved my Dutch drastically. But there was a problem. My school friends started teasing me saying that I spoke like an old lady. I didn't know the nuances to differentiate between what was considered "old-ladies' Dutch" and what was not. This occasional teasing, short of bullying, put a dent in my self-confidence.

After dinner, we would clean the dinner table, Oma would wash the dishes in warm soapy water, and I would dry the dishes. It was always teamwork, and over the years we perfected dishwashing. As Oma continued to clean the kitchen cabinets and floor, I would go upstairs to study again to only come down at exactly 8:00 p.m. for the evening TV news. Then, I would receive a cup of coffee and a single cookie. To be exact, I got one cookie per one cup of tea or coffee. If I didn't take a second cup, no second cookie was allowed. At 10:00 p.m., the second evening news would start. Oma would serve an apple, neatly placed on a small plate with a knife next to it.

Monday was laundry day. My shirts and all of my outfits were washed, ironed, and placed in my cabinet, nicely folded. My bed was made up every day. Thursday was cleaning day. Every Thursday, Oma's daughters came in the morning and deep-cleaned the entire house, including the windowpanes and the floors. By noon, they were done with the cleaning. After that, they would drink coffee together and head home to take care of their kids and families. They provided Oma with reliable support that was incredibly well organized. My least favorite day was Friday. Just before the weekend break, Oma served fish, sometimes she made the classic Haring fish, served raw. Fish was not my thing.

This lifestyle and routine lasted five years. I had no issue with Oma's strict rules. If anything, she helped me reinforce my already decent level of self-discipline that had been cultivated during my years with the ELF.

Oma was a very sweet woman who took care of me very well. I enjoyed her presence and conversation very much. I had found a caring mother in a foreign country. She represented and symbolized what the country of Holland did for me and thousands of other refugees; giving us shelter, love, and support. I am grateful and will remain indebted for all the support and love I received from the Dutch people, particularly Oma Cornelia Nederstigt.

Five years after I arrived in Holland, the immigration authority sent me yet another rejection letter regarding my asylum application, repeating their reason: "You should have sought asylum in Sudan." Eventually, I was asked to appeal and get a court hearing in The Hague. That would be my last step in the legal process, short of Queen Elizabeth granting me a "pardon" or being deported to God knows where. My case was unusual. Many Eritreans receive their approval within a couple of years and some within a year.

I appeared in front of the high court in The Hague to defend my case. Several officers sat around a massive table and they grilled me with detailed questions. Unlike in the previous interviews, they focused on my knowledge of the Eritrean Liberation Front that I claimed to be a member of. They wanted to make sure that I was not falsely claiming to be the child fighter that I detailed in my story. The questions were as detailed as naming certain commanders and the organizational structure of the movement. I was surprised by how much they knew about the inner workings of the ELF. Fortunately, within a few months after the interview, I was recognized as a refugee and granted a permanent residence permit and a passport.

With the new passport in my hand, the first country I wanted to visit was France, the entry point of my journey to Europe. France annually hosted a major airshow in the city of Le Bourget. Now that I was aiming at becoming an aerospace engineer, I wanted to visit the air show. Dawit and I took his old Honda Civic and hit the road. We passed the Belgium border and arrived at the French border.

The French passport control agents told us that Dawit was allowed to enter since he had Dutch citizenship, but I wasn't allowed because I had a passport that required an entry visa. After hours of driving, we were stranded at the border. Frustrated, we pleaded with the agents to give us an entry visa right there. We were desperately begging them. Even though they told us to return, we hung around in our car for more than an hour at the border gate.

Just when we were about to give up and return, while we were sitting in our car, one of the agents approached our car and started talking to us. He asked us, "Where were you planning on staying in Paris?" We eagerly said, "We will be staying in a hotel." The weather was warm and we were talking to him with the car windows open. He followed up with, "Do you have enough money?" We felt there was a chance that this agent would take us to the office and give us an entry visa. Elated, Dawit quickly grabbed his wallet and opened the wallet wide to show him the cash that we carried. The agent then extended his arm inside the car and quickly sifted through the bills in the wallet and snatched the largest bill of 250 guilders, gave us a nod, and headed back to the office. Immediately, I said to Dawit, "Let's go, let's go – we are in!" Dawit didn't get it. He thought the man was going to come back. We argued a little; Dawit, overwhelmed but trusting of my judgment, drove forward and we crossed the border.

This was the kind of agent I was expecting when I had arrived at the airport in Paris from Sudan, but never imagined that I would one day pay a bribe of 250 guilders to enter France illegally again. As always, I wrote to my father narrating the story and told him how shocked I was to encounter an agent who took a bribe in Europe. His reply was, "Nothing should surprise you; corruption is everywhere. It just changes its shape and face."

Magical Year

(Photo Credit EPLF)

X

Magical Year

February 17, 2016. Emirates Flight EK-229, from Dubai to Seattle. The past two weeks have been extremely hectic for me. I visited five airlines on a single trip. The amount of preparation I had to do to deal with each airline addressing unique issues will only be known to me. No manager could imagine how hard I had to work this week. The good thing is, the airlines do. I flew from Seattle to Dubai, Dubai to Doha, Doha to Muscat, Muscat to Dubai, Dubai to Kuala Lumpur, Kuala Lumpur to Dubai, and finally from Dubai to Seattle – in total, 27,000 miles of air travel. This was a busy itinerary. Fortunately, I had a few days of downtime in Dubai where I spent time with my younger sister in Dubai.

This segment is a 15-hour long flight. I have had a chance to relax for few hours and it is now time to continue writing my story and, for some reason, I am thinking about my father a lot. I decided to write about the time I met him after 16 years of separation.

33. *Reconnecting*

Bologna is a picturesque Italian city located near some of the most touristy places in Italy, like Venice, Florence, Rimini, and San Marino. During the summer, the city would be deserted – the Italians love to go on vacation to the beaches. The businesses, however, stayed open to accommodate the international tourists who love to visit not only the beautiful Italian beaches like those in Rimini, but also the beautiful Italian towns with their incredible historical architecture that give tourists an idea of European history. Compared to the other major tourist attractions, Bologna got to see very few tourists except for one special week in the summertime. One week in the heat of July, all able Eritreans who lived in the West flocked to Bologna. We came from the US, Europe, Middle East, and even Australia to spend one week in Bologna. A crowd of more than 10,000 Eritreans visited the town every year and we celebrated the "Bologna Festival."

The festival started as a small gathering of Eritreans living in Italy in the 1970s, but grew to be a massive gathering of people who shared the same fate and dream. People who on paper were not recognized as citizens of Eritrea came to Bologna to claim their identity for one week a year. During this week, Eritrean flags would fly everywhere and Bologna would transform itself into an Eritrean town where music, sports, and conferences would take place 24 hours a day. The local administration of Bologna city supported the Eritrean struggle for independence and provided the necessary logistical support to make sure the festival was able to accommodate the ever-growing crowd of Eritreans.

For us, this was a place where we gained strength and hope that one day we as people would succeed in our struggle against oppression, have the liberty to determine our destiny, and carry an identity that we would be comfortable with. To achieve these goals, the Bologna festival was a symbolic event where Eritreans in diaspora contributed to the struggle by organizing the people and supporting the liberation movement with the cash needed to operate as an organization.

Our struggle for independence was supported by very few countries, with negligible financial contribution. Therefore, we had to depend on our people to keep the struggle alive. Every Eritrean was expected to contribute 15 percent of his/her income every month to the cause, regardless of whether you had a job or received welfare. Beyond that, we made sure we bought every newspaper, cassette tape, or video that was published by the organization to support the struggle. During every seminar or festival, mothers donated their jewelry and others gave whatever money they had saved to make sure the men and women fighting for our independence in Eritrea were equipped with food, medical and logistical supplies. Many Eritreans also volunteered to go back to serve and support the movement in various capacities, some for a limited time and others for good. In addition, we were responsible for raising awareness of our cause amongst the international community.

Although the Bologna Festival was considered a national movement, not every Eritrean was supportive of it because of the differences between the ELF and the EPLF. The festival was organized by the EPLF. The ex-ELF fighters, including me, resisted going there for many years. The ELF even tried to organize their festival in Frankfurt, right after the Bologna Festival ended. For me, having been a member of the ELF and evicted by the EPLF from Eritrea, I felt strong resentment toward the EPLF. Yet, over time, I understood the popularity of the Festival, its momentum, its significance, and its contribution to our only functioning organization (EPLF) that gave us hope for becoming an independent country. So, despite my resentment, I joined the crowd every year by driving from Utrecht to Bologna with my friend Dawit.

Dawit was a devoted EPLF supporter and despite our close friendship we never could agree on political matters, mainly since I was a biased ex-ELF fighter with a strong resentment toward the EPLF. We both agreed to respect each other's position and decided to visit both festivals every year. So, on the way back from EPLF's Bologna Festival, we always stopped at the ELF's conference where I indulged myself in memories of how great the ELF had once been. As the years passed, however, I realized that the ELF Festival and its goals, compared to the populist EPLF and its grand Bologna Festival, were becoming a joke and somewhat a nuisance to the very cause that we all Eritreans stood for.

In the meantime, the political and social landscape in Eritrea was shifting drastically. The time when the EPLF had been cornered in the rugged and impenetrable mountains of Sahel was over. The Ethiopian war machinery, supported by the Russian and Cuban generals, hit a wall and was frustrated with the lack of progress against the resilience and determination of a few thousand incredible fighters. The determined fighters, despite being outnumbered and outgunned, kept one of the largest armies in Africa at bay for several years. The difficulty EPLF fighters had to endure to survive the onslaught was unimaginable. The suffering was particularly harsh to the women fighters who couldn't leave their trenches for several months with limited sanitary provisions and had to endure humanly impossible natural challenges. Their bravery and the role they played in the revolution is a story that I wouldn't dare to attempt to describe.

After many years of defending the mountains and their base, the EPLF fighters started to venture out of their trenches down to the plains of Sahel to attack the Ethiopian garrisons. The progress they made in destroying the Ethiopian army is documented in many history books. Particularly, the attack in 1988 that destroyed the entire Nadew Command, a 20,000-strong battle-hardened and well-equipped Ethiopian army, was a turning point. In the words of historian Basil Davidson, "The victory over the Nadew Command is considered to be the most significant victory for any liberation movement since the Vietnamese victory at Dien Bien Phu."

The rapidly changing events in Eritrea transformed my view of the struggle and I started viewing EPLF as the only organization that could deliver and respond to the Eritrean dreams and aspirations. My resentment toward the EPLF gave way to a sense of pride and belongingness. I started viewing the ELF festival in Frankfurt as a social gathering for ex-ELF fighters, while the Bologna festival was a movement geared toward the liberation of Eritrea. I reminded myself of the pure coincidence of how I had ended up joining the ELF when I was an adventurous 13-year-old boy. It was not a deliberate choice I had made; it was purely circumstantial. While I had joined the ELF by chance, so had my uncles and friends who had ended up with the EPLF. In the end, we were all Eritreans fighting for the same cause. We just happened to have differences in how we achieved our goal. So, to me, the least I could do then was to not become a distraction and obstruction to those who were fighting with the EPLF. There was no need to make their life difficult – it would only prolong the struggle for independence. Eventually, I disassociated myself from the ELF and so did most x-ELF fighters. I started to look forward to going to Bologna every year and I thoroughly enjoyed the resilience and spirit of my people. It became a symbol of unity and a lesson to many on how to wage a popular movement thousands of miles away from home.

Although every Bologna Festival I attended was an interesting event, none was like the last festival that took place in the summer of 1991. On May 24, 1991, after 30 years of bloody war, the Eritrean fighters routed the Ethiopian army and liberated Eritrea completely. The capital city of Asmara welcomed its rightful owners, unscathed. The war was fought and finished outside the city of Asmara culminating in the Ethiopian army leaving the capital on foot toward their homeland, Ethiopia. The military strategy devised by the EPLF to achieve the demise of the largest army in Africa is best left up to historians to analyze, but it was an incredible accomplishment.

The joy I felt after I heard the liberation news in Europe was hard to describe. There was no Internet, e-mail, or satellite TV to announce the liberation of Eritrea – just word of mouth coming from our reliable source of information as delivered by our people. I was left to imagine what this news meant. I was in Rotterdam and ran to the nearest community center to celebrate with fellow Eritreans. The joy, cheering, dancing, tears, confusion, and bewilderment we Eritreans felt that day can never be described in words.

The celebrations were confined to the towns and villages we happened to live in, scattered across the globe. There were no flights to Asmara, making it impossible to celebrate this momentous achievement with our people. We were forced to celebrate our liberation in our bubble in the foreign countries we lived in. The people who had given us refuge didn't know what just happened in this small African country, less so to share with us the joy of a dream-come-true moment. We felt excluded, and we missed an epic moment that is unforgettable to the Eritreans who experienced it.

Yet, amid the celebrations and ululations, on everyone's mind there was a concern about the fate of our family members living in Asmara. In the past, we had seen video footage of how the liberated cities like Massawa were carpet-bombed indiscriminately by the Ethiopian air force which had resulted in considerable civilian casualties and destruction of the cities. What if this happens in Asmara as well?

My father was in Addis, but my entire family was in Eritrea. There was no telephone communication and no one to ask about the fate of our family members. Nevertheless, we kept dancing and celebrating while keeping our respective fears suppressed deep in our guts; frustration, and loneliness mixed with the joy of knowing the biggest dream of our life had just come true. It was extremely contrasting feeling to experience.

In the days ahead, the news of our country's liberation slowly trickled in the media. However, with no video footage and pictures, no one could imagine what was happening back home. Our only hope was that the EPLF media department would work a 24-hour shift to document what had happened and distribute the videotapes for sale in Europe ASAP. Unfortunately, this being a historical moment, they had to make sure the video montage was done properly. The content must reflect the reality as much as possible to invoke the right feelings and emotions. So, the wait was on.

By the time Eritrea was liberated, the preparation of our annual summer Bologna Festival was already underway. For those who lived outside, the festival was our chance to celebrate with our people in the biggest way possible. The Italian government and specifically the people of Bologna who gave us the venue every year would soon witness the joy of people who had been deprived of their identity and freedom for more than a century. The relationship we had built over the years, the information we shared through pictures, seminars, and videos as well as the cultural exchanges during the festival allowed the inhabitants of Bologna and their leaders to appreciate our people, our plight, and our values better than anyone else in the West.

Eritreans were the first people in the continent of Africa to successfully wage a liberation war with dignity, perseverance, and determination without being a puppet or an instrument for external powers. Our motto of self-reliance embodied the essence of what it means to belong to a people that share a common goal and have what it takes to make it happen through collective sacrifice. We won our independence against all odds. The people of Bologna were a witness to all that Eritreans had to endure. It was therefore equally their joy to see our people be free. Against this backdrop, the Bologna Festival of 1991 wasn't just another festival. The festival organizers expected a high turnout and they could no longer count on the venues they had relied on in the past. Now, they had to up their game to accommodate a much larger crowd and provide an experience that would last forever.

During the decisive battle that resulted in the liberation of Eritrea, my father was stationed in Ethiopia and he was equally deprived of the opportunity to witness the historic event. Ironically, the Eritrean fighters' strategy on how to defeat the Ethiopian army was not only to fight them in Eritrea but to bring the war deep inside Ethiopia as well. As such, at the same time Eritrea was liberated, Eritrean fighters together with Ethiopian rebels who fought against the communist regime marched into the capital of Addis Ababa, toppling the government. Just before the Ethiopian regime crumbled in Addis, my father got a chance to obtain a foreign visa to escape the impending fall of Addis Ababa. He managed to take his retirement and left the country safely just days before the fighters entered Addis.

Back in Holland, at one of the celebrations of Eritrea's independence parties, after years of disappearance, standing with her two sisters, I saw Tiblets who was the love of my life. I hadn't seen her for years and didn't know how to greet her and what to say to her. The presence of her older sisters made it even more awkward. We exchanged hugs and chatted briefly. I noticed, although she was stunningly beautiful as always, she had dark spots on her cheeks. These dark spots, called *mada* in our language, are typically associated with women who are going through emotionally tough times. I felt very sad to see those dark marks on her cheeks, but I didn't want to ask her what had happened. With the music being loud and her sisters' presence, there was no place for a quiet moment of reflection. We exchanged phone numbers and we separated. I was puzzled why she had come to the event with her sisters and not her boyfriend (or perhaps her husband by now).

A few days later, I called her and we chatted a little about our lives and how we had been. She didn't disclose anything; instead, she said, "I will tell you more about my life when we meet the next time." This was typical of her – keeping things to herself or not spilling it out easily. Yet, I was surprised that she was open to "meeting next time". I grabbed this opportunity to ask her if we could meet for coffee sometime soon. She lived in Amsterdam and I lived in Haarlem, about a 30-minute train ride away. We agreed to meet at the train station in Haarlem.

Five years before, we had separated at a train station in Amersfoort. There we were now, meeting at a train station and catching up on each other's life stories. I had no idea what to expect, but she looked very relaxed. Instead of coffee we ordered steaks at the station restaurant and started to rewind the tape. She had a great job and was very successful in her career. Her relationship with the love of her life, however, turned out to be a disappointment. Those dark spots on her cheeks indeed were a sign of sadness and unhappiness. So was my relationship with my girlfriend at the time, except I didn't have dark spots on my cheeks. I started to wonder how this was possible that I found myself on the verge of forging a reunion with the woman I had fallen in love with seven years ago. I have always wanted to be with her. *Does this mean I will get a second chance?* I asked myself.

"Old love never dies," my Oma Nedestigt would tell me when I would tell her an abridged version of my love story. My friend Michael, who passed away from a kidney complication, lying in his hospital bed would often repeat that something told him I would eventually end up living with Tiblets. Yes, I admit I did break some of my promises to Tiblets to keep things secret. After the dance floor fight where Tiblets ran into my arms, I told Michael that I loved Tiblets but the relationship never worked out.

Michael's and Oma's predictions kept ringing in my ear. I seemed to be heading toward a love affair with Tiblets one more time. Completely unexpected, a new chapter of romance seemed to have opened again. I accepted the new reality, a second chance to make it work with Tiblets. The new encounter with Tiblets coupled with the liberation of Eritrea added huge excitement and joy to the summer of 1991.

One of Oma's strict rules was that I couldn't bring any woman home. That had applied to her kids and it stood for me as well. As such, I never broke that rule for five years except for a few days in the last month of my stay. With Tiblets back in the picture, we started exactly where we had left, secretly seeing each other. No one knew we had started dating again. Just as I used to sneak into her bedroom through the back window, Tiblets started sneaking into Oma's house through the back door. Oma had hearing issues and used to turn up the TV volume very high in the evenings. I feel guilty to say that I abused these opportunities to let Tiblets come into the house a few times. The timing couldn't be any better. I was about to graduate and ready for the next chapter in my life.

34. *Graduation Day*

After years of the hard work that I had put in to get my life back together in Holland, just a month after Eritrea's independence and meeting Tiblets, I graduated in Aeronautical Engineering from the Institute of Technology in Haarlem. The graduation was a major turning point in my life.

A few weeks before I graduated, I received a job offer to work at Fokker Aircraft Company. This would be the first legitimate employment that would put me in a social class that I had never dreamt of belonging to, a middle class with a stable income in Europe. Shedding off the stigma of an African immigrant dependent on a European welfare system was an achievement that I would never underestimate, particularly given where I came from and how far I had traveled to get there.

The 10-year plan I set out to accomplish had finally come to fruition. This had not happened because I was a genius or an extraordinarily gifted kid – far from it. As seen in my elementary school report, according to my teacher, I was bad at science and mathematics. The teacher had written on my report card, "He has failed in math and science, the kid has no hope whatsoever if he doesn't work harder." But, this time not only did I work harder, I was laser-focused on executing a plan. I feel like I exemplified the resolve, perseverance, improvisation, determination and sacrifice I was taught to endure during my stay at the Vanguards camp in ELF. To a minuscule extent, I consider my drive to succeed and my achievement in education analogous to what Eritreans have accomplished as a people in their struggle for liberation. Hence, the relief and joy I felt were tremendous.

I made an appointment with Oma to pick her up to attend my graduation ceremony. This would be a proud moment for her – to see the African young man she had taken in as a refugee getting the title "Engineer" Officially. Oma used to say to me, "I can see you becoming a successful black man in a black suit, with a black Samsonite and driving a black luxury car."

All my friends and family members planned to attend the event. Sadly, two important people would be missing. I was not ready to invite Tiblets since our relationship was still not public. In addition, my father, who had been invited by the school to attend the ceremony in Holland, couldn't join because he was not able to get a visa on time.

The evening before the graduation event, I called Oma to confirm the pickup time. Strangely, her daughter picked up the phone. I asked her if I could talk to Oma to confirm the time for the next morning. Her voice choking, she told me that Oma had passed away two days earlier and they were not able to get a hold of me. I was paralyzed in shock and didn't know what to make of this news. She said I could come to see Oma now in her home and that the family was there. I was in Rotterdam at that time. I headed to Haarlem immediately to pay my respects. I saw Oma peacefully sleeping in a coffin, surrounded by her kids. I was devastated that after sharing so much of my life with Oma, she wasn't able to be with me at my graduation. She would have been so proud of me and represented my parents who couldn't be there. I had bonded well with Oma and was her son. With Oma gone, as important a milestone as my graduation day was, I didn't feel it was appropriate to have a celebration party that day and I canceled my graduation celebration.

The flight attendant noticed that I have been working very hard on my laptop and suggested that I should take a break and eat something. Some flight attendants are so sweet and caring. You can tell they do what they do because they love it. I agreed and told her "Okay, I will take a glass of red wine and almond nuts." She is right. Everyone is asleep and my laptop screen light is the only source of illumination in the cabin. But this will be my third glass of red wine and anything I write after this might be influenced by the lack of soberness. So, time to take a break.

Less than two months after Independence, Dawit and I were ready to depart to Bologna. This time, my shiny brown Volkswagen Sirocco was upgraded. I installed a more powerful 1.8-liter engine and a five-gear transmission box and I was excited to take it on the German autobahn. I used to love tinkering around with the car.

Dawit always considered my driving skills and how I treated my car as a showoff. True, I was a car enthusiast and made sure my Sirocco baby was in top shape. I probably spent more money than needed on my car when I was a student. Yes, this was the beauty of Holland – you could afford to be a student and still drive a car if you knew how to manage your wallet and you had Oma taking care of you for only 150 guilders a month.

Yet, going to Bologna was a financial burden for all of us. Dawit and I were one of the few that drove to Bologna. Most people who lived in Holland took a bus. Holland was not a country for refugees to make money. The welfare, health, and education system were very good, but everything else was detrimental to immigrants. The system used to be so bad that it made refugees and immigrants live in complete dependency on the welfare system with no way to become self-sustaining. Many people may think immigrants come to Holland to receive welfare, but that is far from the truth. On the contrary, most immigrants are energetic and have survived in harsher conditions, and worked hard before coming to Europe. When they come to Europe, all of them have dreams and aspirations to escape war, find a job, and make more money to support their family members back home. But, once they land in Holland, they get stuck in the welfare system.

Unlike Germany and Sweden, where refugees were encouraged to work and open businesses to survive, the Dutch system was filled with obstacles and regulations that were detrimental to immigrants. For example, it was impossible to open a restaurant or a small cuisine without obtaining a HORECA (Hotel/Restaurant/Catering) diploma. Mind you, the classes were all in Dutch, so as an immigrant there was no way you could open a business without a four year diploma. Driving a taxi was another impossible task while this profession was commonly left to immigrants everywhere else. Getting a driving license, which takes years and lots of money, was in many cases very difficult for immigrants.

The differences between the various Eritreans living in Europe were vividly clear when we all arrived in Bologna. Eritreans living in

Germany and Sweden came with their brand new cars, while Eritreans from Holland mostly traveled by bus or beat up cars. Once in Bologna, the Eritreans who came from Holland couldn't afford better accommodation and slept in tents and cars while others could spend money to stay in hotels. However, to their credit, the Dutch did recognize the importance of going on vacation and getting away from day-to-day life. They gave everyone in the welfare system some vacation money every July and encouraged you to take care of your mind and health.

Dawit and I were no different. We had our sleeping bags ready, and once we arrived in Bologna we always slept in our car for the entire week. Even renting a tent was too expensive for us. This time, however, we were expecting a special guest in Bologna and we had to pony up some money and do better.

My father, whose visa was rejected by the Dutch embassy, was able to obtain an Italian visa just on time to experience the Bologna festival. More importantly, he would get a chance to meet his oldest son who had disappeared from his warm home over 15 years ago. This would also be his first trip ever to Europe. If everything went well, this trip would be an emotional overdose. He landed in Rome a few weeks before the Bologna Festival. The plan was for him to come to Bologna by train.

He knew no one in Bologna and he was counting on me to meet him there. Back in 1991, there were no cell phones, and meeting a person in the middle of a festival after traveling almost two days was going to be very challenging. So, before he departed from Roma, we told him approximately how long our travel would take. My father was a very serious man – he expected us to stick to our plan and arrive on time.

My father arrived in Bologna around noon and has been looking for us. He waited the entire afternoon. Many people who had seen us on the road told him we should have been there by now since it only took a few hours to get from Milan to Bologna. Hours passed by and the darkness set in, but there was still no sign of Dawit or

Mulugheta. Everyone started to worry that we might have been involved in a car accident as nothing else would explain our delay.

My father started to break down and feared that what was supposed to be a beautiful moment might turn into the worst moment of his life. We hadn't seen each other for over 15 years. His excitement turned into despair and a cry for help. It became a waiting nightmare for him. Surrounded by many of our friends from Holland, he braced himself for horrible news. The evening hours dragged, and for many, it was time to inflate the sleeping bags. A few men remained with him, but others started going to their tents to sleep.

The first night of the Festival was typically very chaotic as people try to find a place to sleep and explore where they want to stay within the camp. My father, coming from Africa and having never been to Europe, knew nothing about the festival. Our friends tried to comfort him by telling him all kinds of reasons why we might be delayed by more than six hours, but their faces and tone were not radiating confidence. My father started to become desperate.

Dawit and I, after traveling for more than 14 hours, reached Millan. On our way, we met many Eritreans at gas stations and at the border passport control area who were on their way to Bologna. Unlike Dawit and me, most of them didn't combine the Bologna Festival with side trips for sightseeing. Dawit and I however had a habit of mixing sightseeing activities on the way to the festival. Once we reached Milan, we typically decided to explore Milan and have dinner before continuing to Bologna. Unconcerned about my father's expectations, and true to our tradition, Dawit and I took our time in Milan.

Just before midnight, Dawit and I reached Bologna and parked our car outside the camp at our favorite location. Normally, all the past years we had slept in our cars, to save money. We used to park our car for free outside the camp under a tree so that the sun wouldn't wake us up in the morning. But this time, because of my father, we would have to pay up to sleep in tents inside the camp.

As we walked into the camp, we were received by everyone we knew with concerned and angry faces. Just like a baton in a relay race, we were handed off from one person to another hastily through the camp and were led to where my father was. Those who had heard we were in Millan dining were disgusted by the level of disregard we showed to my father. As we heard more and more outcries, we slowly realized the gravity of what we had done to my father. We finally arrived at the place where my father was.

Surrounded by a handful of people from Holland, my father was standing next to a poorly lit tent. As soon as our friends told him it was us, my father simply couldn't take it and he broke down and sobbed. For me, this was not what I had expected. I had no idea that I would cause this kind of concern and emotional damage to my father. Fifteen years before, my father had been 40 years old and the image I still carried in my mind was of a strong and proud man. Now I was confronted with an emotionally hurt and physically frail-looking man. I was oblivious to the fact that in these 15 years I had grown to be a much taller man than him, not to mention that I had seen so much that emotionally I was not moved easily. Yet, as I hugged him and felt his tears on my cheeks, I did feel guilty for what I had done that evening.

After talking for about an hour in the darkness, it was time to hit the ground for a night's sleep. We went to the tent we had reserved and started expanding the only inflatable mattress we had brought for my father. We did not have a pump, and everyone had to donate whatever compressed air they could generate from their lungs to help inflate the mattress. It took a long time and my father patiently waited until we got the mattress firm enough.

That night, I realized my father did not deserve to sleep in the tent with 20 other people. The next morning, I reserved a hotel outside Bologna. But, for my father, the first impression of his son was disappointing. My father was extremely good at observing people's behavior. That day I am pretty sure I got a big F from him, and my friend Dawit was also not spared.

The first few days, I enjoyed my father's company. As we attended the celebrations, the fact that both of us finally met at an occasion where we celebrated our achievement as a people was a triumphant display of father and son closing a chapter in our life. This celebration was not an ordinary festival entertainment. It was a true representation of what it meant to achieve the impossible as people and as individuals. I spent five precious years in the jungle to fight for Eritrea, my father was put in jail by the Ethiopians for suspicion of aiding the revolution, many of our friends and family members had lost their lives to fight for our freedom. It took 30 years of bloodshed to end the occupation, and in the process, 65,000 young fighters lost their lives, and many more were rendered disabled. Our people endured unimaginable suffering that tested the human limits – a testament to the maximum levels of physical and emotional sufferings human beings could endure to achieve a noble goal. Eritrea's story is a case study that psychologists, anthropologists, and sociologists need to research. Hence, the 1991 festival was the most beautiful celebration I experienced in my life. Cheers, Eritrea!

EPLF military victories in the field in pictures

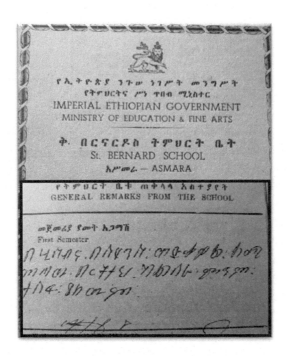

2nd grade certificate giving a bleak prospect

The team in my first job at Fokker Aircraft company – Amsterdam

Fokker S11 Aircraft technician – Amsterdam

Tiblets in 1984, a photo I took in Zwolle, Netherlands

HTS Haarlem, Aerospace Engineering Class 1991

Graduation ceremony, June 1991, Haarlem

Signed, sealed and delivered

Celebrating my college graduation (From right: Michael, me, Senait, Dawit, Adiam, Hanna, Amanuel and Salome)

Fokker S11 – Air show crew 1993

Oma. Nederstigt playing a game with her grandkids.

35. Returning Home

In a heavy East European accent, the announcement rang out from the speakers: *"Ladies and gentlemen, this is your captain from the cockpit. We have just entered the Eritrean airspace. We will start our descent shortly to Asmara international airport. Congratulations and welcome to free Eritrea. Flight crew, prepare the cabin for landing."* Ululation, prayers, laughter, and crying burst loose – feelings that spontaneously caused chaos in the MD-90 cabin.

With Eritrea being free of Ethiopian occupation, Eritreans from all over the world organized charter flights and started flying back home. It was my turn too, after 16 years of leaving my home. I was sitting in a chartered plane from Switzerland heading home. During the descent, stretching my neck as much as I could, I tried to look outside the window to see a glimpse of Eritrea from the air. There was nothing to see in the darkness – just occasional flickering lights in the distance reminding me of my life in the Barka region where scattered fires were the only source of light at night. An uncomfortable and eerie feeling clouded the plane. Finally, as we approached Asmara, a collective gasp was heard in the cabin. We spotted a row of yellow lights surrounded with weak flickering lights of all kinds of colors welcoming us to our homeland.

A loud touchdown followed by hyper-congratulatory clapping heralded a successful landing at Asmara airport – an airport that my father used to work at as Air Traffic Controller for many years; an airport that was off-limits to millions of Eritreans for years; an airport that was converted into a military garrison strictly used to oppress the Eritrean people with Russian-made jet fighters, rockets, and tanks. An airport that sits at 8,000 ft as the crown of our nation and had now found its rightful owners.

Once the airplane door opened, that distinct fresh but earthly air invoked my childhood memories. The airport was much darker and smaller than any airport I have ever seen anywhere; nevertheless, it invoked the brightest and strongest feeling in me. As we made our way down the stairs, the queue was backed up because people started to kneel to kiss the ground as soon as their feet touched their freed motherland. We made our way to the terminal as dark and skinny-looking Eritreans gave us hugs and said to us "Welcome to free Eritrea" repeatedly.

After collecting all the luggage and boxes full of things we had brought with us for our families, it was time to pass a symbolic customs checkpoint and we headed outside. The exit was so crowded it was difficult to find family members. Fortunately, my father, having worked at the airport, was able to enter the airport to meet me inside the terminal. He led me to where my entire family was waiting for us outside.

Tears and more tears.

As I hugged my mother after 15 years, I recognized instinctively the distinct smell of her perfume, hair oil, and everything that was my mother. My mother was overwhelmed with joy and so were my brothers and sisters. For the first time, I met my younger siblings who were born after I left. The siblings I knew no longer looked the same and I had to be introduced to them again. Everyone was in tears.

We took two old Fiat 1100 taxis and headed home. The drive home gave me an empty feeling. It was dark, and the roads were really bad and filled with potholes. The old taxi had no interior or instrument lights and the brightness of the headlights oscillated with the power of the engine. The humidity inside the taxi created a foggy windshield and the driver was using a piece of cloth to wipe it clear. Paper napkins were hard to come by and too expensive to keep using and throwing away. Occasionally, he lowered a squeaky driver-side window to stick his head out to properly see the road. This was my first encounter with poverty since I had left for Europe. This was not the city I knew as Piccola Roma. *What more was awaiting me?*

The next morning, the entire neighborhood came to congratulate our family and welcome me. My mother looked a lot darker and older, a clear difference between age 32 and 47. All the mothers that I used to know looked old and frail. Some of them I didn't even recognize. The churches and schools I used to think were very far, looked so close by. The town Woki Duba, which was besieged by the fighters and had looked very far away when I was young, now looked very close to our home. My mind had difficulty updating the images that I had captured in 1977 and held close to my heart for 15 years with what was presented to me in 1991. It felt like the entire city and its people had shrunk.

There was too much information to process and nothing got captured in my mind and heart. The intensity of the feelings and emotions, however, was hard to describe. Finally, the land that I had wanted to give my life for was free. The land that I had thought would be liberated in a matter of months was liberated after 30 years of devastating war.

The three friends who had accompanied me to Emba Derho in 1977 and returned to Asmara, a few years later left Asmara again and eventually joined the EPLF. Two of them, Fessehatsion and Feresu, were martyred. The third, Johannes, fought for many years and returned home alive. Geremeskel, who accompanied me in my first adventure to Woki Zager, later joined the ELF and was wounded. Fortunately, he made it to Sweden. All the other men and women in my neighborhood who had joined the liberation movement, including my uncles, lost their lives – save three men who returned home safe and sound. In some cases, five or more people were lost from a single family. Eritrea's independence was a bittersweet victory – every family in Eritrea experienced incredible jubilation and deep grief simultaneously. I realized how lucky I was to be alive and to see that day.

While every other liberated city in Eritrea had been destroyed by the Ethiopian air force, Asmara had survived the war unscathed. The final onslaught on the massive Ethiopian army in Asmara was planned and executed with perfection by the EPLF. More than 150,000 Ethiopian soldiers trapped in Asmara surrendered, and the destruction of the city was averted.

I stayed for six weeks in Eritrea. During that time, I visited every corner of the city that had been out of bounds during the Ethiopian occupation. I went to see all the military camps that civilians were not allowed to walk by. In the military camps as well as in the tank cemetery, where all military hardware destroyed during the war was collected, all kinds of guns and ammunition were there for everyone to see and touch. Curiously, I entered the tank turret and for the first time saw the powerful tools these machines possessed and why they were feared.

The cleanup of the city was still ongoing, and it was clear that a lot more than cleaning had to be done to restore the glory of the city known as Piccola Roma. I also visited the port of Massawa that had been destroyed during the war. I looked inside one of the three EPLF tanks that were hit during the battle for Massawa and imagined what it must have been like to be in these tanks and die in the process. I got a firsthand look at the price the fighters paid and the magnitude of destruction that Asmara city had escaped, thanks be to God.

Many returning Eritreans had brought with them various equipment and electronic items for their families. Asmara was flooded with TVs, entertainment units, video players, and such items from the West. Most of the incoming flights were transiting through Rome. Realizing the unusual load the airplanes were carrying, some airport workers in these countries started stealing the electronic equipment from the boxes and replacing them with bricks and other useless objects. I went to the customs area to get some of my items, and one box after another, particularly the video player boxes, were opened and found to be replaced with bricks. Fortunately, my boxes arrived safely, and for the first time at home, videotapes and music CDs played the entire day. The security restrictions imposed by the Ethiopians not to play Eritrean music were over.

36. *Unfinished Business*

L ucky me, after I returned from my visit to Eritrea, I didn't have to apply or look for a job in Holland. I was offered a job straight from school to work on Fokker airplanes as an engineer. During the job interview, even though on paper I was a Dutch citizen, as usual, the interviewer asked me, "Where do you come from?" Some immigrants hate this question, but I had no issue with it. A summary of the journey that had led me from being a child fighter to becoming an aerospace engineer was the most jaw-dropping story the interviewer had heard from an immigrant. We spent more time talking about Eritrea than my actual interest in the job.

I was very proud and happy with my new job at the headquarters of Fokker Aircraft Company, in the Atlas Building in Amsterdam. In seven years, after I arrived in The Netherlands, three years earlier than the original "10-year plan" I had made in Meppel, under the supervision of my father, my goal of becoming a productive citizen had been accomplished. It took relentless effort, dedication, focus, improvisation, perseverance, and iron discipline to get there. I was lucky! The reward was a life that seemed a dream for any Eritrean refugee or an immigrant for that matter. Mission accomplished!

But I still had unfinished business with Tiblets. Tiblets had a stable job in Amsterdam and she lived in a small apartment in Diemen. Since the passing of Oma, I had stayed with Tiblets on and off. Soon, we started to seriously date, and since I had to leave Oma's house and didn't have a home, it was an obvious choice to frequently visit Tiblets' apartment.

Soon, Tiblets and I officially started introducing each other to our friends and families; there was no secret relationship anymore. There was even an opportunity to introduce me to her coworkers. They had an event where they were allowed to invite a spouse or friend to travel to Belgium with company-provided buses and spend a day enjoying various activities. Tiblets invited me to join her, and I proudly accepted. One of the activities was a bowling competition amongst teams. I had never played bowling in my life, but had to be a team player. Surprisingly, although my bowling technique was completely wrong, my scores were darn good. Every ball I threw never rolled – it would slide all the way, like a car skidding on ice, and at the end, none of the pins would be left standing. During a dinnertime ceremony, winners of the various activities were announced. Surprisingly, there I was, the winner of the bowling competition, accepting the prize: two tickets for a Michael Jackson concert! I had delivered, I had made my girl proud.

Life with Tiblets looked very bright and was going perfectly well. After many years of separation, we had to get to know each other all over again. Then, unexpectedly, Tiblets became pregnant and we were confronted with a tough reality. Regrettably, in my view at that time, it was too early to have a baby, and I suggested strongly that we give up the child. Tiblets being a master of not showing her feelings, I wasn't able to read her reaction properly. However, she agreed that without my consent we couldn't have a baby. As unfortunate as this decision was, I judged that we needed to have a stable life first before we could have a child. Now thinking back, I am not sure what I meant by "stable." After all, we both had solid jobs, and Tiblets had a one-bedroom apartment that we could have reasonably started our life in. Tiblets was confronted with a difficult situation and a boyfriend who was selfishly not willing to entertain having a child. Eventually, we agreed to go for an abortion.

I was not sure what I was thinking to suggest an abortion at that time when I loved her so deeply. I know with certainty my reluctance to have a child had nothing to do with not being committed to Tiblets. I was deeply in love and was the happiest. Yet, with no other option on the table, Tiblets made an appointment with the abortion clinic.

On a Sunday evening, the day before the appointment, I called Tiblets to confirm if her appointment was still on and provide my support by phone. Tiblets told me a piece of devastating news. Her mother had unexpectedly passed away in Addis, at just 55 years old. My father and I had met her mother about six months before when she had visited Tiblets and she had looked perfectly healthy. Her death was hard to believe because she had taken various medical and physical tests while in Holland and the doctors had found nothing wrong.

I was very sad for Tiblets and immediately concluded that there was no way I would let her go to the abortion clinic the following day. I asked her to cancel the appointment and suggested keeping the child. Spiritually speaking, it almost felt like Tiblets' mother had left this world to correct our stupid decision and spare our first daughter's life. Had we not decided to make the appointment for an abortion, would Tiblets' mother still have lived? Was this a telepathic choice we had to make between the life of our daughter and Tiblets' mother? Only God knows. Either way, it pains me deeply to write about this.

The unfortunate passing of Tiblets' mother sealed our fate and made us reaffirm and expedite our plan to commit to each other and start a family. Our first baby was born six months later and became the affirmation of our love. Tiblets, I am sure, saw our baby girl as a reincarnation of her mother, and as such the event had a deeper meaning than just having a child.

After a year, we bought a house, and our second daughter followed, and a happy family settled in the outskirts of Amsterdam, a place called Diemen. My 10-year life plan that had never included a love story now was accomplished with a woman I loved and had two beautiful children with.

Now that I had accomplished my plans, I started to think about the other things I had had to forgo to focus on my education, like playing music in a band. I bought a guitar and keyboard and started playing music with local Eritrean artists like Gidewon Beraki and Okbay Mesfin. A year later, with Gidewon, I recorded the first CD ever by Eritrean artists. I toured Europe and performed at various venues while enjoying my family life with Tiblets.

Life was stable and good in Diemen. We lived in a new middle-class neighborhood. We fully assimilated to the Dutch lifestyle and its middle-class way of thinking. We made many Dutch friends.

One day, Dawit came to pick me up from work. He arrived earlier and was waiting outside the Atlas Building, Fokker Aircraft Headquarters. As I entered his car, he said "You know, every person that I saw coming out of the building was white, while every person that was going into the building was an immigrant." He continued, "Do you realize how lucky you are to be one of the very few black people who came out of the building?" It took me a while to make sense of his observation, then it hit me. He meant that all the people who were going into the building were immigrants who worked for commercial janitorial services cleaning the office after hours. I was walking in the "wrong" direction with the "wrong" crowd. It made me realize how far I had come in life. Sometimes, simple observations like that were needed to remind me that I was very privileged to be where I was. Yet, it was not a privilege handed to me by anyone; I proved it to myself that every immigrant that went into that building as a janitor could come out as an engineer few years later.

37. Immigrant For Life

Fokker Aircraft Company, established in 1912 in Germany, was one of the oldest aircraft manufacturers in history. It was founded by a Dutch engineer, Anthony Fokker, and was moved to Holland in 1919. The company boasted an array of commercial airplanes ranging from 50-seater turbo-prop airplanes to modern 100-seater jets. Nearly 77 years later, in March 1996, the company went bankrupt, and circa 15,000 employees lost their jobs. Sadly, I was one of them.

Just when I had thought my family life had started to take shape, my first life test was presented to me in the form of a layoff. We had purchased a house two years earlier, and with two daughters, two and three years old, the layoff couldn't have come at a worse time. Finding a new job was difficult since another 15,000 former Fokker employees, many with similar skills, were looking for a job in the limited aviation industry. Although the Dutch had an incredible social support system, the idea of being dependent on government handouts once again was upsetting.

Despite the grim situation I found myself in, there was a life lesson I learned that kept me going. After all, the defeat and devastation of the ELF in Eritrea was a sad event that had opened the door for me to end up in Europe. Sometimes, bad things happen for good things to follow. I embraced this concept diligently. My desperation was replaced with hope. With a positive mindset, I started applying for multiple jobs at KLM, Transavia, and Martinair airlines as well as Schiphol Airport. Many responded with "You are overqualified for the job you have applied for." For the first time I learned that in some cases being educated can work against you, but I didn't give up and kept applying.

A few weeks later, I received a letter in the mail, and the sender was The Boeing Company. With extreme curiosity, I opened the letter, and to my surprise, it was addressed directly to me and was an invitation to meet with Boeing recruiters who had flown from Seattle to Amsterdam to meet with Fokker engineers who might be willing to go to the US to work for Boeing. At first, I resented the thought of moving to another country with my family. After living in Holland for 13 years, I was not ready to immigrate again. Also, I realized the probability of being accepted for a job at Boeing was remote, considering the availability of more than 3,000 qualified engineers seeking job opportunities. Skeptically, I accepted the opportunity as good news and casually shared it with Tiblets and my family.

The reactions I received from all of them were uncompromisingly negative and discouraging. It damaged my desire to apply for a job at Boeing and move to the USA. I called my father in Eritrea to tell him about the opportunity and to ask for his opinion. His response was, "Going to America is the greatest opportunity God could have presented to you." He added, "The only people we see engaging in useful investments in Asmara are Eritreans who live in the USA," implying that I would be financially better off to move to the US. Given that my father's advice had always served me well, I was excited about the opportunity.

"Seattle is not your typical American city. It is more like a European or Canadian city with the low crime rate and is voted the best city to live in. Coming from Europe, you will have no problem adapting to the culture of Seattle Washington," said one of the Boeing senior managers. On two massive projectors, he presented slides showing beautiful pictures of Seattle's iconic towers and the Space Needle. More than 400 engineers and managers were packed in the Hilton hotel ballroom listening to a sales speech from Boeing.

As I was watching the presentations and the beautiful pictures of Seattle, I couldn't help but become intrigued and excited. I was familiar with Washington, but it was the first time I was hearing of Seattle. I simply assumed that Seattle was in Washington DC. At the end of the presentation, those who were interested lined up to hand over their resumes. A quick glance at the resume by the administrative personnel qualified applicants to make an appointment with one of the nine Boeing managers for a follow-up interview in the coming days.

Three days later, I showed up for an interview with Terry Garrison, who was a senior manager of the Technical Publications department at Boeing. After reviewing my resume, one of my certificates caught Terry's attention – a certificate I had received from CFM International (jet engine manufacturer) for a two-week engine-troubleshooting course I attended at Transavia Airlines. Terry said, "If you are interested, we can use your engine expertise in our Power Plant team responsible for writing engine maintenance instructions." He added, "You have 40 days to think about this offer. Please discuss with your family and let us know."

I didn't know how to react; it was an amazing moment! Further details were provided by the HR person and I learned even more exciting news. In addition to what seemed a generous salary as per Dutch standards, the offer would include no income tax for the first year. The job would be offered through an employment agency of my choice, a Dutch agency Randstad, or a US company called CTS International. In short, this was an exciting offer worth serious consideration.

There were no cell phones in those days. I couldn't wait to tell my skeptical family that I had a lucrative job offer. Cruising on the highway, I talked to myself loudly and giggled many times. The wheels of fate and destiny, through invisible forces, were set in motion once more to guide me to an unfamiliar destination. I found myself on an unthinkable path that could lead to immigrating to the US, entirely changing my life trajectory and that of my family. Twelve years earlier, in Sudan, as a helpless, uneducated, and poor teenager, I had applied for the American Resettlement Program to immigrate to the US. I was a refugee then seeking shelter and protection. Now, an American company was inviting me to come to the United States as an invaluable immigrant under the H1B visa rule, accorded only to rare professionals deemed critical to major US companies and the US economy.

I had never harbored any dreams of immigrating to the US. Although my father's view of the US was great, mine was very different. Most TV documentaries we had seen about the US in the

Netherlands depicted a country where humans perished daily at the whims of gun-toting policemen and criminals. The stories of slavery, racism, and the US's bullying foreign policies, visible to everyone but the ordinary Americans, gave nobody a reason to dream about immigrating from Europe to the US. Immigrating to the USA was reserved for desperate refugees escaping war zones, I thought.

Granted, we also thought there was something special about the US. Dawit and I had planned to tour the US in an RV (Recreational Vehicle) for several months as our final goodbye to the West before our eventual return to Eritrea for good. But "living in the US" was never on our minds. Yet, we had heard the US is an intriguing country and the land of opportunity. "In the US, if you dare to climb, you can make it high, and if you fall, a concrete floor awaits you – there is no mercy. In Europe, you can't climb high, and if you fall, there is a nice cushion on the ground." That is how Dawit and I had summed up the contrast between American and European life.

Nevertheless, considering all the financial advantages, I warmed up to the idea of moving to the US, a sellout. It was a different story for Tiblets. Despite my excitement and the compelling financial numbers, she didn't want to go to the US. Leaving her family behind and quitting a well-paying job was not something she wanted. To make the decision even more difficult for me, 10 days before the expiration of the Boeing offer, I received a letter from KLM offering me a job at their power plant engineering department. My main motivation to move to the US was unemployment. Now that I received a job offer from KLM, there was no justification to go to the US other than to follow my father's advice. A mild confrontation ensued, my father and I on one side against the rest of the family on the other.

Faced with a dilemma, Tiblets and I decided to find a middle ground. We agreed to take a risk and decline the KLM job offer and accept the Boeing offer. However, we wouldn't move the family to the US. Instead, I would go to the US alone for three months to try it out, and after that my wife and the kids would join me for three months on vacation and to check out life in the US. If we both liked the US, then we would sell our house in Holland and move. If not, we would go back to Holland and I would have to look for a job. With this compromised plan, I accepted the Boeing offer and visa processing started.

I bought several maps to study the US and Seattle. I was shocked to find out Seattle was not in Washington DC but five hours away. This was bad news. We needed to do more research about living in Seattle. The salary might be higher than in Holland, but what if the living costs in Seattle were higher as well? The Internet was in its infancy. I was a member of an online Eritrean community group called Dehai, and I posted a request for someone in the US to answer my questions. Surprisingly, I got a reply from an Eritrean who worked at Boeing in Seattle. He gave me a detailed breakdown of the cost of living which was very helpful. CTS International also did a fantastic job of making the move to Seattle easier for me by providing detailed information. Later, I found out that superior customer service is a uniquely American strength.

In the summer of 1996, I arrived at the Seattle-Tacoma (SeaTac) airport in Seattle. I rented a car and put my navigation skills to the test. I had studied the city map and knew the main highways and arteries of Seattle pretty well. The low speed limit of 60 miles per hour combined with a very loud road/tire noise however felt like I was driving a tractor.

My first day at Boeing was very pleasant despite the unfamiliarity with culture, language, and people in general. A few Dutch engineers had already arrived a week before me, which made the transition that day a lot easier. Later in the afternoon, I called the Eritrean engineer who had given me information about the cost of living to tell him I had arrived in Seattle. "Where are you? Do you know your building number?" he asked. I told him "Duwamish 11-14." "Are you kidding me? Which tower?" he sounded excited. I said, "The North Tower on the fourth floor." He couldn't believe his ears. He worked in the same building, floor, and department! What were the odds of that? Just like that, I added a new Eritrean colleague to my list of friends who contributed tremendously to making life in the US easier.

Three months of my bachelor-like life passed very fast. Daily lunch and dinner at the South Center Mall food court did some serious damage to my waistline! I kept buying new outfits to fit in. My distinct Eritrean features of prominently displayed cheekbones also took a hit and started to look round. Confronted with the unusually high number of overweight people strolling the mall, it was important to pull back on mall food.

Every day I learned something new about America. I was shocked to learn that the teenagers we saw in the mall pushing the baby strollers were mothers – unthinkable in Holland. Equally shocking was how incredibly friendly the people were. I remember, a Dutch friend and I were looking for shampoo in the Safeway store and the store manager noticed we were struggling to find what we were looking for. The only shampoo that we recognized was Head & Shoulders. After a short chat, he quickly realized we were newcomers to Seattle. A few minutes later, while we were waiting at the cash counter, he came to us with a big jar of ice cream and said, "Welcome to America! This is free of charge." What a gracious man! Wherever we went, people asked us, "How is your day going?" and engaged in conversation. "Where did we know these people?" we wondered. Why were they so friendly? It was astounding, to say the least. I fell in love with the people in Seattle.

Coming to America!

Before the September 11 attack on the Twin Towers, the international arrival hall in Seattle airport was separated from the waiting area only by a glass wall. Standing outside the security zone, I could see a pregnant woman and two kids standing at the customs desk. I didn't have my eyeglasses on, but squinting hard, I recognized them as my wife and daughters. My wife was engaged in a discussion with the officer and didn't see me, but I was able to attract the attention of my two kids. Excited, the kids wanted to run to me, but soon they realized they couldn't do that. The kids kept looking back at Tiblets and that was when she noticed me. But she had to continue talking to the officer.

The customs officer wouldn't let my family enter the country. He essentially told her, "You came to the US to give birth so you can have an American citizen baby." In addition, he didn't trust she was Dutch, he wanted her to prove that she was a Dutch citizen. He requested a Dutch translator to test her language skills. Although she told him that her husband was standing right there on the other side of the glass, he refused to let them in. My kids, tears streaming down their faces, together with their mother were dragged away to an immigration office within the airport. Helpless, I could only squint harder until I couldn't see them anymore. What was supposed to be a happy moment turned into hours of agonizing wait. In the end, despite verifying that she was Dutch, the customs agent rejected the one-year visa that had been issued by the embassy in the Netherlands. Instead, he revised the entry visa to last only six months.

Despite the unpleasant experience at the airport, our family's experience in the US for the first few months was incredible. There was no discussion about moving back to Holland. The Dutch were one of the most tolerant and friendly people in Europe. But we felt at home in Seattle. The fact that no one in the US asked where we came from by looking at the color of our skin was an incredibly liberating feeling. I had never minded people in Holland asking me where I came from, but, as innocent as the question sounded, it was simultaneously a gentle reminder that I was an outsider. In the US, the land of immigrants, however, even when my English was not American, no one would ask where I came from. I felt at home, I was accepted as an American, and enjoyed listening to this song with my kids.

This land is your land, and this land is my land
From California to the New York Island
From the Redwood Forest to the Gulf stream waters
This land was made for you and me.

As naive as I might sound here, I realize well the dark history of the US always overshadowed these lyrics, and the US, as I found out later, was not as pretty as these lyrics make it sound. Nevertheless, while living in Seattle, I didn't experience the sad racism stories and the ugly police brutality that we used to see on TV when in Holland. Life for our family was as beautiful and happy as it could ever be.

The work culture at Boeing was very relaxed compared to the tense and serious nature of the Dutch. Americans are lighthearted, easier to talk to, and just look happier people. The birthday parties of my kids were full of coworkers and few Eritrean friends. It was summertime, and the natural beauty of Seattle and its surroundings, compared to the flat fields in Holland, was breathtaking.

A bonus to all of this was that most of my ELF friends had somehow ended up in Seattle. Unlike in Holland, most of them were successful men and women. Just like Maasho who became an engineer in Canada, many of them turned out to be engineers, technicians, teachers, nurses, and professionals. Some were even working at Boeing as design engineers. Others had taken up tough jobs and worked two shifts to make ends meet. The common trait amongst all was the willingness to put in the effort it took to succeed. All had a story to tell how they managed to avoid PTSD, overcome life challenges, graduate, and find a job in the US.

In the first few months in Seattle, I made more friends than I had ever made in Holland over 13 years. With great coworkers, friendly people all around me, a relatively luxurious lifestyle, big air-conditioned cars, big houses, recliner sofas, garbage disposal, plenty of parking areas, cheap gasoline, no speed cameras, no income tax, etc., and above all the amazing evergreen city of Seattle and its natural beauty, we were sold, and it was time to make the US our permanent home. So, three months later, we flew back to Holland to formally say goodbye to our friends and family, sell our house, and move to the US for good.

Now that we had decided to move to the US, we visited the US Embassy in Amsterdam to process immigrant visas for the family. At the embassy, I was told I could only take my kids to the US, not Tiblets. The reason was that Tiblets and I were not officially married, therefore, according to the US Embassy, she was not my wife. This was something I had never expected. A formal marriage meant nothing to me – it was a waste of money with little practical meaning. I believed, if you can divorce so easily, what is the point of marriage with so much fanfare? My commitment to the person I love would not in any way be affected by a "married" status the society forced me to carry. My concept, as odd as it sounded, worked perfectly fine in the Netherlands – living together was as good as getting married. But the US embassy insisted that I get married before Tiblets could even request a visa. After some back and forth, the embassy agreed to give Tiblets a one-year visa provided we got married in the US within six months.

I have heard people talk about forced marriage in Africa, but what the US embassy did to us felt just like forced marriage to me. With no other choice, we agreed. Now that I think back, my rebellious attitude toward the widely accepted traditional norms and values might have to do with the fact that I grew up in the revolution where backward cultural values and conformance to these values were rejected as reactionary. I was brainwashed with progressive concepts of life and I took it a step further. The progressive and open Dutch culture didn't help either. Also, my love for Tiblets was so unconditional and unwavering that the standard marriage protocols felt an insult to my relationship. Not sure if Tiblets agreed. Nevertheless, that was an occasion where I learned that marriage has some value.

About 150 Dutch engineers who used to work for Fokker Aircraft Company had accepted job offers at Boeing. Just like me, they immigrated to Seattle with their families. Most of them worked in the same Customer Support department in the Boeing building I worked at, located near the Duwamish river. Daily, during lunch hour, we would all get together at the table and chat in Dutch. We almost had a dedicated set of tables where we sat together. In a way, we were not fully disconnected from Holland. Looking back, if a bunch of immigrants would sit together during lunch every day, it would be a major controversy in Holland. They would be blamed for not wanting to integrate with the Dutch people who hosted them. I raised this topic with a few of my Dutch friends and asked them if they understood now why immigrants tended to stick together in Holland. It is not because they do not want to integrate or they hate the host country, it is because they are so far away from home they miss their unique social and cultural interactions. When they occasionally get together, they can exercise their culture and interact in a way that provides them with a feeling of happiness and familiarity. They got it – it has changed their perspective.

As good as life in the US was, there were many things we missed about Holland – the cheese, the fresh bread from a neighborhood bakery, the delicious cakes, the meticulously designed and maintained highways, the dependable electrical power, the Dutch humor and, of course, the efficient social and medical services. However, it is not fair to compare Holland to any other country. Regardless of how much materialistic comfort I obtain from these countries, Holland was a home where I was born again. Just like the way a baby is delivered to this world with pure innocence and so much to learn in life, my life in Holland started with a blank canvas and it was God's chosen destination for my life. The Dutch gave me a chance, in every way possible, to find a place I could proudly call home. With the effort, money, and compassion of so many Dutch people who touched my life, I was able to navigate the confusing and treacherous social avenues that many immigrants, unfortunately, get lost in.

My life was steered by many individuals: the volunteers who helped refugees under the VVN umbrella; the many warm-hearted individuals who did everything possible to make immigrants feel at home; Oma Nederstigt and her family who took care of me as their family member for five years; the many public officials and officers who were very helpful to immigrants; UAF who gave a chance to me and those who otherwise were unable to get a scholarship; Mr. Karthaus who wrote me a recommendation letter; the youngsters who left me alone and never bullied or bugged me when I was an alien student in college ... The list is very long.

It is difficult to put in words the gratitude I feel towards the Dutch people. I know things have changed and the immigration process is no longer what it used to be for understandable reasons. But I am 100 percent sure that the good Dutch people still are taking care of many refugees. With their help, I am hopeful that many refugees will still find a way to succeed in life.

Equally, before arriving in Holland, many individuals played a role in keeping me out of harm's way and took care of me when I was young and vulnerable throughout my journey of becoming who I am today. My fate was in the hands of so many known and unknown generous people from all walks of life guided by higher powers. Holland however will always have a special place in my heart.

De Telegraaf newspaper wrote a multi-page article on how Fokker employees were coping in the US. (Left lower corner: Frank Bindels, Paul Manoch, myself and Pim Hogens.)

38. *Never Burn Bridges*

In 1998, two years after I started working in Seattle, Boeing decided to lay off thousands of people as part of a large-scale plan to cut airplane production in the face of the Asian financial crisis. The first group to go were employees who worked under a contract agreement, like the 150 Dutch engineers who had risked coming to the US to build a new life. The H1B work visa we had obtained didn't allow us to work in any profession other than in the Aviation industry. In addition, our spouses were not allowed to work in the US at all. The layoff, therefore, was disastrous for all of us who had come from Holland. The majority of the Dutch engineers had no choice and returned to Holland. Especially those who were hired through a Dutch employment agency couldn't find other options.

A few of us, however, didn't want to go back, and tried hard to find ways to stay in the US. Fortunately, through my contracting agency, CTS International, I found a job at BF-Goodrich Aerospace (TRAMCO) as a Modification Engineer, which was a huge relief. My Boeing friends were happy that I was able to stay in the US. By then we had expanded the family – our third daughter, Haben, had been born. Terry Garrison, the manager who had hired me in Holland, organized a farewell party for my family. The event was well attended and made me fall in love with the beautiful people at Boeing even more. Concerned, a few American friends offered to sponsor me for a green card so I could stay in the US permanently, a gesture that I am very grateful for. Despite the layoff, I genuinely felt part of the Boeing family.

Back in Eritrea, the year of 1998 was not a good year either. Seven years after Eritrea's independence that opened the door for hopeful and stable progress, war broke out again between Eritrea and Ethiopia ostensibly over border issue. When the war erupted, we were in Asmara on vacation introducing our children to our families. The unexpected nature of the war was apparent. In a matter of few days, thousands of youngsters were mobilized and loaded on busses and trucks to go to the front. Chanting and singing, they headed north towards Keren. It seemed like the entire city was being emptied. I stood there processing what I was seeing while at the same time getting flashbacks.

The chaos, excitement, and commotion reminded me of the exodus to *Woki Zager* in 1974. This time however, I was not in a position to hop on the busses or follow the crowd on foot, like I did when I was 11-year-old man. Instead, my three youngest siblings were called to go the front line to defend the country. What was supposed to be a short-lived conflict had no end and was more deadly than the 30-year liberation struggle. My two sisters and my brother spent years in the army. A depressing circumstance that would consume my thoughts for many years ahead.

A day before the Asmara airport was bombed and flights were interrupted, with a deflated morale and sense of hopelessness, we left Asmara on June 3rd 1998 and returned to Seattle. Then, I got a call from my former manager Rex Douglas asking me if I wanted to return to Boeing. I wholeheartedly accepted and returned to the mothership as a contractor. Ironically, I was asked to lead a project between Boeing and Fokker Stork, the remaining part of my former employer in Holland. A few years passed and I moved positions within Boeing. In the meantime, my two kids grew up fast. The Dutch language was replaced with English. In 2011, in the aftermath of 9/11, the cycle of another layoff at Boeing started. This time the impact was massive, and Boeing laid off more than 30,000 workers. *No escape.*

At that time, I was involved in a special project that involved a very small Boeing team. The project had major strategic importance for Boeing and a decision was made to spare the team. This, however, didn't apply to me since I was a contractor. A blanket layoff of all contractors was contractually a must-do for Boeing before they could lay off other unionized engineers. Human Resources and my senior leadership frantically explored all avenues to save my job. Eventually, HR gave the verdict: the only way my department could keep me under the radar was to directly hire me as a Boeing employee effective immediately.

Hiring a new employee at a time where thousands of employees were being laid off was a difficult thing to do. However, given the importance of the project, they were able to get approval and I got an offer. To make things complicated, I had signed a contract with CTS International in which they would sponsor an application for permanent residence, and in return, I would work three years for them after receiving my green card. The Boeing offer, if I accepted it, could jeopardize my green card process with CTS International. There was no time to think, things were moving fast, and I had to make a decision. Thankfully, CTS was understanding of the circumstances and agreed to rescind the contract. Over that, they graciously agreed to finalize the green card process as long as I refunded them all the expenses. Given the options on the table, this was a fantastic outcome! So, instead of being laid off, on February 22, 2002, I became a permanent Boeing employee. Since then, I have moved on to a different position where I have had the honor of working with incredible people and have played a key role in designing, marketing, selling, and deploying world-class products that airlines across the world have used to transform their maintenance operations. I have visited over 100 airlines and traveled the world carrying the Boeing name proudly. Some people are just that damn lucky.

These events reinforced my belief that for every bad thing in life, there may be more good things coming to tip the balance. Having a positive outlook in the face of challenges is an attribute that is very helpful in life. I am fortunate to have experienced this time-and-again in my life that it shaped my view of life in a way that is reassuring and keeps me somewhat worry-free. If things are meant to happen, they will. It is not all about what you do. I believe there is a higher power that you have no control over but which has the ultimate say over your life. I have seen too many lives cut short in many ways to make me believe that it is not all about "what you do." Yet, you have to do the right things in the best way you can to mine your luck, and leave the rest to the higher power – God, Allah, Buddha, Jesus – or any other power you believe in.

I am a very religious person in my way. Yet, I do not conform to what society has created for us in terms of religion and beliefs and I don't pray to anyone's god. I pray to my own god and am thankful for all the protection my god awarded me. I used to joke saying, "I have a perfect relationship with my God and he is protecting me extraordinarily well. Why should I disrupt that relationship by joining a bunch of others who pray to their own God? What if their God is different than mine and not performing well?" In addition, religion seems to be the main reason why civilizations have killed each other and still kill each other. So, I tried to raise my kids with that in mind, but without depriving them of the liberty to go to any religious institution of their preference. My wife, Tiblets, on the other hand, is a firm Catholic. Yes, you read it right, she is my wife officially. We took care of the title as requested by the US embassy.

It was Christmas in 1997. Dawit and my sister, Senait, had come from Holland to visit us and we had a surprise for them. One evening after work, we invited two of our Dutch friends and a special guest, a female colleague who worked as an engineer at Boeing. As soon as our special guest arrived, she unpacked and wore her official wardrobe, a beautiful blue gown with a long golden cross in the middle. She brought a single vibrant red rose with her and she placed it on the dinner table together with a few documents and a pen. She was there for a mission. We were asked to gather around the table and the two Dutch friends knew exactly what was about to happen. Dawit and Senait, however, were sitting on the sofa, clueless, wondering what was going on. Although they spoke English reasonably well, their ability to follow American accents in a setting where there was no context kept them in complete darkness. "Mulu, where are the rings?" our special guest asked. I don't like wearing rings, but our special guest had requested them ahead of time and I had bought two simple rings for the occasion. I pulled out the small box and gave it to her. That was when my sister and Dawit realized what was going on. Tiblets knew what the result would be, but she wasn't involved in any of the logistics of the event.

"I take you, Tiblets Melles, to be my wife, and these things I promise you: I will be faithful to you and honest with you; I will respect, trust, help, and care for you; I will share my life with you; I will forgive you as we have been forgiven; and I will try with you better to understand ourselves, the world, and God; through the best and worst of what is to come, and as long as we live."

The whole ceremony lasted probably about 20 minutes and just like that we were declared husband and wife, a phrase that meant nothing to me but was a prerequisite for us to live in the US. Our two Dutch friends, Paul Manoch and Fatma Sahin, were the witnesses, and the wedding minister was my colleague Caroline Peraullt.

After all was said and done, Dawit commented: "This is the first time I understood what I signed up for when I said 'I do'. With all the stress and chaos in the church, I didn't process anything during my wedding, I was just repeating what the priest said!" "This is deep stuff I committed to," he added with a twinkle in his eye. Yes, in a daring move, my best friend Dawit married my sister Senait in Eritrea and thereby downgraded our relationship from "best friend" to "brother in law".

My sister let her tears pour uncontrollably, tears of happiness mixed with sadness. She was happy that I had finally got married, but she was extremely sad and disappointed about the protocol, or lack thereof. She sympathized with Tiblets.

Our two toddler daughters had no clue about what was going on. They played around and ran from one room to another, just like on any other day. While our newly born daughter peacefully lay in her crib, Tiblets took the entire process bravely. She was dressed in her casual daily outfit and there was no makeup or preparation for a photoshoot, there was no photographer. We signed the paperwork on our kitchen table and we were done. A few minutes later, Tiblets went back to complete what she had started – cooking our dinner. She was as jolly and bubbly as she always was. We enjoyed the evening with our Dutch friends and the day ended uneventfully.

Looking back, Tiblets probably thought that day was anything but a wedding day. She wiped it from her memory and moved on with life as if it was just another day. But the story didn't end there for her. The next day she was confronted with another bizarre request from her newly married husband. I asked if I could have the wedding rings back. Although she knew I didn't like rings, she didn't expect that I would suggest returning the wedding rings to the store the next morning. Yet, for her, this wasn't a subject worth arguing about a day after we had got married. She took the ring off her finger and allowed me to return it without any resistance. In many ways, she accepted that day to be my day, allowing me to do whatever I wanted. She on her part just needed to check this off her To-Do list and move on. I returned the rings and exchanged them for a gold necklace for her.

I am sure for Tiblets this event was a fiasco and an utter failure on her husband's part. My inability to comprehend and follow basic cultural values and norms that bind a society together was made abundantly clear to her. This is just my guess. Tiblets' true feelings that day were only known to Tiblets. True to her nature, I am afraid she will not talk about it for life.

I understood the peculiarity and eccentricity of my behavior very well, but it was not strong enough to overcome my "jungleman's" behavior or tilt the balance against my long-held views that a wedding is a waste of money. Reaffirming my view, a few years later, the wedding necklace I had bought for Tiblets was snatched from her neck by thieves in Addis Ababa while she was sitting in a car with the windows open. With the only wedding memorabilia that she kept going, the wedding day diminished its value altogether and is now never celebrated, to the annoyance of our kids.

EriAm Sisters

Performing in Stockholm, Sweden July 2010

XI

EriAm Sisters

August 17, 2016. Air France Flight 355, from Seattle to Dubai. I am heading to Dubai through Paris. After boarding the plane, I was sitting comfortably in my seat. The seat next to me was empty and I was waiting for my flight partner to join me. Normally, I am very easy to talk to. I like to chat with anyone who sits next to me and tell them stories about Eritrea, my family, and where I come from. Often, the conversations tend to massage my memory and help generate content when I write my book. A middle-aged Frenchman came to sit next to me. As I was preparing to welcome him, he declined any eye contact, sat in his seat, fastened his seatbelt, and immediately pulled forward the panel that separates the seats to indicate he wants nothing to do with me and needs his privacy. Disappointed, I started to mind my business. A few minutes after we leveled off, a flight attendant came by with her cart, full of welcome drinks, and accidentally poured the entire ice bucket on his neck. All hell broke loose. I don't know how she managed to do that but I said to myself, "That is karma," and went back to writing my book.

39. Speaking of Our Kids

I am blessed to have three daughters: Lianda and Salina, born in Amsterdam, and the youngest, Haben, born in Seattle. Salina, in her closing speech at the UN environmental conference in Paris, said, "I am Eritrean by heritage, Dutch by birth, and American by schooling." She was right – they carry multiple identities and passports. The same is true for their parents. I proudly display five flags at my work desk: Ethiopian, Dutch, Eritrean, European, and American – in the order of how I received my citizenships over the years. Speaking multiple languages and being a "world citizen" at least covering three continents is a fantastic feeling. It helps me connect with people easily and with a less prejudiced attitude. I see beauty in other cultures and ways of life. However, like most things, it also has its drawbacks. It makes mastering a language challenging. It is said, "Your primary language is not your mother tongue, it is the language in which you think." In my case, after living in Holland for 13 years, no translation was taking place in my mind when I spoke Dutch. I used to think and speak in Dutch. Once I moved to the US, many translations took place, which slowed my ability to speak English fluently. After many years of living in the US, I gradually stopped thinking in Dutch and converted to thinking in English. In the transition process, my standby vocabulary started to decrease drastically.

Consequently, I noticed I became very inefficient in using my standby vocabulary. Just like when I used to consult multiple dictionaries during my college years in Holland, multiple translations took place in my mind to get to the right English words. Sometimes I translated words from Dutch, other times from Tigrinya (Eritrean), and occasionally from Amharic (Ethiopian). In addition, as I aged, my brain's processing ability slowed, making it even more difficult to master any language, including my mother language. This was particularly true when dealing with infrequently used words. This challenge doesn't apply to multi-linguists in that they always think in their mother language proficiently and have direct access to vocabularies of multiple languages.

The language issue inevitably affected how we communicated at home as well. We used a mix of Dutch, Tigrinya, Amharic, and English depending on the situation and mood. Therefore, our communication in our household was not as clear, causing unnecessary arguments and prolonged debates.

In addition to the language barrier, as immigrant parents, communicating with our kids became harder due to the major background and cultural differences with the kids. As my kids grew up, there was a clear conflict of perspectives in many aspects of life. The many topics like multiculturalism, racism, boyfriends, politics, money, family values, culture, LGBTQ+ rights, pets, music, language, women's rights, connecting to Eritrean roots, sleepovers, parties, religion, immigration, police brutality, human rights, identity, white privilege, materialism, social media, marriage, therapy, mental health, suicide – the list goes on and on – wreaked havoc at the dinner table.

As our kids grew older, when dinner was ready, the five of us always gathered at the dinner table without exception. This allowed us to open up to each other and create a family unit that many people say is "unheard of" these days. After years of hot debates at the dinner table, I realized that the challenges I faced in life as an immigrant did not apply to my daughters. My way of thinking and the actions I take to deal with many of the seemingly common challenges that immigrants face simply didn't resonate with my kids. At first, I had a hard time understanding them. Gradually, I realized that their generation is so different from ours, my solutions couldn't be prescribed to them.

In my world as an immigrant, I had taken the following as a fundamental reality to deal with.

- I have to adapt to my host country.
- I have to work harder to prove to my host country that I am worthy of the shelter they have provided me.
- If they see me as different and alien, I have to accept that I am different and alien; after all, I come from another country and continent.
- The country I live in has permanent owners and I am not one of them, I am a guest.
- I can understand that some people will not like immigrants because we intrude on their way of life. So, I have to adapt. "When in Rome, do as the Romans do."
- I have to behave in a way that highlights positive images, and shouldn't attract negative observations. I, as an immigrant, should not in any way be found doing illegal things.
- As much as I love my host country, I love Eritrea more than any country on earth.
- I have succeeded in life by conforming to social rules valued by others.
- I cannot succeed as an immigrant by confronting the hosts and demonstrating for change.

The list goes on.

Essentially, I had mastered the act of reaching high by laying low. As an immigrant, I lived in a single-dimensional world where the other side could never be wrong. It was always my responsibility to fit in, however difficult that might be. I strongly believed that I alone would make or break my image. I felt it was my duty to change the bad image that might exist in other people's minds about immigrants. It became my goal to engage strangers with my ethnicity and where I come from being the center of our discussion, in the hope that the stranger would say, "I met a nice immigrant from Eritrea." Every time I made someone believe that there were good, hard-working immigrants in this world, it was a win for me. The burden of proving to others that I was a good person was part of my daily routine, and to some extent, it still is in my daily routine.

I was also quick to resent immigrants who pointed fingers at others. I believed that one only had the right to point fingers after exhausting all possible solutions within oneself. Despite all the wrongdoings perpetrated during the era of slavery and colonialism in Africa, I believed the burden was on us to somehow pull through. The topics of police brutality, the Black Lives Matter movement, white privilege, and racism especially required me to dig deep to understand different angles. My journey and experience as an immigrant did not equip me to reason objectively with my kids on these matters.

When my kids told me they had joined the Black Student Union in college, having never heard of such a union, they got a reaction of shock from me. I never understood how such a union based on the color of skin could be allowed to exist. "What if there was a White Student Union?" I countered. I simply didn't understand the history and racial dynamics in this country. All these years, I was isolated in my immigrant shell where I was happy to be given a chance to live in someone else's country. No resentment whatsoever against "white people" existed within me. If anything, it was the opposite. I had high regard and respect for white people (the Dutch people) for allowing me to stay in their country, sheltering me, holding my hand to guide me through a new life, paying for my education and living expenses, and offering me a job. How could I possibly think otherwise? Even with all the geopolitical and colonial historical facts, my personal experience with the average white person was too powerful to assume anything "evil" in white people to the extent that I could harbor hate. I got troubled when a discussion pinned white people against immigrants or black people.

As I befriended more African-Americans in the US, I started to hear the phrase "white people" more often. For the first few years, I made it my goal to not "infect" my kids with that phrase. It was almost banned at the dinner table to raise the topic of race. I felt that if one is obsessed with assigning blame to skin color, life would turn into unbearable and consistent misery. This was highlighted by my personal experience where a janitor at Boeing used to stop by my desk after hours and ask me, "Do the white people here leave you alone?" – a horrifying question to hear. How could this person ever be able to feel free and excel in a work environment where white people are the majority? It would be miserable and felt very bad for him.

This was a reminder to me, however naive, that I had to raise my kids to not talk or see the world in terms of color. Instead, I wanted them to see the world in terms of cultural diversity. I rigorously attempted to make them feel that they are first Eritrean, second American, third Dutch, and last their skin color. But outside our home and on social media, life in the US was making them feel first their skin color (black), second Eritrean, third Dutch, and last American, a difficult reality to reckon with.

The deep underlying history and systemic racism in the US were considered somewhat a distant history in my world. With Obama becoming president, I convinced myself that the US had buried its history for good. I never educated myself on the plight of black people in the US, specifically African-Americans. I generalized the experience and didn't understand that the social challenges faced by immigrants were very different than that of African-Americans. Based on my ignorance of this issue, I could have easily passed for a far-right Republican with no connection to what black people go through in this country.

I had to be educated on the history and purpose of the Black Student Union, Black History Month, Black Entertainment TV, and anything that starts with the word Black in the US. The idea of police killing unarmed black men was so remote in my world, my lack of awareness could have easily made me a victim.

One night, as I was driving with my Dutch friend in the Renton area, I saw a police light behind me and pulled to the side. Out of respect, as one would do in Holland, I opened the door and immediately came out of my car to greet the police officer. Right away, I was blinded by a powerful floodlight. I never felt any danger of any kind. It was cold and I reached out to both ends of my open jacket to close the zipper.

What followed was a terrifyingly loud yell. The officer ordered me, in an aggressive tone, to keep my arms off my jacket and immediately return to my car. Confused, I returned to my car, and, out of respect, I kept the driver's side door open. Again, the officer shouted and ordered me to close the door. It still felt odd to close the door when we needed to talk. So, I didn't fully shut the door and left it slightly open. I wish I could see what the officer was doing or if he had a gun drawn. The floodlight was so powerful that I couldn't see what was happening. Fortunately, the officer approached the car and saw how confused my white friend and I were. He didn't escalate the situation and I got away with a life lesson. When I think of this incident now, I realize that my ignorance of the US police culture could have cost me my life. This illustrates that I had very little knowledge of American culture and society, beyond the few documentary films, and definitely not well equipped to raise three black kids in the US.

As the kids grew older, instead of me guiding my kids, my kids started educating me on the history of the US, the lingering impact of slavery, segregation, redlining, systemic racism, police brutality, and the intricacies of racial relationships in the US. Regrettably, it took me a long time to understand that their challenges and perspectives were much more complex than my simple one-dimensional immigrant world. They are not immigrants! All my firmly held beliefs and guidelines on how to survive as an immigrant in the West made no sense to my kids and those who were born here. As such, I will be the first to admit that I failed my kids during their teenage years in preparing them to understand the US as it is and to recognize their role and position in this society.

Nevertheless, our contrasting experiences and opposite views have allowed my daughters to be well-grounded and pragmatic individuals with a wide periphery on various social and political topics. We have made frequent trips to Eritrea with the goal of helping my kids understand and appreciate where their ancestors come from. We also wanted to instill in them a sense of belongingness by not only visiting family members in Eritrea but actively giving a helping hand to those in need. During their "McDonald age", every year they used to collect all the happy meal toys they received and at the annual Eritrean festival they would organize a game where children pay to play a game and win a toy. They would then donate the proceeds to a good cause. In addition, as part of our plans to visit Eritrea, the kids would collect clothing as well as their Halloween candies to donate to the orphanage in Asmara. In the process, they spent a day with the children at the orphanage developing compassion and empathy to others.

During a trip they made without me, my wife even took them to a remote village to see the birthplace of my father, which I must admit I have not seen yet. They consider the trip as one of the most memorable trips they made. As they grew older and started performing on stages, they travelled twice to Eritrea to perform, including at the training center Sawa that allowed them to connect to thousands of Eritrean students as well as youth that came from all over the world. Salina went even further and conducted her thesis research at the Bisha Mining Company in Eritrea where she studied the impact of mining on the environment and particularly impact on women in Mogoraib, the place where I was stationed first as a prison guard in 1977.

The extreme emphasis on our cultural values, where respecting others is at the center of who we are, contrasted with the inward-looking values in the US, helped them land somewhere in the middle, achieving a sense of balance. They turned out to be relatively respectful and decent. At the same time, although we occasionally debated the solution, I embraced the fact that I can no longer limit my periphery to the challenges of an immigrant but must expand to include the wider issues that people of color face in this country. After all, to the outside world, I am a black American man, not an Eritrean immigrant. I could still picture the faces and voices of my kids as they were angrily saying, "Daddy, here in the US you are a black man, you are not an Eritrean man".

Particularly a few years after the election of President Barak Obama, it started to hit home that the US, despite the election of a black president, has a long way to go to shed its racist past. If institutionalized and covert racism is not obvious, the execution or near execution of unarmed black men and women in the streets of American cities in broad daylight made it clear to people like me who lived in their bubble and to the world at large that the US has a long way to go to live up to its ideals.

That being the reality, as a family we agreed that education is the greatest equalizing asset and key to success in life. We agreed that completing high school was no reason to celebrate. We always told our kids, "You can't throw a party because you met the minimum requirement in life." Yet, in the US, the reality is different. Many kids in the US don't complete high school, and those who do definitely throw often a large party to celebrate the achievement. For us, no party was justified for completing high school. I remember during the high school graduation ceremony of my youngest daughter, a good friend of mine, struggling to keep his tears from flowing, said, "I am very emotional. This is the first time in my life I am witnessing three kids from a black family complete high school." I was shocked to hear that but, at the same time, it reminded me that as people of color, we have many more mountains to climb.

Sept 2, 2016, Rome to Amsterdam: On the way back from Dubai, I visited Alitalia where, together with other three team members, I attended a two-day workshop aimed at reviewing their maintenance operations and presenting products and services that could improve efficiency. The Alitalia team was impressed with our work and it was productive. But, moreover, a comment they made during the meeting stood out as memorable. "America is really beautiful; I am impressed," one manager said in a thick Italian accent. "Look how diverse the Boeing team is!"

At first we were confused – then it hit us. The Boeing team consisted of an Eritrean, a Vietnamese, an Indian, and a Canadian – all representing the US and one of the greatest companies in the world. What a beautiful observation that highlights what a great nation America can be if we all give each other a chance to excel.

The EriAm Story

My daughters understood that higher education is an important part of eliminating the disparity and the negative perception of people of color. Acting as role models in their rights is the best contribution they can offer to the younger generation. They are blessed to be in positions where they can effectively reach out to younger kids using social media and other platforms.

My youngest one appeared on national TV as one of the most talented American kids at age 10. As sisters, their singing talent allowed them to appear on the TV shows like "America's Got Talent," and they made it to the semi-finals. They were selected as the top 100 YouTube Black Influencers in the US by YouTube. These opportunities provided them with a platform they could utilize to change the world for the better.

Back home in Eritrea and Ethiopia, they are well known and can play a critical positive role. The name of their singing group was "EriAm", short for Eritrean-American (or as my Dutch friends call them, "Eritrean Amsterdamers"). The idea of highlighting their identity and being proud of who they are has had a tremendous effect on young Eritrean kids living in the diaspora. My kids have received many messages from young Eritreans who wrote "Thank you for making me believe in myself and that nothing is impossible." That alone made their singing careers worth it.

In the last thirteen years, the sisters' music career had dominated our lives and taken us to venues and places that we had only seen in movies and TV shows before their limited stardom. Having shared tables with The Osmonds, Steve Harvey, Craig Robinson (the brother of Michelle Obama), Hall of Famers like Lenny Wilkens, performing with David Foster, and the extraordinary musicians who used to play for Michael Jackson, reminded us that we have tasted the American Dream.

As I write this, my youngest daughter Haben just signed a management contract with XO Records and Q10 management, managers of the renowned artists The Weeknd and DojaCat. Salina, on the other hand, joined Harvard University pursuing a Master in Public Policy with full scholarship including International and Global Fellowship Affairs. At the same time, she works for the UN and World Bank as a strategic Advisor. Her passion to connect to her ancestral land is so strong that she accepted a temporary assignment in Nairobi, Kenya. Lianda, my oldest daughter, received her BSc Degree from University of Washington and is currently working at Washington Students Opportunity Scholarship (WSOS), a foundation that helps minority students obtain financial assistance to excel in STEM. Lianda seems to prefer to stay closer to home. Although, she did go to Peru on a research program that led her to explore the Amazon and she is also a world traveler and an adventurous tourist.

Overall, in addition to their common love for music, the sisters found their individual passion and interests. I could write a separate book about their musical journey but for now stardom at a modest level while maintaining humbleness and wholesomeness are the best things that have happened to my daughter's musical career. After all, in Dawit's words "In the US, if you dare to climb, you can make it very high, but if you fall in the process, a concrete floor awaits you."

March 13, 2018. Delta flight DL-143 from Kiev to Seattle through Amsterdam.
It has been a while since I wrote anything in my book. I am returning from Kiev, Ukraine, where we inked an airplane and services contract to the tune of more than USD 1 billion. Early in 2017, I accepted a new position within the Sales and Marketing department of Boeing. I am now a regional marketing director for Boeing Global Services responsible for the Middle East, Turkey, Africa, Russia and Central Asia regions. This job moves me away from my previous technical role to a more sales-oriented position. It is a shift that I took as a challenge and so far I am enjoying it. But, on the home front, 2017 was not a good year..

The last picture my mother took at my brother's wedding. She is in the middle between the groom and bride

40. Regrets

My Mother – Lemlem

The year 2017 was a difficult year for me. My mother, whom I had so many plans for, passed away unexpectedly. She was 72 but lived as if she was 55 years old – young-looking, energetic, and full of life. So much so that the year before she died, I was telling my kids that I was going to bring my mother to the US to live with me. I wanted to catch up and compensate for the years I had missed enjoying my mother.

Sadly, my plans were trashed and I lost her before I had a chance to enjoy time with her. Every time I realize that she is gone, my heart sinks with disbelief. She was a major happiness-generating human being who disappeared from my life without warning. She was a person who was deeply connected to everything I do in life. But, I make peace with the fact that she died happily. Just six months before her passing, for the first time in our life, she saw all her kids in her home when we all returned to attend the wedding of our youngest brother. She was the happiest, and that was the last I saw her.

My Country

The choice to study aerospace may have been mandated to me by my father but the focus on airplane maintenance was chosen by me purposefully so that I can go back home and serve my country with knowledge that is useful to Eritrea. I have always dreamt of going back home to contribute in some capacity. The closest I have come to that was when the Eritrean government decided to establish a national carrier and invited all aerospace professionals to attend a conference in Eritrea to help setup the airline in the best way possible.

Many Eritrean aviation professionals who worked in the airline industry, regulatory authorities, Original Equipment Manufacturers (OEM), Maintenance Repair & Overhaul (MRO) and other relevant areas of the business around the globe went back home to attend the conference. The President of the State of Eritrea opened the conference and gave the attendees a clear mandate of the mission. His understanding of the aviation business and aerospace technology was astounding. The background information he provided to justify the need for establishment of the airline and the challenges our country faced gave us a clear picture of the situation. His desire to listen to our recommendation was empowering and we started working enthusiastically.

We grouped the attendees by domain, elected leaders for each domain, and went to work for several days. I joined the team that would establish the vision and program guidelines for airplane maintenance, safety and training. At the end, each team presented its plans to the larger group and eventually reported out to the President and Minister of Transportation. The plan was comprehensive and yet pragmatic enough to align with the reality of the country. However, it required significant resources and talent to execute.

After listening to the plan and recommendations, the President, true to his words to listen to the professionals, asked the team how to address the resources issue. He also indicated his expectation that key members of the conference will contribute in one way or another, ideally in leading the establishment of the airline and managing the execution. This was where our commitment to help Eritrea was tested.

Unfortunately, some of us had to resolve many personal issues and adjust our life plans before we can commit to quit our jobs and move to Eritrea to help establish the airline. However, many experts, especially from the flight operations and pilot community, committed themselves to return to Eritrea and work for the airline. They complemented the existing airline employees already working in Eritrea. Captain Asres who at the time worked for Boeing and volunteered to assist, was elected as the man who would lead the challenging work of establishing an airline under a difficult circumstance with limited resources and finance.

We celebrated the successful end of the conference and I returned to Seattle. In the subsequent weeks, I worked closely with Captain Asres in preparing detailed presentations of his plans to procure assets and develop network. Yet, it bothers me that I didn't come close to what I was expected to do for my country in this regard. Yes, like many Eritreans in Diaspora, I spent considerable effort to engage on matters pertinent to Eritrea. Every evening after work, I ran the now defunct community websites like Ertra.com for more than 10 years. I set up and managed a remittance service to help continue the flow of hard currency into Eritrea when the US blocked our government from providing money services business. I created a language tutorial software to teach our kids their language. However, I regret that I couldn't do more to help in the field that I am supposed to contribute the most.

I learned that there is no perfect time to return to your country, there is always one or another reason that holds you back. I took comfort in the idea of "I will return later by taking early retirement". Unfortunately, as practical as it sounds, tomorrow is not guaranteed; I learned it the hard way.

As if the passing of my mother was not enough, just weeks after she passed away, I was diagnosed with a difficult disease at age 53.

This terrible news disrupted any plans I had for early retirement and returning back home. At first, I received the news with denial, but slowly, as the symptoms are becoming stronger, I have come to accept that my life will no longer be the same and that I have to adjust my expectations and plans for the remaining years of my life.

I am now at a stage where I am trying to figure out how to be strong and live a life that is as close to normal as possible while hiding the sickness from everyone except my closest family members. Yet, I understand this disease is not one I can hide for long.

Dealing with a disease that is not curable is consuming my thoughts these days. However, I do not want to burden my family by telling them the details of the limitations my sickness is causing me. I am receiving great support from my wife and kids as well as from my sisters in Holland. Especially my daughter Salina who is living abroad. I feel like she feels my pain more than I do. My sister-in-law, Kedest, puts more effort into finding the best doctors than I care to do. So, I am blessed to have such support, nevertheless, it is a piece of devastating news that may alter my destiny.

As much as I would like to keep working on my career, return back home or make plans to run my own business during my retirement, if I don't succeed I will not feel deprived of anything. I will accept whatever may come with gratitude. The life I have lived so far is such an incredible one that, even if this disease wins, I feel like the relatively short life in the way I have lived is much better than living a longer life with a credible lifestyle. I will not take anything for granted and plan to live life to the fullest extent possible and keep mining my luck with utmost gratitude and optimism.

For my mother, I was still a young boy who needed to be fed and entertained, even kittens are not off the limit

My sisters Lia, Simret and Rahel.

The first time I was introduced to them was during this trip. We spent good time visiting Massawa, the port city of Eritrea. The tank in the background is one of the three tanks EPLF damaged in the battle of Massawa. The three tanks are now put in a memorial display in the center of the city.

Our wedding: The witnesses Paul Manoch and Fatma Sahin

The coolest daughters in the world

Mission accomplished, kids are grown up, it is time to be just the two of us again

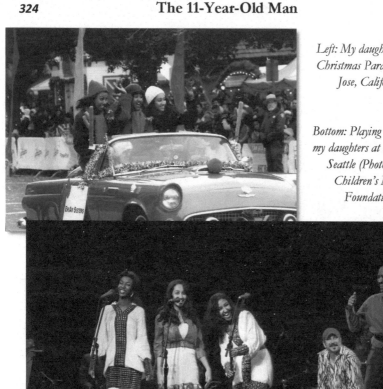

Left: My daughters at the Christmas Parade in San Jose, California

Bottom: Playing Kirar with my daughters at an event in Seattle (Photo credit: Children's Music Foundation)

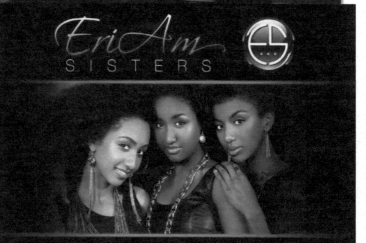

All grown up: Salina, Haben & Lianda

Left: With President Isaias Afwerki (2ⁿᵈ from left) and the late Foreign Minister Ali Said (2ⁿᵈ from right) at Eritrean Airlines conference in Asmara May 2002

Right: The team that travelled to Eritrea to attend Eritrean airlines conference touring Sawa training center

Bottom: Standing in the middle, Minister Andemichael serving honey from his own bee-farm in his backyard with a big smile

2002, Moscow USSR, All Russian airlines conference

Nairobi, Kenya 2018: A selfie at the African Airlines Association conference

Beijing, China Dec 6, 2013: All airlines conference, one of my favorite trips

Top: With my colleagues Kurt Vandermolen, Rex Douglas, Aime Do, & Brian Lund

Middle: With Darlene Wilson & Larry little in Moscow

Bottom: With Kamil Gaynutdinov

In Loving Memory

Of my beloved parents-in-law
Abrahatsion Melles and
Tesfaghiorghis Gebremedhin

In Loving Memory

Of my beloved mother
Lemlem Tseghay

Acknowledgement

I am grateful to all individuals who played a positive role in my life. As you read the book, I hope you sensed my deepest appreciation by the way I wrote the stories. Therefore, I will limit the list to the people who contributed to the creation of this book:

※ My beloved daughters Lianda, Salina and Haben for encouraging me to take the writing of this book seriously.

※ My wife Tiblets for allowing me to spill the beans.

※ Khalil Walji and Vera Haile for being the first to read this book and giving me invigorating feedback.

※ Mriga Jammu for her professional effort in copyediting the content.

※ Kassahun Chekole for providing professional and encouraging feedback

※ Barth Poage, Daniel Morgan, Damien Gallet, Darlene O. Wilson, Jim Baqai, Don Galvanin, John Maggiore, Robert Cann, Rourke O'Brien, and many other friends and colleagues for listening to my story and encouraging me to put it in writing.

Photograph credits

With the exception of the family photos, many of the pictures included in this book are not mine. EPLF and ELF fighters took most of the pictures during the struggle for liberation of Eritrea. Some of the photographers are martyred. In doing so, they have left us a legacy that enables us to pass Eritrea's history to the next generation.

The photo-book titled *Eritrea - Down After a Long Night*, published by EPLF's Department of Information in June-1989, contains incredible depiction of Eritrea's struggle for independence. Some of the photos I used as chapter dividers are taken from this amazing book.

M-Abraham.com

Shabait News

Asmara UNESCO

Battle of Afabet

EriAm Sisters

Kagnew Station

Printed in the United States